Back o' the Hill

Highland Yesterdays

JOHN G. GIBSON

BIRLINN

First published in 2008 by
Birlinn Limited
West Newington House
10 Newington Road
Edinburgh
EH9 1QS

www.birlinn.co.uk

ISBN 13: 978 1 84158 638 0
ISBN 10: 1 84158 638 2

British Library Cataloguing-in-Publication Data
A catalogue record for this book is available from British Library

Typeset by Hewer Text UK Ltd, Edinburgh
Printed and bound by MPG Books Limited, Cornwall

Back o' the Hill

Contents

Acknowledgements

I must with pleasure acknowledge help from the following people, Mrs Fiona MacLean of Ardgour; Alistair Gray, Blaich, Ardgour; Alasdair Roberts, Bracara; Pat MacBrayne, Edinburgh; Eileen O'Rua, Tearlach MacFarlane and Ronald MacKellaig OBE, Glenfinnan; Maggie MacDonald, the library, Armadale, Skye; Rory MacDonald, Blarour, Spean Bridge; Chris Doak, Glasgow; Hugh P. MacMillan, Ottawa, Ontario; Sally MacPhee, Brisbane, Australia; Dr Robert C. Cameron, Leura, New South Wales, Australia; Bruce Cameron, Ardachie, NZ; Kurt Duwe, Hamburg; Tessa Spencer, NAS, Edinburgh; Peter Milne and Laragh Quinney, map library, National Library of Scotland; Sally at NLS; John Guthrie, Scarborough, England; Florence and Andrew Nisbet, Kinlochiel; Alex Du Toit, Highland Council archivist; Sue Payne, historian, Perth Museum and Art Gallery; Steve Connelly, archivist, Perth and Kinross Council Archives; Andrew Nicol and Caroline Cradock at the Scottish Catholic Archives in Edinburgh; assistant curator George A. Woods of Inverclyde Council; Mrs Rhian Wong at the Print Room of the Royal Library, Windsor Castle; Seumas Watson, Queensville, Cape Breton; Nadia Barsoum PhD, Alice Holt Lodge, Farnham, Surrey (forestry); my sons Seumas and Michael; my brother Tim D.S. Orr in Australia. That Alasdair mac Iain [Alasdair MacLean] the poet, born Glasgow *c.* 1926, and later crofted in Sanna, Ardnamurchan, was the real name of Donald Cameron, author of *Field of Sighing* was deduced from several electronic sources.

I must also confide that a sense of confidence and delight given me by a fellowship from the J.S. Guggenheim Foundation for 2005 loosened any diffidence I might have had in writing a text such as this; indeed a few dollars found their way into some of the research reported below and I am humbly and proudly grateful.

Resentment memories are long and heritable, so I have changed one person's name to avoid litigation.

Why do so few memories lie so clearly and powerfully, even in their fragments, their disjointedness and sometimes their deceptions?

Introduction

A little burn that flows south over the tunnel of what began as the West Highland Railway used to mark here the ancient watershed boundary line between Cameron of Lochiel's estate and MacDonald of Clanranald's. That little burn joined the Callop River and the Callop there marked off Inverness-shire to the north and Argyll to the south. In Argyllshire there were two countries northwardly bounded here by the Callop – Sunart to the west and Ardgour to the east – and their roughly north–south line of division, a watershed, joined the Callop a little to the westward of where the little burn dividing the Cameron and MacDonald holdings did. So, four old Highland estates almost met there in what is a tight and wooded cleft in the mountains.

To the west of the cleft lay the old Clanranald village of Glenfinnan with its relatively recent Jacobite memories, to the east the most north-westerly of Ardgour's farms, Callop, and for ages one of the most westerly of Lochiel's farms, Cregag. All of these lie to the west of the great seismic fault that severs the north from Lorne to Moray and therefore are in the West Highlands.

This book is about, and inspired by, a boyhood spent in that marchland just after the Second World War. From that boyhood came interests about Highland people, interests that were later fanned by anti-Highland attitudes that were never far from the surface in the Edinburgh I knew – it is the anti-Highland reactions and remarks that I remember. Luckily, or maybe unluckily, the weight of anti-Roman Catholic Highlandness in Edinburgh meant that the thought of getting some formal, post-school learning in Scotland about the Gaelic world, never occurred to me. Looking back, I am saddened to note that I was even preoccupied enough not to have recognised kindly overtures from Highland folk in the city.

For a complex of reasons, including a need to assess my interests, I went to Canada. As I settled into myself it became inevitable that I would find the last main Gaelic-speaking places in the then Dominion, in Cape Breton and north-eastern Nova Scotia. With a few very short breaks I lived there from 1972 till 2007. There were cultural strangenesses to which I was introduced that summer of 1972 and a need to fit them into the social world of Gaelic Scotland, then the wider Gaelic and European world, have flavoured my curiosity about us. I even learned some Welsh with a view to seeing how an old, declining language was being encouraged. Where David Hume was open-minded about Gaeldom at the time of the Ossian controversy, Samuel Johnson was peremptory and often derogatory, and later Walter Scott sought to profit from Highlandism without enough understanding. Had the last two not accepted that the Saxon branch of Germanic civilisation was by then superior to the Celtic one; had they stopped to consider the much greater antiquity of the latter, and its vast influence on all European peoples, even its remarkable geographic extent once upon a time, we might not have been so slow in our own realisations. Iain Òg Ìle and Alexander Carmichael and other Scots might have had other able colleagues on whose works we might build a more complete understanding of a very old and durable society.

So this book looks first and last at the effects of a few years in the West Highlands but really depends on a broader group of adult ideas, an assemblage acquired elsewhere that to me is a main basis of my perceptions. My sons have asked me about India, or the Crimea, or the East or West Indies, Australia, or New Zealand, or out West on the prairies, even the vice-regality of Peru, and my answers are often stimulated by some knowledge of a Highland regiment, a clearance, some happening involving a Scotch Gael. I haven't been to most of those places. I make no claim to Gaelic's persistent, overlooked or even derogated genius throbbing through one empire then another in a cunning, kin-centred, non-centralist political concept. I just notice that language and consciousness are linked in such a way that poesy and kindness at many degrees of cleverness should always be encouraged, never condemned. New words in the old tongue, not imposure or unthinking acceptance from outside of some foreign *lingua* lock, stock and barrel, the one I write in for example. For me, even in English, thoughts and knowledge of the Gaelic world are an important platform for considering the world of man.

From its personal approach this is sometimes a book about what probably was, just because there aren't many historical records to refer to and none that are fundamentally contradictory. In doing this, an outsider's imagining of that older consciousness is the heart of what I have to offer, clad in knowledge gained mostly in and from Scotland and the Maritimes of Canada. I enjoy the use of footnotes – Michael calls them 'under-story' – and have indulged that pleasure, I hope convincingly and informatively. The book relies a little on cartography both because maps have interested me since my days at High School Yards in Edinburgh (which is where geography was in the early 1960s), and because these documents can often be very informative; they were often all I had to go on for approximate knowledge, and for lack of knowledge.

There must be examinations of the persistence of Gaelic thought, balance of thoughts, and life through so many genera-tions, so many centuries, so many ages, so many oppressions, so many superficial changes, and this one of that older consciousness, is radically fortified by what I have learned about it in the last Gaelic-speaking *Gàidhealtachd* in the province of Nova Scotia.

John G. Gibson
January 2008

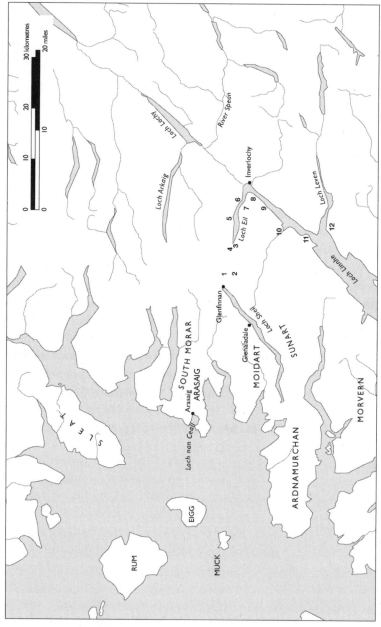

1 Craigag 2 Callop 3 Drumfern 4 Drumsallie 5 Fassifern 6 Kilmallie 7 Blaich 8 Treslaig 9 Stronchregan 10 Aryhoulan
11 Corran 12 Baile Chaolais

The lost negatives of Callop, Ardgour

Although I have an enlarged, grainy, black-and-white photograph of Craigag Lodge from the same old strip of browning negatives that I remember beside me in Judique in Cape Breton, I have lost or misplaced the negatives themselves. They included exposures of the Callop farm in Ardgour, taken with an old leather-clad, thirty-five millimetre camera about thirty-six years ago, between 1970 and 1972. I knew very little about photography and cameras then, but still those Craigag and Callop exposures were simple daylight scenes and were sharp likenesses taken from near a fence on the tongue of land south-west of the lodge. I regret losing them because they were made only about twenty years after I had been taken away from Craigag near Callop, and Glenfinnan a mile or two to the west, and not much had changed physically from just after the war when I lived there. They actually, and now almost unimaginably, showed the place much as I remembered, and still remember it (although many details have taken leave of my recollection), and, although my search for them has not been exhaustive – and I have looked at other people's collections of photographs – I have never seen another photograph of the two buildings at Callop nestling under the Ardgour hills with the little hayfield nearby. And, as for years I thought fondly back on the memories that I had simply enjoyed and had not studied, with only a little more general information, I argued, with irrepressibly naïve conviction too, that not much had really changed for the century and a half since the little road had been built as far west as Glenfinnan sometime maybe as early as 1799 (more likely post-1804 for the demanding Cregag and Callop to Glenfinnan section).

That of course was wrong. Although the dominant, overall theme of the change that had happened was a local population decline, the movement away of Highland people, emigration and a dissipation of a distinct folk o'er the world, and the neglect of the land as a primary and direct source of sustenance in favour of a nationally integrated system of agri-business and commerce – often ovine monoculture – there are other facets of the overall decline that I knew almost nothing about. Mine was not wishful thinking so much as thinking that fitted into a simple model that involved a general knowledge of the great intra-empire emigrations from the Highlands to North America (c. 1770–1840) as considered from an isolated, culturally conservative overseas, once-colonial *Gàidhealtachd* in Cape Breton and Nova Scotia where many Gaelic-speaking emigrants had chosen to settle, and where Gaelic is still spoken by a few.[1] This thinking turned less to what happened in Gaelic Scotland after many of the original folk had left or been shifted (because the time had to be spent learning about the overseas anachronisms). I would have said that what happened had concerned the post-emigration, skeletal residue of people in Locheil and Ardgour, and that they were the objects of intensifying Procrustean economic manipulation and Anglification, which is in large part true of many rural Highland populations, including these.[2] Not men with whips and torches. Men with accountants and managers, new churches with teinds and a court of teinds, and proscriptive ministers.

The majority of people who left North Ardgour and Glenfinnan for overseas did so in the later emigrations of the late 1830s, the 1840s and 1850s, most to Australia and New Zealand. They appear to have preferred and been able to stay home till then for two main reasons. The first and earlier was because of understanding from estate owners who overlooked or tolerated the older agricultural population – Alexander MacLean of Ardgour (1764–1855) in particular was a kind and sympathetic landowner-cum-chief.[3] The second was the availability of work on the new roads and canal. On account of the latter, when quantifying identification of the poor/maladaptive/unfortunate had become a sophisticated and national economic phenomenon, given the good fortune of many British 'empty' spaces, emigration of one sort or another was inevitable. The notion of cruelty, or of the discountenancing of various apparently unquantifiable elements of human life – some concept of waste, an optimum people/acre scale, a sensitivity to notions of ownership in common, least harmful land use – were always overruled, or mitigated at least, by the argument that most of the displaced people were simply shifting, almost certainly to their own benefit, within one huge, expanding juridico-political kingdom. As we refine the practice of improvement so shall we evict. Many reliable documents, including the six-inch-to-the-mile Ordnance Survey maps of the Glenfinnan and Callop area, which were surveyed in the 1870s, and to which I will refer, *inter alia (et inter documenta alia)*, point generally to a later leaving, to a change of people, occupations and lives, all within a general rural decline and the radical conceptual shift, varyingly conceived, from kin-ism to nation-ism, from hospitality and social bonds to un-remitting commerce. But, in some ways, there was also the retention of more local Gaelic society than I had imagined, or had the interest or ability to investigate when I lived there. The accuracies of various maps also show subtleties of place names and (stone) house positionings of which I could not have been aware as a boy (and nobody thought to teach me). While I knew from *Moidart or among the Clanranald,* by the priest Maighstir Tearlach MacDonald (1835–1894), that most of the Catholic Glenfinnan people who emigrated did so late, after the potato failure year of 1846–7, and to the east of the Australian Bight, I knew almost nothing of any emigration from Callop and the mile or so of land between Kinlocheil and the Glenfinnan line at Allt na Crìche [Boundary Burn].

There were many more people than I imagined living there into the 1880s. The dried cow dung I dug in for worms on the old pasture below Craigag was an unimaginable thing of the past by 1960, and only twenty-one or two years before I set foot in Craigag Lodge three names of farms near Calap were still in use (Altlaig, Dalriach and Mealdamh) that I have never heard spoken.[4] My photographs showed the early days of the last agricultural neglect.

With more information from *documenta alia* – archival documents, church records, maps and photographs – there is now a much more complete historical description of the place, over more than twenty decades going back from 1953 to 1743. With that knowledge, for me there springs more surprise than anything else, surprise that my childhood place was even as Gaelic as it was in the 1940s after all that had happened there. Indeed only a faint reverberation of the old consciousness was left by the middle of the twentieth century. The old bare stretch of boggy land where Lochan Dubh Tòrr an Tairbeirt [Black Lochan of the Hill of the Isthmus] is, and the land on the left of the photos, Blàr Creagach [Rocky (Peat) Moss] (which the little road (to the isles) skirted to the northward, and which extended south from solider land to the lochan),[5] is so much changed today.

It all has a much more eloquent past which has sunk into its peaty and riverine soils, a world of farms and pendicles of farms, shimmerings in long-gone sunshines, early wafting smokes on crisp winter mornings, glows of peat embers in the darkness. Certainly homes and traditional Gaelic farming life, involving perhaps as many as thirty people, probably reflecting subdivisions as favoured families became extended families, have disappeared, and had probably just about disappeared by 1840, and not just in a quadrilateral marked by Craigag and West Drumsallie, Callop and Drumfern. There and in the wider Ardgour–Locheil area there have been incomers and changes in tenants, but more outgoers from the land – my assumptions were accurately, but only generally, described by the general Highlander migration and emigration theorem. Readings of the censuses and other latter-day papers show that the deepening touch of commerce in this corner of Gaelic Scotland forced dyke-building, shepherding and gamekeeping on local Gaels, and also mobility and speculativeness on those who chose not to move away or to emigrate.[6] There have been changes in the uses of the land, all leaving hard-to-find links with the old, more Gaelic past, which I confess fascinates me.

For the moment though, the startling observation is that by 1980 many of the traces of my old boyhood world of only a few rugged but local horizons were on the way to obliteration, in part because of the influences of a pulp mill near Corpach opened in 1963. It was far from the first industry to be introduced to Lochaber, especially to Fort William, but it brought in what appears to me, understandably, to be abnormal continental forest in a west coast temperate environment.[7] It also brought in new people, blanketed a few old country places with houses, council housing 'estates', and other buildings, leaving what felt to me like neglected, no-man's-areas (like Camaghael and Corpach Moss); it deepened the commitment to the automobile and commerce, and added new chemicals to that physical world, and turned many a rural hand from the cow's teat, the flaughter spade, the peat-cutter, the plough, the pick and spade, and the scythe (Flemish or not[8]).

There is a black-and-white photograph by Donald MacCul-loch,[9] in Somerled MacMillan's *Bygone Lochaber,* taken in or not long before 1951, from somewhere on or near Joe MacLeod's property, between Corribeg and Kinlocheil, looking to the more Gaelic, and Catholic, west. Joe MacLeod was much more of a cultural focal point than I knew.[10] Although there are telegraph and/or telephone poles by the railway line, the old photograph still evokes and conjures the old soft, humid, and lovely myrtle-y world I knew, with its old human markers and relics tucked away, neglected and crumbling, harking back to ever more Highland days, but I still wish I had all of my own pictures. Perhaps Gavin Maxwell made some like them – he lived at Craigag Lodge for a while before we got there[11] – but I have never seen any of Callop but my own. Robert Moyes Adam (1885–1967), the ornithologist, botanist, Highland mountain and tree lover, and photographer, to whose extensive work I make reference, made many exposures of Glenfinnan, the Callop River and Loch Shiel over the years, but none of the Callop buildings or Craigag Lodge.[12]

The old one-storey Highland stone farm at Callop, a speck in the photographs, stood under the north Ardgour hills a mile off to the south, beyond the Callop River (the main part of which Somerled MacMillan (1909–1977) wrote had marked the shire boundary since 1633 when Archibald, Lord Lorne had it altered from the Sound of Mull to suit his purposes[13]). It was not like the roofless byre I remember seeing somewhere near Torebane [Torr Bàn] or Kinlocheil [Ceann Loch Iall], from the height of a vehicle (I don't remember any bus service past Craigag, although one might have run; there had been a coach service between Mallaig and Fort William before the railway opened on April Fool's Day 1901, and a new stone coach-house). That old, thick, double stone-walled, derelict byre – perhaps Hebridean, using an old simple classification of black houses – stood on the north side of the road and I did not see it in 2002.

The latest road had been made the master of the scene as though nothing else mattered. It had changed the old course, levelling little hills and hardwoods, dismissing old turns, rationalising anew, and funnelling traffic at speed, east and west, at the same time no less. Once or twice I spied the old road to the right on its way to disappearance. The old building I remember was chimney-less and had rounded ends that were typical of a solid old Highland house of tacksmen and the well-established main tenantry before the architecture was changed, much longer ago – perhaps it was an old MacPhee home, there were MacPhees in that part,[14] now almost a haunting, like the MacVeans. The building marked just to the north of the road on the Langlands map in 1801 is surely the same building.

When I was boy at Craigag I didn't realise that the poorer folks' homes had lang syne disappeared for ever. Sadly too I had not realised that those people's less permanent, cruck-type, as well as simpler turf and stone and withy homes with thatched roofs had still been a widespread feature of the local landscape into the 1890s. When the railway building firm of Lucas & Aird advertised for Highland workers for the West Highland Railway in the 1890s it wrote that 'comfortable hutting is provided, but Messrs Lucas & Aird will gladly give every facility for those who prefer it to erect Turf Dwellings.'[15] The reporter who covered HM Queen Victoria's drive, with John Brown and others, from Lord Abinger's new Inverlochy mansion to Kinlocheil, reported in *The Scotsman* of 11 September 1873 the thatched cottages dotting the Ardgour side of Loch Eil. A few days later, when the queen drove further west, to Glenfinnan, the reporter wrote of the 'several beautiful woods' she drove through on the north side of Loch Eil, and of 'a number of small cottages built in a truly Highland style, a hole in the middle of their thatched roofs serving as an outlet for the smoke which curled lazily upward.' The report was telegraphed to Edinburgh for inclusion in *The Scotsman* of 16 September 1873.[16]

Economic changes, though generally not including evictions, had driven many of the earlier generations of those folk hither and yon in the great empire, and their physical remains had decayed and merged with the forgotten and the lost.[17] There were also among the travellers, the shrewd, ready to imitate their old superiors, and get rich far away where old social and economic stratifications could no longer tether them, in the Carolinas and other American states, in Nova Scotia, out West on the prairies, in Australia, in New Zealand, in Bernice (in British Guiana), in the West Indies, and other places. The echoes and traces of the simpler folk however are only for the thoughtful and the archaeologist, although many of the needed deductions about them stand out from old statistics, if not yet from the earth itself. There is still a lot to be discovered about the Old World in the New, in Callop and Ardgour and Glenfinnan's case, in Australia.

Behind the Callop farmhouse there was a speckle of shrubby trees among the ubiquitous heather and bracken up between the two main Callop tributaries, given on modern, post-1950, Ordnance Survey one-inch maps as Allt na Cruaiche [Stream of the Rounded Hill] and Allt na Teanga Duibhe [Black Tongue Water]. These tributaries rise in two complex peaks to the south, Sgur Craobh a' Chaoruinn [Crag of the Rowan Tree] and Meall nan Damh [Hill of the Stags] (names that were transcribed/given in 1815 by surveyor James Wingate, Alloa, as Scur n' craobh Cousin and Mealldamh in RHP89887, and then repeated in 1820, Scur n Craobh Cous[/r]in and Mealldaimh, by John Thomson the map-maker whose atlas of Scotland was published in 1832, before the Ordnance Survey). There is only the Allt an Fhaing sheep reference[18] to mock the memory of the older cattle society of the Gael, and it appears on the six-inch OS map of the 1870s. The people's music and tongues are silent now and it is often only from analogues that the old world begins to show its face again. Too late, why bother about it, say some, but not I.

Perhaps in the lost photographs, against the southern-western sky, there was a line of mountains, called by twentieth-century OS mappers, Meall na h-Àiridh [Hill of the Summer (cattle) Pasture], Meall a' Bhainne [Hill of the Milk], Sgòr nan Cearc [Crag of the Hens/Grouse], Sgòr Craobh a' Chaoruinn [Crag of the Rowan Tree], all of which divided the Callop and its tributaries where they

flowed northward, from their ultimate destination, Loch Shiel, to
the west, just beyond. Since those hills' western steep slopes rising
from Loch Shiel were only indented (and to no great depth) at
Giuthasachan [Giusachan], the names, at least the names of the
northerly two hills, Meall na h-Àiridh and Meall a' Bhainne belong
to the Callop farm and give it a power and command in black cattle
days that it never had when I lived at Craigag. If there were any
serious consideration for early boundary makers it was that the
Callop turns west and flows into fresh water Loch Shiel (the
potential dispute being whether Calap lay in Sunart or Ardgour).

   What were the pre-1633 bounds of the Callop farm – did they
reach, at an early time, as far as the Loch Shiel shore and include the
precipitous land from Giuthasachan (also given sometimes as
Guesachan) up to the Callop (at Sgeir an Rò[i]n [Seal Skerry])?
(Not for the sun sat they on that rock.) The answer was no in the
1790s, and no in 1815, except one must note that one 1870s
MacVean place name lying on the Loch Shiel/Sunart side hints
otherwise (for some time unknown – an Allt Feadan Mhic
Bheathain drains into Loch Shiel), since at least one prominent
MacVean family was associated with Callop, but only briefly that is
known about, in the early nineteenth century – I have found no
earlier records. In the sketch of the Calap property, part of the
Ardgour estate in 1815, the boundary is the same as the Ardnamurchan (and Sunart)–Ardgour parish line (excluding the upper
Loch Shiel shore-land from the Callop property – this was owned
by 'Sir James Riddell'). The six-inch OS map of *c*. 1870 shows this
division running a little east of south from the Callop River,
through Lochan Dubh Ghlaic [Black Hollow Lochan or Black
Valley Lochan], following Allt Dubh Ghlaic, then running via the
summits of Meall a' Bhainne and Scur n' Circe and Scur n' Craobh
Cousin, a watershed line. This demarcation is more detailed than
the description given in the mid 1790s (Old Statistical Account
[OSA]) and 1840s (New Statistical Account [NSA]), but in 1902, it
appears that this watershed line still marked off the western limits of
the Callop farm (and Kilmallie parish). This boundary gave the
Callop farm small-vessel, freshwater access, via Loch and River
Shiel, to the Atlantic.[19] James Riddell bought Ardnamurchan and
Sunart and Kinlochaline in 1767 from James Montgomery, who

had obtained the lands from the lead miner, Sir Alexander Murray of Stanhope in the same year (neither the traditional Highland owner).

Assuming that the Ardgour estate, by some undiscovered definition, was bordered by the watersheds of fresh waters that drained both northward into saltwater Loch Eil and eastward into saltwater Loch Linnhe, then the Callop farm, lying in land that drains into freshwater Loch Shiel, may have belonged originally to Sunart and become a later bone of contention, or perhaps it always was slightly contestable, mountain versus river as prime definer. With very steep mountains rising out of upper-east-side Loch Shiel it is conceivable that this northerly, Sunart part of the Ardnamurchan parish was seen as trespassable by the occupants of Callop (and others), and/or as a neutral outlook point watching a main cattle trade artery, hence perhaps the MacVean place name on the Loch Shiel side of the watershed. Perhaps there was even some right of way allowed or some sense of neutral guardianship inhering.

From the point of view of Catholic Clanranald country, the wooded Callop pass was the one obvious entry point for enemy soldiers from Fort William, and undoubtedly Mac Iain Òig's Glenaladale, as guardian of that pass (owning land on the north of the Callop River), would have maintained at least potential control over the Sunart corner on the south shore of the river where it meets the loch – how the Gaelic Ardgour MacLeans stood in this guardianship is not known. In commercial years the pass had a droving significance to be discussed later. In any case, given the importance of placing strong families in borderlands, there may have been a simple military explanation for the part played by the MacVeans or a particular MacVean.

Was the main old Highland farm building at Callop, in 1800, on the same site as the main building I knew, or was it somewhere else? I don't recollect cattle of any sort on the hills behind Callop, although at least one cow was milked in the stable part of the stone farmhouse, and there was a family of domesticated goats. I remember no sheep. Calum Lowrie the gamekeeper was the only working man I was aware of. Certainly in the photograph, shown to the south, were the rough hills, Meall na Cuartaige [Hill of the Little Circle], just a degree or two west of south, Meall nan Damh

[Hill of the Stags], much taller, to the south, then Glas Bheinn [Grey Mountain] and Meall nam Maigheach [Hill of the Hares], to the south-south-east and to the south-east. I never saw a hare in Craigag or Callop.

Beyond the hills south of Callop farm lay what to me was the mysterious, soft-sounding Cona Glen − I don't remember that I realised that Craigag then was part of the 'lands and estate of Conaglen';[20] I used to hear Cona Glen talked about at home but have never seen it, except the western, high land part in latter-day climbers' digital photographs where it was rough sub-arctic pasture near the summits. It ran as west–east as Locheil. I wanted to go to Cona Glen and other places but my two older half-brothers didn't have the patience when they were home from Dollar to wait for a sprat to catch up. In any case, at Callop in those days there was another house, which must have been a lot more than a bothy though it seems in my mind's eye to have had no well-worn, permanent aura to it. It stood near the main old farm building, but to its west a little. It was the other dot on the one-inch Ordnance Survey, and other maps of the day, and is still represented on the 1997 Landranger sheet 40 (1:50,000). It's as though it had a long story attaching to it, and as though some day it may have a usefulness (if indeed it is neglected just now). I don't know when it was built. It would not have had much definition in my old photograph, although the buildings' positions had a hydrological significance that I have not noticed until recently. The other building stood near a tiny tumbling burn I've long forgotten about which fed into the Callop near where a ford had been in olden times and yards west of where in 1970 there was still the wooden footbridge I had crossed many times from Craigag to visit the MacVarishes − in retrospect I see the footbridge as having been fairly new, and I can see the shingly crossing at the joining two streams just west of it. Sarah MacVarish lived in the little home (and somewhere between Mrs MacVarish's and the little tributary was where the midden was). That newish wooden bridge near the ford, perhaps even the little house, may have been built, the latter perhaps on an older house site, to accommodate Sarah MacVarish and her family of displaced children during the last years of the Hitler war. If that were so then the farm at Callop never merited a bridge approach in all its Gaelic centuries. At least since 1633 Callop was probably approached, not from the north or north-east but from the east, perhaps from the farm at Drumfern. In this case the Callop would have been forded upstream. The road that Thomas Telford improved and built in the 1800s made the radical intrusion. In the 1872 survey for the six-inch map there is a footbridge crossing the Allt Dubhaidh a hundred yards to the east but still only fording access to the main farm at Callop. Presumably most of the *drochaid* names belong to the improver-road building age. Geographically the Callop farm was defendable Gaelic border-land, better unimproved.

I'm sure there was an aura of emptiness to both buildings in 1970 because we didn't walk over to explore. That was when, visiting from Toronto, I first showed M the place that was increasingly inspiring my deepening interests in Gaelic Scotland. The old, dignified Cameron man living in the main farm was gone by 1966; I remember in Edinburgh my mother telling me that one day she had met him in Tollcross, far from his home. The Callop farm was sold by the Earl of Morton in 1953 and that is surely when what I knew withered awa'. One of the houses at Callop, for a time (for two or three years from about 1980), was the home of the fiddler-accordionist Farquhar MacRae.[21] I know that Sarah Mac-Varish had moved away from the other home by 1954 or 1955 because I spent part of a summer with her, her two foster children and some of the adopted family I had known from Callop – perhaps they were orphans – at Torlundy [Tòrr Lunndaidh], a stone farm-steading owned by the Canadian rancher Joseph Hobbs, not far south of Lundy Bridge, all a few miles north of Nevis Bridge on the Fort William to Spean Bridge road.[22] I had cycled on my three-speed channel-derailleur Dawes, there and back, about 138 miles each way, through Glencoe and Glenorchy, through bonnie Strathyre of the little rose gardens, a day each way. I still remember the first miles leaving Torlundy that day so long ago – it's that memory of there that I must cherish. The grass began at the road's edge, no wasteful shoulder, and there was that old Highland country aroma, unique; I remember it immediately.

Going north I remember the keen pleasure climbing the hill on the bicycle, and later on a motorcycle, out of Lowland Callendar with its gentle meander, into Highland Scotland. Hilly turns in old hardwoods, cats' eyes on new black-top, a barn owl's silent swoop on an innocent motorcyclist. I remember the wet grassy and heathery roadsides from Loch Lubnaig to Glenogle and from the Glenogle Pass, and all the way to Glenfinnan, all somehow mine, no one else's even in the marrow of my bones. I can still smell it all in a thoughtful pause, the bell heather, the rushes and nodding bog cottons, the myrtle, the harebells, the fragrant orchids tucked away, cinquefoils, all the profoundest poignance. I remember the gloomy half-finished lochans near Achallader, the great, lonely Campbell northern outlook farm guarding the old drove-road south. I still hear the rivulets' musical tinklings and see the crystally cold waters over the rounded granite cobblestones somewhere at the top of Glencoe. Even by bicycle, my memories of Gaelic Scotland have something strongly in common with the deepest concepts of home and small communities that are ingrained in the old walking and riding days when a mile was much more than a minute. Automobiles were by no means yet the corrupters of distance and locale, and the skies, even if often packed with amorphous cloud, were pure, and dark, dark and silent on winters' nights. Many people were alive then whose memories were of days when the only hearable engine was in a steamboat. Man's mind has changed.

In about 1970, only about fifteen years later (although it seemed an almost unbridgeable age) M and I visited Mrs MacVarish at 4 Carn Dearg, in a small, grey, drizzled council housing estate of stippled two-storey buildings at Claggan, over the Nevis river, on the northerly edge of greater Fort William – that was the last time I saw her. The image of the profile of her kindly, wrinkled old face, and of her arthritic, crooked old fingers entwined around a glass of whisky lingers in my mind's eye. Although she was old, she immediately controlled one inadvertent slip into gossip that a thought of mine, and the drams, had evoked; she was ingenuous and staunch and much more motherly than I had known, and knew. I see remarkable resemblances between her and a number of older Gaels I've photographed in rural Inverness County: Katie MacDonald (of the 'Anthony' MacDonalds from Eigg) at Sam Batherson's in Troy when she was over a hundred; old Maggie

MacEachern (Hillsdale), Duncan Peter Campbell's wife, in Glencoe; and Lisa Kennedy, the old travelling spinner I met about 1977 in the senior citizens' home in Inverness in her last years when she was well over a hundred. Those aged faces fronted consciousnesses that I imagined and that intrigued me almost to the point of enchantment. Something of my own unexplained mystery lay in those thoughts.

To me Sarah MacVarish had always been old; even in the 1940s she may have been closing in on sixty-five. She is the first of all the people I remember immediately when I think back on Craigag and Glenfinnan (just as Margaret 'Blue' MacLean from Orangedale and Valley Mills is the first of the women I remember when I look back on my early days in Inverness County, Cape Breton[23]). Thinking back to the visit at Carn Dearg, and to the kindly old face of Maggie Campbell from Glencoe in Cape Breton, it is conceivable that Sarah MacVarish was about ninety in 1970, which would mean that she had been born perhaps as early as 1880, only thirty years after the emigrations to Australia, and among a small number of people whose memories included direct memories of Waterloo. If she were a local person, she would have remembered Locheil-side before the railway. She would have known what happened at Lochan Dubh Tòrr an Tairbeirt on the order of MacAlpine's son. She would have perhaps seen the valley of the Finnan before the official opening of the Mallaig branch of the West Highland Railway and its spectacular concrete viaduct over the river, in 1901. Were there one, she would have seen the last droves of cattle along Loch Eil-side and in Ardgour – the Kyle Rhea crossing from Skye was last used by drovers in 1906.

When I last met her I was only there to explain wordlessly to her that she had meant a lot to me and to say farewell. I was too innocent then of what had happened to Gaelic Scotland, too innocent of the knowledge that the complex world of the ordinary folk of Gaelic Scotland was still in many ways untold and was not to be simply unearthed from a book in any library, and that few, and largely ignored, were the memories of the last Gaels like Sarah MacVarish. I had yet to discover the psychology of fear and guilt that underlay such national ignoring and derogating, in large part because a sophisticated and domineering national educational system was at the heart of the superficial side of the problem. The older Highland Glenfinnan, and Callop people, however, gave me much more valuable things from native kindnesses, which I could only absorb unconsciously, and then for a reason which sometimes I might have disparaged as inadequate on which to construct an adult lifetime of curiosity, one that I still live. There is no plane beyond kindness.

The day we were sitting in her living room, dark it was and plain, I had forgotten the name of the peat cutter I remember her using when she and her family were out on the bare moorish stretch near Lochan Dubh Tòrr an Tairbeirt, between the Callop and the Dubh Lighe [Dark Water], about where they *dos à dos* (doe-see-doe), about at the fifty-foot contour. After a moment's thought she told me the word was *toiresgian*. How selectively the memory works, and sometimes how tormented by later experiences and re-rememberings. I cannot forget the powerful heat from Mrs MacVarish's fire in her little house at Callop. I remember the bannocks she made on the girdle over that fire, and the thick barley broth in blue-decorated pottery, I remember the hens straying in, but for some reason any memories of the reek of peat that must have been everywhere in that little home, have gone. Sarah MacVarish almost certainly could have burnt nothing else. If coal was buyable from a lorry from Fort William (we didn't buy any, that I recall) she would have had to carry the hundredweight sacks from the road, as far away again as the peat source itself. All I can guess is that my older Callop memory of such a powerful Highland aroma had been replaced by the later recollection of that distinctive smell as my mother and I approached Lewis and Harris on the MacBrayne ferry from Uig in the north of Skye. That was in or around 1970. I didn't miss Scotland greatly, but a few indelible Highland images and thoughts were fixed even then and as near to magic as the boyhood ones. Almost all the homes in and near Tarbert in Harris must have been burning peat about 1970 because that oddly acrid aroma reached out to us, intimately, over the salty Minch. I had completely forgotten that smell at Callop and it was as distinctive to me as the sharp tang of myrtle I had not forgotten, and can never forget, from the treeless slopes of Druim Fada [The Long Ridge], from Kilmallie to Fassifern.

There must now be many years, perhaps as many as forty, since peat was burned at Callop. I have no memory of looking out and seeing the first smokes on a clear day. The peat hag I remember going to one spring or summer day over near the lochan is no longer visible, although perhaps one could find a depression amongst the conifers. I remember the moist shiny face of the peat to be cut, facing east. I remember the foot-long L-shaped metal cutter. I have never been to any other peat hag although I saw several in Lewis from the road, sometimes cut right down to the grey acid-schistose bedrock of the world. (When in those days I thought about Excalibur, I thought of the possibility of Jacobite basket-hilted swords' having been tossed into Lochan Dubh Tòrr an Tairbeirt in 1746 by some Gaelic hero, so affecting was my childhood, in English, but touched by an imagined Gaelic world of yesterday, the world that had absorbed so many Norse, Normans and Flemish.[24]) The Craigag photograph beside me shows that in front of the place there was what looks like perfectly good peat. I'm not sure that we ever cut or burnt it. Neither we nor any home at Callop had electricity and I would be surprised to learn that there was running water at Sarah MacVarish's, except from the nearby stream. I have no memory of any outhouse (or peat stack). Looking over the Callop River to Callop farm in those days you only saw shrubs and trees near the river; the country was exposed, heathery and alone, with a faintening echo of its past.

The Callop photographs – there were at least two in the strip – were clear enough because it was a shot that called for a small aperture. They were of no artistic merit, or so I thought the last few times I stumbled on them in some collection somewhere in Cape Breton. I would love to see them again, and the tiny snap of Joe MacLeod and his fellow railwayman, Joe MacVinish, posed, each on one knee, with their heavy work tools, somewhere on the incline in the railway line near Kinlocheil – it is misplaced too – how little I knew them. (I have found no record of Joe MacVinish to this day, 20 June 2007). Joe MacLeod made me a wooden whistle once, from a sappy branch, and showed me how to do it; he was only fifty-two when he died in 1953, and a great loss to local lore according to Calum MacLean – Joe had also given Somerled MacMillan information. (Another old snapshot, the one of me standing beside Pat Monaghan, in the midst of an adult (male) pipe-band on a broad playing field in Fort William, is also too well hidden – I couldn't even find the field in 2002 because the new town road system had made such changes, in propitiation of a strangely mutated power.)

The Callop shots were taken from a treeless but sheltering and almost-hiding-the-lodge shoulder of land, a *sròn,* on the Inverness-shire side of the Callop River which divides Inverness from Argyll (which line, with a vast but accidental eloquence follows the Allt Dubhaidh [Stream of the Black Goddess],[25] and then bisects Lochan Dubh Tòrr an Tairbeirt, a very ancient *portage* perhaps). The exposures had been made from just about where I accidentally found a yellow-hammer's nest in the heather when I was a little boy, the only one I have ever seen, just above where the path from Craigag Lodge to the road was met by the much narrower and rougher and older one from the south-east (the old trackish approach).

Like old Cameron, and Calum Lowrie, Sarah MacVarish was one of the last of the old generation of Gaels in Callop, but that she was a Gael at all was something I never noticed when I was a boy and that only began to fascinate me when I crawled out from under the mental burden of Presbyterian Edinburgh and wondered free.[26] Maybe everyone in Callop spoke English when I was around and reverted to Gaelic in private, although perhaps not all of the four home children who lived with Sarah MacVarish beginning during the war, picked the language up – they would have heard Sarah MacVarish talking to her two Cameron foster children in their mother tongue. I don't know yet when the others were moved from Clydeside but imagine that the Battle of Britain had such an effect, and perhaps also the Nazi atomic bomb project in the war's later years – at least one boy from Edinburgh who still lives in Blaich in Ardgour to the east, was boarded out from Edinburgh in 1945. It is apparently known beyond doubt that there were no unilingual Gaelic speakers from Kinlocheil east to Fort William by 1931 – goodness gracious, widespread bilingualism among the young was recorded by the minister of Kilmallie, the 'Reverend Mr Alexander Fraser',[27] as early as 1792, before, and probably explaining in part, the Gaelic caricaturisms of Walter Scott's friend, Alasdair Fiadhaich [Wild Alasdair] (MacDonell of Glengarry), the man who hated Telford's Caledonian Canal and started the Club of True Highlanders – I am unaware of his reaction to the road to Loch nan Ceall on the Atlantic coast from the Lochy. To some degree as yet unascertained by me, this threat on the older language probably also explained the sympathetic population policies of Alexander MacLean of Ardgour of the Royals, who spoke Gaelic. In this too there is the early powerful, improving influence of John Cameron, first of Fassifern, which will some day fit much more clearly into an understanding of Cameron land expansion south-ward and the spreading of trade in the West Highlands. (The Fogo and Campbell Loch Etive Trading Company based at Inveresragan, 1729–1754, dealing in brandy, tobacco and other things – alum, hoops, buckram, nails, linen among them – had creditors from Lochaber to Edinburgh and Glasgow[28]).

This whole story, a study in places, more and more a study I admit, begins with and comes from memories remembered and remem-bered again, loved and inspiring always, simply because they had to be, desperately needed sometimes, and in ways that I have only come to understand lately. Of consequent importance is the inadequate-ness and misleadingness of some of those memories, so from those fractions and blurs I have found myself prompted to try to reconstruct a little of the history of the place where I was a boy. That history interests me as no other local history does and, pre-1800, much more must be inferred from known larger-scale events than read in any local person's writings. Where ordinary, illiterate people are con-cerned, the depth and breadth of an older consciousness (including perhaps many relics of an ancient legal system, a coexistent found in customs of overlooked worth) is only ever to be inferred, alas, although the power and value to history of folk memory is at last being acknowledged and summoned from its dim-lit corners.

It is from that deep-seated local interest, for me, that all Highland Gaels, the Gaelo-Pictish period, the ferment of the Gaelo-Norse period, Clan Donald and the Norse, the infiltration and plantation of Normans and the Normanised into medieval, non-Norman (but polyglot) place we call Scotland, the varying rate of Gaelicising of Norman landowners and their manipulation of their hero-story-inspired Gaelic tenantry, and the Lowland Christian Reformation become vitally important, and my starting point for enquiry. The Gaels and western Gaelo-Norse on one hand, and the Franco-Norse and Saxon on the other, embodied different understandings of inheritance of land and power, the power of religion, law,[29] kinship structure, politics, country and kingship, and the distinctions, and more important, the unidentified distinctions, remain inadequately imagined and emphasised in much writing of Scottish medieval history. The war for Lowland 'Scottish' Normano-Saxon independence of English Normano-Saxon power (perceivable as a partial civil war), the linguistic subsumption of the Picts and the Norse into Gaelic society, the Gaelic Lordship of the Isles, with its own Gaelic ideas of independence (and its rise during the first phase of the English–French Hundred Years' War), the effects of the plague in the Saxon-Norman lands on MacDonald expansion policy, Scottish Gaelic and Irish affairs as a primary socio-political consideration, the long and brutal anti-Catholic and anti-Episcopal period from the sixteenth to the nineteenth centuries, all develop, always with the potential to confuse, if not approached with very keen objectivity or, if necessary, pronounced Gaelic bias.

The greatest difficulty has long been, and for most remains, that western Gaelo-Norse and Gaelic affairs in Scotland have to be extracted by inference and deduction from a paucity of contemporary primary documents (written by the winners who, in the case of Edward I of England, surely among many, also destroyed what he found of the Gaelic written legal record in 1291, such as it was or may have been), as well as from the many later works that try often, in my opinion, hopelessly and often thoughtlessly, to make Scotland (or Ireland for that matter) one.[30] Many of the anti-Campbell military savageries by Gaels, in the seventeenth century, are explainable as having been, at heart, the product of the radical conflict of two linguo-cultures and perhaps elements of two legal systems that began in the time of the Canmore kings (1057–1286) when an organised just-post-Gaelic regal minority exploiting new European, Franco-Norman monastico-political concepts and techniques, spurred by overwhelming greed, managed, eventually, to dominate what became a new eastern heartland in the land of the Briton, Pict and Scot. When is a Scot not a Scot?

From the simple questions that come up, about Callop and

Craigag, a tiny Highland locale, come larger questions about Ardgour as a Gaelic (and MacLean) wedge between the Gael-ruling, arguably Flemish/Norman-in-origin Campbells of Argyll and the Norman-Gaelic Cameron chiefs (with their Gaelic followers, and with their more deeply adopted Gaelicness[31]). For centuries, on paper, all was in the control of various earls of Argyll, but a level down from superiority under the non-Gaelic Crown lay another, more personal consciousness which was never far from self-expression, called, at convenient times, by the usurper, rebelliousness. From that grasp a perspective deepens and you often see validity in what had been publicly presented, deliberately or thoughtlessly, as inexplicable, or savage, or unintelligent and disjointed events (not that savage, inexplicable and unintelligent events did not happen in the Gaelic world). That is a broad enough framework for a knowledge of Europe from long pre-Christian times, at least from the Hallstatt salt times, a history that reaches tantalisingly to the borders of China, and later everywhere the English empire and its armies reached. (The Maya and Cherokee evolved a similar political notion of independent, interlinked states or nexuses assembled with an urban core, with language in common which made their final suppression by the Spaniard invaders complicated and protracted.)

There were long periods when my own memories and thoughts lay dormant as I was preoccupied with other things, but there were times, one summer in particular at a common pasture in Cape Breton, contained by mixed maple-yellow birch-dominant forest on all sides, when, at no bidding but my imprisoning mind's, they became the only refuge from mental confusion and anomie, a gathering of ineffably delighting fragments laid down early, just by accident, un-understood, never interpreted, which afforded me peace enough to conceive that there might be another, more tranquil path to follow. Thus does one put down intellectual roots and develop assignments. I don't think I have changed those memories in the slightest, but of course, checking what is easily checkable, I see that I have, but never radically; some orders and dates are askew, little more. Perhaps I have not enough for you.

Some time in the middle to late 1970s, probably when an old friend was in the last stages of his graduate research work for the

Celtic department at an old once-Presbyterian American university, I was introduced to his professor, Charles Dunn (d. 24 July 2006, aged ninety, in Boston), who was visiting him in or near Glendale, Cape Breton. We were sitting in a car somewhere and the well-known, Scots-born Harvard scholar naturally asked me what it was that had attracted me to Highland affairs and studies. I felt nervous – it had been his book *The Highland Settler* that had decided me to move to Cape Breton in the summer of 1972. Besides I hadn't even really thought I was.

I told him simply that I had been a boy in Glenfinnan.

He thought for only a short moment and said, 'Yes, that would do it.'

I don't know what ran through his mind, but ever since, he (like his student) has been an intimate part of my thinking about Gaelic Scotland, part of a small world of people who, among many projects, try to understand what really happened to so many people, many, but by no means all, poor, vulnerable nearly all of them, and seldom understood perceptively for what they were and how they applied humanity to their physical world. So I have had, till recently, a Highland foster-brother in my thoughts and imaginings with whom I shared some fundamental imperative, an imperative for which I would sacrifice greatly. I have more than one, but not many, and they are all as close and as tight about me as many a Highland company facing an alien enemy. Something of that imperative still exists in strength and it contains a radical not easily shrugged.

This story, however, is also about a background cultural and linguistic persistence into the middle of the twentieth century that I had learned, one way or another, to assume to have been relatively uncomplicated and more than a little pervasive. Until John Mac-Donald (Mac Iain Òig, known to me now just as Captain John) left Glenaladale in the sheltered heart of Muideart [Moidart] for St John's Island (Prince Edward Island) in 1771/2, I had assumed some old-world stability for the ordinary people. I had assumed that it really wasn't until the great emigrations that began in the 1790s that much changed for EveryGael, and, where Glenfinnan was concerned, I had thought that it wasn't until the emigration to Australia in the late 1840s that the fabric of the old society was finally dismembered and allowed to drift and swirl far away on the salty breezes and the seagull's cry. And I was by and large right. And yet it is the Gaelicness of Glenfinnan that I remember – most of the older Highland folk, just a handful there actually were, were bilingual – perhaps there was one who spoke only Gaelic – and you could sense in that misty, pregnant pause between tongues another civilisation, one which did not hide its measure and its mannerly kindness from a boy. The current notion, a laudable one, 'let's make next year [2007] a year when Glenfinnan people learn to speak Gaelic' cannot but strike me as surprising – if they only knew what it was like, and I only glimpsed the tail end of that. Perhaps they do.

There was indeed, linguistic conservatism through the old patrimonies, from Lochiel and Ardgour and Sunart to Moidart lasting till the present, but the tale is far more complex than I had early thought. Economic changes had been going on since Ewen Cameron of Lochiel's time in the 1680s, and then particularly inspired by his grandson John Cameron of Fassifern starting well before the Forty-five, in Loch Eil and Ardgour. Urban Fort William, beside old Achadh an Todhair [Manure Field], on the heaving, but naturally controlled Atlantic, grew to be a strong fifth column – Norman power from *c.* 1250 concentrated in thick walls at Inverlochy, and maybe a little later at Glen Urquhart on Loch Ness, had precluded any pro-Gaelic capacity to stop invaders at Lismore or the Corran Narrows (the 'Current of Argour' for John Swettenham in 1750[32]), if there were such a desperate sense. In Moidart to the west, to some extent with the financial failure of the South Morar MacDonald family shortly before 1784, there was also an emerging native Gaelic commercialism and profiteering by people like the MacDonalds of Borrodale and Glenaladale which touched every man and put places like 'Raitland' and 'Inver Rosse' and 'Ardlash' and 'Oban [and] a Cave'[33] and the woods at 'Alny' in South Morar on current maps for about the first and last times.[34] There was also a Cameron presence in the new commercial sheep culture in South Morar and elsewhere. Captain John himself commented wryly, from Prince Edward Island, on the spread of alien sheep-farming practices, and the steal of greed. He was aware of the direction that his chief, Clanranald, had chosen, and he was right in detecting its break with Gaelic tradition; that chief's descendant, Ranald/Reginald George MacDonald of Clanranald (b. 1788), through his managers, especially the factors Robert Brown and Duncan Shaw, became a ruthlessly greedy kelper before divesting himself of almost his entire estate by 1838. On 30 January 1804, for a minor example, John MacDonald of Borrodale wrote to Robert Brown about his (Borrodale's) experiments to sell 'hoops and watlings from his estate in Morvern[,] in the Long Island.'[35] That Gaelic capitalist exploitation generally didn't last long (and perhaps was at its most successful in the Montreal-based North West Company) but emphasised the passing of the Gaelic subsistence community with its old cattle economy that did so well for many but was burning its last mad brightness during the Napoleonic Wars. In the early nineteenth century, estates had become investments and inevitably the outsiders (including Catholic gentry and people not at all unaware of many old Highland values and understandings, taken from Alasdair Fiadhaich MacDonell perhaps, or Walter Scott, or David Stewart of Garth's *Sketches*), more equipped perhaps to be ruthless, replaced the Highland would-be improvers, and the few club farmers,[36] and performed economic excisions from which the old folk suffered one way or another (often only remembered, distortingly, because the improver was not a local Gael). The Camerons of Glendessary, after the Duke of Argyll, had the largest estate in Morvern from the first decade of the eighteenth century until they went bankrupt in 1775–6 (Morvern is peninsular, part of old Gaeldom, and separated from Ardgour to its north by another Tairbeart). Other Camerons were earlier in Ardgour. Often it is only from old letters and maps that the older world demography can be conjured, unless like me, you remember Sarah MacVarish, Joe MacLeod, John 'the post' and Chirsty, Angie 'the bar' MacDonald, the MacKellaigs and the Gillieses. From them there sprang thoughts of another world altogether. Ah, such simple and forlorn echoes!

My most positive, influencing, early memories, of the years before I reached about eleven were very seldom of Edinburgh and almost always of Craigag and Callop and Glenfinnan, and other local places I was taken to in the area (Giuthasachan in Ardgour, Loch Ailort in

Arisaig, Morar silver sands and Lochan nan Sleubhach in Glenaladale's Moidart). The warm scents of the country, dew beading on primroses, particular little hazel trees, sense of distance, the mighty heights of mountains to a small boy, the sense of home and future, for me are Highland, and so shall I die. Any important parts of my adult work have been the result of the power of those often disjointed memories of well over fifty years ago when I was a boy dreaming of having a Highland farm and living and dying among the Highland mountains of home. I assumed that there would be a lifelong continuity. Like my mother tongue, those few, early memories got very deeply ingrained. Most important was my sense of kindliness from Gaels. My fundamental concepts of a mountain, a stream, and a stream bank, for decades were, in some ways still are, West Highland – the mighty Canadian Rockies are gauche, staggering, strata-tilted and unbelievable exaggerations, hardly old enough to handle whisky. The rivers in Cape Breton are wild, uncontrolled profligate things in the spring, ever-changing courses, drowning bottom-lands with the dross of time, unsettling, nomadic – to me Highland mountains and streams, riotous and changing as they undoubtedly were, are forever fixed, integrals of an older world, and my standard. The ancient bard lying by the stream, near the old oak tree in my Sar-Obair is I.

> *O càraibh mi ri taobh nan allt,*
> *A shiubhlas mall le ceumaibh ciùin,*
> *Fo sgàil a bharraich leag mo cheann,*
> *'S bi thus' a ghrian ro-chairdeil rium.*

> [O lay me by the banks of rills,
> Which slowly flow in measures mellow;
> In the shade of branches lay my head,
> And wax thou, sun, thy warmth on me.][37]

I've outgrown most of my shame at not speaking Gaelic; the strong traces of some geographical and cultural distinctness laid down in my mind from that far-off place, in English, have qualified me independently, and I am by no means alone, although lonelier as the years pass on and a complex, proud old tradition slips away from this world for ever. Knowledge that I am still building up, the significance of the occasional floodings of the Callop River, and furrows high on Tom na h-Àiridh (photographed by Robert Adam on 21 September 1920[38]), for example, often show my lack of perception, till I grew older, till I grew into my seventh decade, but that shortcoming has not yet dampened the enthusiasm so simply triggered. My work has nearly always been, and is, in grateful acknowledgement of my memories' calming and stabilising effects (and at times it has been strident because of a deep sadness I have always felt about what happened to the old, extraordinary, kindly folk I knew). Little things like the yellowhammer's eggs, so unforgettably scribbled in brownish mauve, like the eleven tiny speckled eggs I found, and could not find again, in the wren's nest in that little tuft of grass on the pasture over the road between Craigag and the Callop River, like the outline of feral goats with their long swept-back horns and matted, shaggy coats against the southern skyline of Ardgour, like an Attlee friend of my father's visiting to spy the rare gold-crested 'wren', these are among my indelible mental collection. Although none of these were photographed, and I have memories of other lost photographs, that doesn't matter and never has. Atlee meant next to nothing to me. Sarah MacVarish and John 'the post' and others left unforgettable traces.

2

Craigag/Cregag/*Creagag*/Craigegg

Whatever he knew about the actual building, older farm and acreage, 'Craigag is mentioned, with his interpretation of the name, in Somerled MacMillan's *Bygone Lochaber* in his appended list of place names. Elsewhere in the text, if carefully read, one finds what can only be honest and misunderstood hints about the place. MacMillan used basic primary sources for his book, Acts of Parliament, sasine records, Privy Council records, exchequer records, Lordship of the Isles records, local lore, among many others, and in years to boot when there was no easy access to indexed historical documents as there is now. In his bibliography he did not cite *Memoirs of Sir Ewen Cameron of Lochiel* in either manuscript or published (1842) form. He cited in a general way, making an editorially undistinguished text, which very often lacks specific attributions. With a welter of names and material to deal with, MacMillan did not use the 1872 Ordnance Survey six-inch maps pertaining to Craigag and Callop, and, to my knowledge, he did not use the censuses. He left out an unknown amount of the subtenantry, canting later superficial thinking in favour of the slightly powerful, majority bilingual middle class. Yet, no matter those and other shortcomings (the Presbyterian stance is transparent as is the strange almost schizophrenic readiness to excoriate Cumberland and his troops and almost proudly trumpet that two MacMillans sought to rat on the bonnie prince for the money), it is a remarkable Highland work on Lochaber in English, a collection of genealogies of the main families, many tantalisingly incomplete, but weighted with sound background genealogical and historical research, privately presented. It is useable, interpretable and amenable to revision, and I respectfully revise some of it here.

MacMillan proclaimed that the Camerons of Locheil were Norman, not Gaelic in origin. They were latterly clearers in the nineteenth century, and this plausible supposition, perhaps conceivable as an author's bias, is a *sine qua non* for the genealogist and the student of Gaelic affairs from late medieval times who seeks for understanding of local power balances, placings of tenant farmers, overlooked explanations of behaviours, and contemporary conceptualisings. The work is less concerned with the great changes of the Victorian era than it might be. 'Craigag' however is listed in one of the many subheadings under Fort William in the 1841 census and is marked as Cregag on the 1872 survey for the six-inch maps, as well as in earlier maps and documents in the nineteenth century. The most informative, the 1872 six-inch map shows three buildings not far from the north bank of the Callop. On the modern, post-World War Two twentieth-century Ordnance Survey maps, 'Craigag' only appears as part of Craigag Lodge, the same home we lived in high on the shoulder above what I knew as an old cattle pasture, at least the riverside part.

The older Cregag is gone, was gone in 1946 with no self-explanatory trace obvious to a boy that I can recall, or to a researcher-cartographer.[1] The name Cregag/Craigag represents a post-1876 reversion to the old north-of-the-Callop River name for a farm. I don't remember outlines of houses or other buildings near the river, although I often passed that way. Then again, racking my memories, when you were near the height of land on the road near the bridge to Callop there was, perhaps, a rubbly irregularity of the unwooded surface, but it meant nothing to me and I can barely recall it.

The posh new Craigag Lodge high on its shoulder was built between 1874 and 1876 as a shooting lodge for the late-Victorian gentry, before the one-track West Highland Railway extension was driven through from Fort William to the fishing port of Mallaig in North Morar, passing close behind Craigag *c.* 1900.[2] (Craigag/Cregag and Craigag Lodge were undistinguished in the four homes listed under 'Callop' on census day in 1881 – it must have been unoccupied.) Craigag Lodge is not marked on the 1870s' OS six-inch maps while many drystane-dyke sheep fanks are elsewhere, showing neatly that the intenser, Victorian deer-hunting, tweedy gunners on the hills, final phenomenon (to that point), in some places, still lay just ahead.)[3] Among the papers of the D. and J.H. Campbell firm of solicitors in Edinburgh are the accounts of the estates of the Earl of Morton for 1874–6 which include a record of work on the 'Calass' shooting lodge (a clerical felicity over the geminated 's', the first written as the old non-terminal 's' was, duly changed to Calap).[4]

My father rented Craigag Lodge for fifty pounds a year, he told me, just after the war when there was rationing, little or no tropical fruit anywhere in Britain, general economic depression and little regenerating interest in hunting and shooting lodges.[5] Craigag Lodge was a big one-storey, double slate-roofed building, the biggest house I have ever lived in. It is somewhere recorded that it was over a hundred feet long and nearly eighty wide but that is perhaps an exaggeration. The building, like Glenfinnan church, was built on a raised, levelled plinth at the north of a little flat land a hundred yards deep, perhaps more, deep enough to allow the building to be almost hidden from all but above, and later the eyes passing by on the old steam train. The inverted double-Vs of the roof, seen best in the gable ends, are unusual – the only other similar roof that I know in the area is also on Morton land, the two-storied house built in 1858 at Aryhoulan in the lands and estate of Conaglen in Ardgour.

Craigag was oriented roughly north-east to south-west, although the doorway I knew and used was on the east side of the building, toward the back/north, beyond the long multi-paned Jack Frost window, looking to the giant *roche moutonnée* of Ben Nevis behind Fort William. Only on clear days could you see the great mountain, and from the two gable-end windows the same went for the tops of all the Ardgour hills over the plot of rhododendrons at the west of the gate through the fence – perhaps rhododendrons are a reliable marker of something. Between the back of the house and the line there used to be a tall old birch tree, perhaps there were two; the image of a hammock lingers. We had a chopping block, which was by the closer birch. An old hen-house was also behind the house though to the west a little – I remember it because some of our hens preferred to lay in their own scrabbled burrows and we had to hunt for the eggs in strange strata of fowl detritus. There was a flattish area to the Glenfinnan side of the house where the stags butted heads and belled in rutting season. They even signalled their knowing of the passing of the deer hunting season by occasionally taking shelter hard against the west side of the house on the raised ground. To a Lowland city person like my mother, deer began as baleful, alien monsters. I don't remember exploring the flat area to the westward, but it was part of the mountain tongue that the railway tunnel cut through. To narrow the perspective, Craigag Lodge's primary view was south into Ardgour but with glimpses openly to the east and much less so to the west.

Very few were the cars on the little old road in those days. The roof of Craigag Lodge leaked and all the rooms except the living room (where we had an open fire, and the China-couple nodded silently on the mantle) and the kitchen (where the black range was) were almost always damp, but I was only told that. I have only happy memories of Craigag. Paraffin lamps, tiny to large, mine with a blue glass shield, mustard-coloured earthenware hot-water bottles with places for your feet on either side of the filling neck, the long horizontal window of about a dozen panes looking east, near the kitchen, where Jack Frost occasionally formed ferny swirlings, stags belling, the train puffing hard up the incline from Kinloch Eil, past Joe MacLeod and Joe MacVinish's bothy in the cutting (just west of the stream/burn), always at roughly the same time, at least one firing the bracken with its sparks and lighting the darkening sky in the autumn, filling the air with charcoal scents I only knew as a boy. In my mind at Craigag I could circle high on the breezes like the ragged-winged buzzards that hunted the heathers; the wind was a magical power. Galloping through the heather gave one legs of steel. Midges, and clegs, and driving and drizzling rain only hint now and again at the fringes of my recollections. Even in the soft Highland drizzles those were the sunny and halcyon days of joys and peace and nearby enchantingly powerful yesterdays. I don't remember the mystery darknesses of the nights but they must have conditioned me to dislike city lights and urban shadows. I don't remember watching the moon. I never saw the Perseid Shower or the northern lights till I got to the Dominion, much further south, and I knew no real winter.

Only the tops of the M-shaped roof of Craigag were visible from Mrs MacVarish's at Callop across the river, six furlongs off, and you only saw that much if you knew where to look. It had been hidden. Perhaps little wonder that MacMillan missed it. Looking north from Callop, on a clear day, there was a mighty extent of heightening mountains behind Craigag, craggy outcroppings, scarce, unmajestic, scrabbling trees, tracts of heather and bracken, and patches of bare rock that glinted after a rain, ostensibly deserted of people. A great power somehow gone by. The eye casually scanned the whole *massif* scarcely registering the little plateau that almost hid the lodge, and beyond it, Meall Clachach [Stony Hill], which hid a lochan (Lochan na Càrnaich),[6] which I have never seen, and then to a dominating almost south–north line of bare, exposed heathery peaks that nursed the clouds, and faced the sheets of driving rain, higher and higher, Beinn an Tuim behind Craigag, then Stob Coire nan Cearc [Stob of the Corry of the Hens (Grouse?)], and lastly the dual peaks of Streap [Struggle], and Streap Comhlaidh [Struggle's Other Half(?)], both just under 3,000 feet. To a boy, embracing, enchanting, liable to delay an objective view of folk who lived on flatlands and never climbed and really breathed the subtle, noble airs.

To the east of this brave mountain brotherhood the streams drained, in Cameron of Locheil country, eastward into the wooded cleft of the Dubh Lighe [Black Water], which drained into salt Loch Eil. To the west, invisible from Callop and Craigag, the little mountain streams drained over almost treelessness, when I was there, into the Finnan, which emptied into freshwater Loch Shiel in old Clanranald's Moidart and Àrasaig, and Sunart in Argyll. That watershed was the divide between two countries, north of the Callop. The 1872 survey marks the southern few miles of this watershed as lying in Allt na Crìche [Landmark or Boundary Stream],[7] which joins the Callop in the old woods a furlong or so to the west of the big rock at the Craigag new lane-end. The line had just bisected a tiny lochan to the north of the road (which I do not even remember – maybe it had been drained).

The Callop, o'er which the lodge looked, is the dominating oddity, as others have noticed; it rises in Ardgour hills, in full view of Craigag, little white tails here and there in the storms, but instead

of turning from its northerly course to the east into saltwater Loch
Eil, it flows roughly north, falters not, then curves to the west of a
slight height of land (*cnap*) with two hills rising above boggy land
where the lochan lies, and then ambles, south of the old Cregag
height of land, through a pasture to the rugged wooded cleft of
what I have called the Callop pass, westwards into Loch Shiel. In
the woods, coming from Callop, where the biggest curve begins,
there are suddenly no more shingly deposits and the water is ten
feet deep and mysterious. There the Callop actually permanently
becomes Loch Shiel. Under prolonged heavy rains on rocky, thin
and unretentive soils, with south-westerly winds, Loch Shiel
naturally expands its shores, temporarily, eastward through that
cleft, meeting the raging hill water of the river and its tributaries
where the shingles gathered. The coarse Callop riverine silts and
the loch deposits make for two patterns of vegetation through the
cleft. Unconsciously for us it was the river's loch-ish character that
defined us as almost in Glenfinnan, not Kinlocheil. From near
Craigag itself I only remember seeing the immediate hillside to our
north with its dotting of hardwood trees, only rising a few hundred
feet. Looking north-west, though, you could see the naked peak of
Fraoch Bheinn [Heather Mountain] behind Glenfinnan. I never
climbed it but walked for years, a boy, under its powerful auspices. I
understand the profound sadness of the many who had to leave
these thoughts behind.

Other thoughts mostly about wood and water

Writing those thoughts takes me into the outer room of a quite
different world I know existed, although I can often only share
glimpses that must be left implicit, or that are only tangentially
supported from data from nearby, and I don't always know how to
express the degrees of obviousness in that language of suggestion. My
boyhood sources, in retrospect, were not all unselfconscious. Many
of them I admit were mostly Jacobite, a draught from a well of what
was largely superficial Victorian Bonnie Prince Charlie-ism, which
touched Gael and Saxon alike and which was not without an
important, deeper potential value for the interested imagination.

The older maps I've used to explore Craigag, Callop and Glenfinnan, for example,[8] leave me wondering many simple geographical things. Was the distribution of deciduous trees in this clefted borderland that the lodge almost guarded, much broader before the great spread of sheep, or even in the mid nineteenth century than I remember it a hundred years later? Glenfinnan (and Knoydart, Moidart, Arisaig) was 'almost Void of Cover or provisions' in December 1747 according to Allardyce, a Hanoverian source.[9] What were Cregag and Callop like before the sheep-farms came? What were the reasoned forest policies of the old powerful Highlanders, Cameron of Locheil, John Cameron, first of Fassifern, MacLean of Ardgour, the owners of Sunart, and the Glenaladale MacDonalds (before Ranald MacDonald of Clan-ranald sold the woods of Moidart and Àrasaig 'in the parish of Islandfinnan and shire of Inverness,' oak, elm and ash excepted, 'for such term of years as shall be necessary for one regular cutting of the said woods at the rate of 400 dozen [sacks of] charcoal at the least yearly' to Hartlie, Aitkenson and Company, Cumberland, in 1772[10])? How did they place pines and other conifers, and oaks, willows and alders? How did they border any plantations?[11] A *doire*, for example, is given by Edward Dwelly as 'an insulated grove of trees, properly of oaks' [*darach* is an oak], after his more general and first definition of a wood or thicket. Queen Victoria passed through several impressive woods on the north bank of Loch Eil in September 1873 – I remember naturally well-spaced old deciduous trees at Annat and then at Drumsallie. There is a Doire Mór named on a map, behind the farm at Callop, between the two main tributaries and high on the track to the pass that cuts over to Conaglen to the west of Meall nan Damh, and nearby there's a Doire Bàn (given in the 1872 survey as Doire na Cruaiche) although I can't say I remember any large clumps of trees behind Callop.

The hillside north of Craigag was not well wooded; indeed it is the bracken and heather that I remember first, specially the razor-sharp dry bracken. I remember old oaks (and a holly[12]) to the east of Craigag which seemed to have straggled out of a dense enough wood at Drochaid Sgainneal/Sgainnir and nearby Dail na Sgain-neal/Sgainnir [Dell of the Scandal/Scattering] of the Dubh Lighe

(Gleann Dubh Lighe) where the old grey, unmarked, speckled road
I knew crossed the Dubh Lighe a mile and more south of the
Olivers' home deeper up the glen.[13] The greater detail from the
six-inch map calls this wood, on the west side of the Dubh Lighe,
Coille Tom Ruadh [Red Knoll Wood]. If Peggy Oliver, or
anyone, used that term, I don't remember. To old Highlanders
in 1883 the oak was *righ na coille,* king of the wood; it probably still
is, with Graves's *White Goddess* as a reminder. Where Moidart,
Sunart and Ardnamurchan are concerned, what might have been
seen as of great importance to pre-1772 Gaelic subsistence society
was minimising the effect of Loch Shiel flooding, but to my
knowledge there is no evidence of inter-family (Catholic, Episcopalian and Presbyterian) cooperation to ensure, by shore-line and
hillside forest planting, the slowest possible rising in loch levels in
torrential rains – there was no dyke and *boiteau* at Glenalladale. The
ability of the short (about two miles), navigable Shiel river to
disgorge the flood of a large rainfall catchment area is limited –
Loch Shiel is 11.4 feet above mean sea level (and here and there
over 300 feet deep) and prevailing ocean weather inevitably
encourages rapid loch water-level rise in prolonged rainy times.
At a certain point in the subsistence period, cattle grazing must have
discouraged forestry at both the depositional and the shieling levels.
Later, between about 1800 and 1838, although commercial sheep-
farming generally had replaced subsistence agriculture, and had
displaced many traditional families, there was a notable increase in
forestation in the Protestant and Presbyterian parts of Ardnamurchan and Sunart by men like James Riddell.[14] In those flooding times
the old farms at Callop and Cregag, but particularly the latter, must
often have stood guard on flooded pastureland.

The six-inch maps of the Cregag, Callop and Glenfinnan area,
made from the early 1870s surveys, show clear boundary lines
around unmarked white areas (farmland and sheep 'folds'), around
white and rough ground areas, around acreages of trees, around
treed areas within broader woodland, and around treed and rough
areas in which dotted lines demarcate the treed parts. There are also
various road delineatings using unbroken and broken as well as
bold face and plain type font, surely bearing on ditch and bank
types given in the James Donaldson job description of the Com-

mission for Highland Roads and Bridges in 1804.[15] There is no explanatory legend for what is deducible enough. The bathymetrical maps of Highland freshwater lochs, surveyed around the turn of the twentieth century, three inches to the mile but based on the six-inch OS maps, show (probably misleadingly) unbroken lines around the wooded areas.[16] These boundaries, whatever they were, may indicate either some sort of walling protection for important woodlands in the seedling stage, or careful guarding, with continuous foresters' care later. Forestry was obviously an integral part of the life of the old traditional farm and land holding,[17] and, as the records show, was valued by many later, post-Gaelic landowners, to the point of plantation culture, and the taking of protective litigation against simpler needy folk helping themselves even to off-cuts – Archibald Clerk noted the value put on oak bark in particular (OSA, vol. 7, p. 150).[18] The obvious collateral note is that landscapes were subject to varying amounts of forest-cutting at intervals of from a few decades to much longer periods, as needs were met. Whether or not the old Gaelic owners clear-cut or maintained their forests/woods by selective cutting, I don't know – I have read no study of buried tree stumps from which opinions might follow concerning harvesting practices. Neither have I read any record of Highlanders' forest policy clearly enunciating long-term appreciation of climate variation. The Robert Adam photograph referred to above, from Tom na h-Àiridh in Glenfinnan, shows what look like thirty-year-old *Pinus sylvestris* [Scotch pines],[19] most of which I do not remember in any concentration in the 1940s, but some straggling members of which remnant may have only recently been chopped down from around the church.

To the east of Craigag in sometime latter-day woods, oaks and willows

Clearly do I remember the dappled sunbeams through the green and golden leaves of the old hardwoods overhanging the bridge, Drochaid Sgainnir or Sgainneal east of Craigag.[20] It was a flat wooden bridge when I was at Craigag, doubtless because of the nearby mill – I seem to remember that it was tarred and that nail heads showed through. Nearer that bridge than the Olivers', however, was Drimsallie (saw) Mill – my oldest brother worked there one summer (and bore a scar to his dying day) – and Drimsallie Mill is first in the records of the National Archives of Scotland in 1770 although I cannot for the life of me re-find the papers. I read that Drumsallie left Locheil ownership in 1951 when death taxes forced its sale.[21] Lying at the lower end of Glendylie, the mill was part of the 'property' of John Cameron of nearby Fassifern (d. *c.* 1785) in 1746, or might have become so in his post-1746 period of continuing acquisitions.[22] The question will be dealt with further on. Coille Tom Ruadh must have fed the old mill. John Cameron was nothing if not the risen and rising local power, and a thoroughgoing capitalist with a sharp eye for a business deal, locally, nationally and internationally. He was a brother to Donald Cameron of Locheil of the Forty-five and a great user of land, at whatever level of holding and occupancy was available to him (he held Fassifern on wadset for example).[23] Besides Fassifern on the north shore of Loch Eil, at the mouth of the valley of Gleann an t-Sùileig [Glen of the Willow(?)], in 1746 he possessed or otherwise controlled the glen of the Dubh Lighe, and Wauchin [Uamhachan] deep up the glen of the Fionn Lighe,[24] as well as land on the south shore of Loch Eil, and Cona Glen and other parts of northern Ardgour in 1746 – he was granted written immunity from Hanoverian predation for 'Fasifern, Wachin, Glendylie, Inner-Skahadill, Conglen & Achafuboill. With the Inhabitants and farmers thereon and there [*sic*] Effects.'[25] Many of those imagining his hidden Jacobitism in 1745 probably underestimate his then-modern, and very shrewd acquisitiveness. Cregag, perhaps for a lifetime before the first Fassifern, going back to the 1690s, perhaps for less, was a buffer between Cameron East and Clanranald West.

The 1872 survey shows that there was a *coille* [wood], up Gleann an t-Sùileig (the Fionn Lighe glen), Coille Cala nan Creagan [Wood of the Haven of the Rocks]; there were also at least two *doirean*, Doire Shomhairle [Sorley's (Oak?) Wood] and doire an Rathaid [The Road (Oak?) Wood], up the same glen. From wherever Fassifern's residence was (he lived as a court-decreed exile in Northumberland for a decade from either 1753 or 1755 and used, in 1757, Alexander Cameron of Dungallon as his factor,[26] he would have carefully controlled his woods at Fassifern and elsewhere – he had shipping interests – and may well have controlled, or later have got temporary tenanting control of Callop and Craigag, possibly from MacLean of Ardgour, date unknown. As a note, it is remarkable that in 1746 Drimsallie farm, a rich enough one standing on the lowland almost at the head of Loch Eil, between the slow-flowing Dubh and Fionn Lighean, was held on wadset, not by Cameron of Fassifern but by an Evan Cameron (d. 1750, with Fassifern as executor);[27] the 1774 forfeited estates drawing of Drumsallie leaves the location of the mill uncertain; were the mill on the east bank of the Allt Dubh Lighe it lay within the Drumsallie farm – it also included saltwater frontage from the mouth of the Dubh Lighe north to the Fionn Lighe. This may represent a consolidation made by the improving managers of the forfeited estates. When Cregag was a holding north of the Callop, east of Allt na Crìche, under the Camerons of Locheil I can see no reason to believe that the higher ground was not much more important as a forest land, and like Drumsallie.

The forest theme for the area of course is dominant at Drimsallie, only a walk from Craigag. 'Druim' means a ridge, or a keel; the second element may derive from the Gaelic *sail* (f) meaning a willow tree (and woody symbol for S in the old Gaelic alphabet. The Latin cognate *salix*, is also feminine. *Sail* may be the root involved in Sùileag, used above. For whatever reason, the latest English Ordnance Survey map still calls the area from Kinlocheil to the wooden bridge, Coille Druim na Saille [The Wood of the Willow Ridge], although I don't remember seeing willows from the road in my days gone by.[28] Here, still, *na saille* is a feminine form of the definite genitive. One obvious significance of the willow, perhaps on both sides of the height of land, Cregag and Callop, and Kinlocheil, is that withies split thinly and used in the turf-and-wood homes, the creel houses (lived in perhaps by the majority of mainland Highlanders), as well as for horse panniers, were often made from willow (hazel, another locally growing under-canopy tree, was also used). As figures given in a note below show, horses were common in this area. The various species of

Highland willows mentioned in John Cameron's *Gaelic Names of Plants* (1883) include *Salix viminalis* or Cooper's Willow (the Osier), and *Salix caprea* (Goat Willow) and *aquatica,* the latter two of which were used for 'tackle of every sort' as well as ropes and bridles; *Salix caprea* in Gaelic is also given as *Suileag*.[29] The willow is also the tree species that is best able to deal with freshwater flood conditions. Then comes the alder (and there are alder trees still thriving in the Callop Gap).

Where oaks and willows and other valuable trees are concerned, I am surprised that there was a relic of an old hardwood forest at the wooden bridge and around the mill as late as the 1940s; perhaps Fassifern or some other middle-class Cameron monopolised the willows in his day, perhaps for coopering purposes. A John Cameron, (not of) Fassifern, 'brewer', wrote to Alexander Campbell of Barcaldine in 1789 about the sale of barley and, among six letters (1763–7) from a John Cameron to Duncan Campbell of Glenure, later of Barcaldine, again the supply of barley came up.[30] Four brewers are named in *No Quarter Given* in the Cameron regiment that fought in 1745–6, one a sergeant at Corpach. Brewing and barrels went together, friends of the oak and maybe too the willow. There is no record yet found that shows the raising of barley on any of the Craigag and Callop farms and, in my time, there was no local beer maker. The more intriguing possibility, the provision of boat and ship timber from the Drumsallie mill will be considered at the end of this book.

In our time too, further up Gleann Dubh Lighe forestry and sheep coexisted with a walled divide. The only inhabitants up that lost valley were George Oliver, a Lowlander, and his Highland wife, the red-headed, big and tall, Peigi Oliver – we got our milk from Peigi Oliver. I associated George with shepherding for some reason although the available record doesn't. Perhaps he just kept them from the trees. Hundreds of sheep and their indiscriminate close-cropping habits would have been death to unprotected forest seedlings – with the mill still running, one man, probably a 'parker', would have tended the dykes and been charged to keep them from the seedlings and saplings. I have never sought diagrams of local forested areas, showing dates of planting although records certainly exist for Ardgour, in NRAS3583.

*Where the road and the railway part a while,
enclosing the lower old Cregag farm*

From where it crossed the Dubh Lighe, south of Drumsallie Mill, a little south too of the road there, the West Highland railway had to climb its first important incline since leaving Fort William, the long climb to Glenfinnan Summit. Had it shared the Callop Gap with the road it would have faced an insurmountable grade out of the headland of Loch Shiel. From Kinlochiel it laboured up to the west, over the old road which ducked south and swung round the broad tongue of higher land, over the little cresting height of land of its own – I remember the clearance sign painted on the arch of the stone bridge, in black and white I think, but forget the footage and inchage. At the bridge over the road there was an embankment where the brambles, one autumn, were so plentiful we gathered them in grey galvanised pails (the blaeberries on the hill were got in cups, paltry compared to the Shadow's field in Long Point, Cape Breton or at Roller's (Gillis) farm in the rear of Judique on plateau-ish land that has been exploited by the pulpers.

The line almost immediately drove through a cutting and it was there Joe MacLeod and Joe MacVinish's railway bothy nestled on the south side of the line. In spare moments there, perhaps when the driving sheets of rain were just too numbing and penetrating, Joe MacLeod carved *cromagan* from sheep horns – in those days I had no sense of profit and profiting, but later knew that my mother presumed that Joe was satisfying some market, would-be Highland gentlemen, or visitors, for tall walking sticks with crooked horn handles. Joe had a reputation for financial shrewdness that his home bespeaks to this day. Across the line, on a little ledge of exposed grey schists, they had an old cup standing gathering whatever liquid chemical mixture seeped out of the rock, yellowish and foul-tasting – maybe he used the substance to harden wood, or horn for that matter, although the rain must have diluted it. The answer to what it was, however, is found on the 1872 survey, which shows a 'chalybeate' (iron) spring at the spot, almost thirty years before the first steam train went through.[31] Some medicinal value perhaps.

The bothy was only a short walk east from Craigag, completely hidden from the road and only exuding the tiniest wisp of Lowland

company power which its occupiers absorbed with Highland sense
and knowing. The line then all but brushed the north of Craigag
Lodge, as Douglas Earl of Morton knew it must (which angered
him, an irritation that fits into a longer story) and just to the west of
Craigag, the line disappeared into a tunnel that ran under the
Lochiel–Clanranald line of Allt na Crìche. The tunnel had little
alcoves on its sides and from not far in you could see light at the
other end, where it emerged less than a mile from the Glenfinnan
viaduct which arced in its long concrete curve across the Finnan up
the glen a bit, where the hills came nearer together, Beinn an Tuim
[Mountain of the Round Knoll], to the east, and Tom na h-Aire
[Look-out Hill] and Fraoch Bheinn [Heather Mountain], to the
west. The old railway house was almost under the viaduct. The
tunnel was long enough that I never walked to its western end; for
some reason too I never hiked across the surface, over Allt na
Crìche, to or from the Finnan. From Kinlocheil the line had
climbed over 100 feet, leaving no much greater climb through
Àrasaig of the ever-subtle summer warmths of honeysuckle and
fox-gloves in woody, bielded nooks and turns near where the
Màmaidh MacGillivrays came from (to Nova Scotia c. 1790), and
the Gillises from Gaoideal a little to the west later came to Cape
Breton. A gnarly old golden hardwood beauty was lingering in
Àrasaig in October 2002. Then the line went on into the Moss of
Keppoch, beloved Morar (with its odd last 'ch' phone heard on
Margaree Gaelic) and the heaving salt seas the old Gaelic Lordship
had commanded, gateway to Tir nan Òg, away for ever.

MacMillan, for whatever feature he thought he was describing,
gives the place name as Creagag, which he translates as 'perch', the
fish (not the *spiris* that birds, expensive Victorian 'chapels' and posh
Victorian shooting lodges roost on). He explains his 'perch' as
probably being related to a nearby stream, and indeed there is one,
the very small one nearby cutting diagonally across the pasture –
the 'Burn' mentioned in note 2 (p. 225), the one Sholto George
knew well. Creagag, in Dwelly's dictionary, means 'conger' before
'perch' and having fished the Callop countless times I know that
eels were common at one time of the year – they had come a much
longer way than I knew, from the great Atlantic, perhaps reaching
up Allt Dubhaidh [The Black Goddess's Stream] (translation from

Seumas Watson, Queensville, Cape Breton) as far as Lochan Dubh
Tòrr an Tairbeirt. I never saw anything else but brown trout,
salmon and salmon parr, and eels in the Callop and I would have
remembered handling a perch; I never fished that little burn that
cut diagonally across the pasture below Craigag although I know
salmon went up it to spawn, for Corrie our collie caught one.
Insofar as I don't remember any obvious stream on the flat plate of
land where Craigag lodge stood, or just to the westward, Somerled's definition of Creagag is probably astute, if, as I think,
incorrect.

There is no evidence yet extant that the MacInneses in 1841
(census), or anyone, lived higher up where the lodge was later built.
Perhaps where Morton built the lodge was out of the way garden
land or part of a summer pasture. There is a still better explanation
than 'perch', or 'conger' for that matter.

Creag first means a rock. It has the simple synonym *clach*, from
which one has diminutive *clachag* and descriptive *clachach*. A little
rock would be *creagag* (feminine). When I thought about it later,
what I always took as the inspiration for the name Craigag was the
giant schistose boulder that lay just north of the road at what we
knew as the end of the main lane to the house and, abutting the
lane, just to its east. To a boy it was huge, although easy to climb. In
Gaelic, as in English humour, big things could easily become small,
in a Celtic litotes. The main (post-railway) lane to the lodge began
by cutting almost directly north from the road just west of the
creagag, just east of a little descending, treed shoulder. Not far up,
the lane had to zigzag right and left and then, at the top, merged
with the older grassy path heading west-ish. Then the path
described a curve to the right up to the gate in the fence, then
alongside, to the east of the block of tall rhododendrons and on to
the east side of the lodge. The lane was perhaps too steep for horses
and carriages; certainly none used it during my time there – I am
not sure that anyone nearby owned a horse.

I can't see the Sholto George burn near the railway bothy. I have
forgotten how we got our water at Craigag. I don't remember a
stream from under the line, a well or taps (there was no hot water
except via the top of the range, if we had wood or coal enough; I
remember a copper hip-bath but not having used it often) but there

must have been at least a trickle getting in, other than through the
roof; seldom did a stream dry up in the West Highlands; there was
no rain shadow in those rugged mountains – Craigag lay deep in
the ocean weather's primary obstacle – and often the serried
cyclones produced condensed banks of cloud, unending (and
yet I do not remember raincoats, only sou'westers). To me the
nearest stream, only a foot or two wide, but deep enough for a
spawning salmon, the little nearly invisible one, came down off the
hill, under the railway line somewhere, reaching the old pasture
maybe two or three hundred yards away south-east of the house
and a hundred from the zag. It was never near the house. There was
a building down there when we arrived. I have no photograph of it
and remember only that it looked like a sort of windowless,
uninhabited storage place; it had almost certainly been built as
the stable and storage for the people renting the shooting lodge up
the hill. The burn emerged from the hill behind it and there took a
westering turn diagonally south-west across the pasture, under the
road, almost invisible because it remained narrow and cut deep. At
times it filled and overflowed with Loch Shiel but there were no
meanders. Down-cutting trumped deposition. The building had
been built, I'd say, beyond the flood-water's reach. The little
stream must have flowed under the road in some ancient Dick and
Readdie drain, and on into the trees to join the Callop just beyond
my twin hazels, one on either bank, still only a boy's long step
across, but much deeper now. There must have been a continuous
uprising of the land after the ice.

What I remember with greater clarity is that a short branch road,
which had been paved at one time, led in towards the storage
building from the south-east, from the main road from Fort
William just after the latter had made a rightward turn and breasted
the little height of land (part of the Locheil–Loch Shiel watershed).
This would certainly be in keeping with the plans of someone
hoping to profit from building a shooting lodge, and no such
branch is shown on the 1872 survey. The great majority of visiting
guns would have come via Fort William or salt water. I know the
road and the branch north-west to the lodge's outbuilding yet
because I walked and cycled the little dips and curves round to the
brambly railway bridge. A little eastward of the junction, near the

height of land there was the track that led to the wooden bridge over the Callop and thence to Calum Lowrie's and old Mr Cameron's farm and Mrs MacVarish's wee house. This track, according to the six-inch map of 1872, led first to (and by) the three-building, pre-shooting lodge, 'Cregag' or 'Craigag' farm complex, the real guardian of the Callop Gap. If my memory of the rubbly contours there is right, this was what was left of the early, and very old, medieval Cregag farm.

Almost certainly it was here that the MacInneses lived in 1841. The memory of the lodge's storage building and the road leading to it are most powerfully fixed in my memory, especially the road, because, when I was big enough to use an old bicycle, I was brushed by a car as I skilfully turned in there just after the short downhill from the little knobby height of land. I wasn't hurt, but the moment was unforgettable and mental patterns were etched there and then. That was when a man I didn't know angrily explained hand signals to me. I hadn't known about them – what conceivable use were they with scarcely a car on the road (and those drivers that were were there without exception considerate and on the look-out). Had I had the gift of impudence I would have explained the rareness of cars (and that we all but owned that stretch by virtue of living nearby), the nearness of a hill which made cars undetectable to a junior biker planning the joy of a turn, and the average driver's weakness on one-lane roads of trying to get to the next passing place, or at least past halfway there, before someone driving in the other direction, not to mention guilt turned to anger at an innocent.

I have no clear image of the storage building in my mind although I used to go to Mrs MacVarish's that way. At the sharp zag in our lane at the top, just a few feet below where I found the yellowhammer's nest in the springy heather, a rough track had been worn on a diagonal up from the storage building where I remember a big steel H girder on its side for a bridge. The track was rough, you had to skip carefully down it (if you were chasing cowardly, thieving redcoats), and had been expanded a little to give a testing mountain diversion to the motorcycle riders who competed in the Scottish six days' trial. I remember the muddy, numbered, noisy trial bikes ripping up the track and then down the broader main lane, at least once. Before the railway, the track up from the stable/storage building must have been the main approach to the hidden lodge on the hill, just a narrow path, somewhere. After the railway allowed speedier access from Vladivostok to Glenfinnan (and Mallaig to the west), the wider driveway/path must have been cut to the north just west of the big stone, and cutting into the tongue of land to meet the old track up the hill.

Sholto George Douglas, the Earl of Morton's was one of several loud voices petitioning against the first railway projection, from (industrial Glasgow, via) Fort William, on to Roshven on Loch Ailort in March 1889. He, like Professor Hugh Blackburn (1823–1909), whose Roshven property would have been radically altered to accommodate a terminal and pier, was standing against the published wishes of the Crofters' Commission of 1884, which had expressed the need for a mainland terminal to handle daily Hebridean and west coast mainland business to the southern industrial area. In a *Scotsman* report of 27 March 1889, the Earl of Morton's lawyer, Mr Monckton, was not reported in detail, but obviously Morton knew that any line to Glenfinnan would have to run very close to his shooting lodge at Craigag and was naturally alarmed about his investment and profits. Reported in some detail, however, was the response to legal questioning of Donald Cameron of Lochiel (1835–1905, *reg.* 1858–1905). Inasmuch as his opinion retold some local historical knowledge, here is a simple introduction to one of the two events that have earned Cregag the reputation it has, and the stories I enjoy. Cameron, who was in favour of a railway that would skirt the north shore of Loch Eil, through some of his better woods and fields, told the committee of the House of Lords that Morton lived seventeen miles from that area of his Ardgour estate (Craigag) that would be affected, that this (Craigag) was but a small triangle of land, and that it was really part of Locheil and not Ardgour. Locheil's history of Cregag, and his almost claim to it, will be considered in detail below.

Considering the railway, let's look at the Ordnance Survey one-inch Sheet 62 of the area that had its first revision (from the original survey of 1866–76) in 1895 and was published in 1902. It shows the new railway and the branch road into a building (my stable or storage building) at the little stream, with no track beyond it. It shows also the other road up to another unnamed building standing just south of the railway line, certainly Craigag Lodge. Thus the vouchers of George Glendinning, the factor of the Earl of Morton estate, for the building of Calass/Calap shooting lodge between 1874 and 1876 find confirmation. So, the 1745 term *creagag* where people are concerned, began describing a farm or older holding on which there must have been buildings, lying to the north of the Callop River on the little height of land. Such a farm complex, of three buildings, lying south of the old *c.* 1803 road and just north of the river Callop, separated from it by a fringe of trees, is shown on the six-inch map surveyed in 1872. Called 'Craigag', the buildings stood close to a thirty foot recorded height a matter of twenty yards north of the Callop about where the bridge was that I knew, just west of where Allt Dubhaidh joined the Callop. This old farm-building complex, like the Callop buildings, stood above the highest flood-waters of the Callop/Loch Shiel. When the rich man, Douglas Earl of Morton, knew that deer stalking and shooting might be combined with the older sheep-farming to yield a better income, he built the lodge and kept the name of the local farm Creagag for it.[32] Cameron of Locheil's shooting lodge was built at Achdalieu in 1885. MacLean of Ardgour (who charged £150 for the Ardgour shootings in 1844),[33] built a lodge before 1858, at the crofting township of Blaich, so, if Blaich was still operating, after 1885 Morton's new lodge had two other gunners' lodges within a few miles of his, and of each other. The deer have survived and blend into the sporing brackens; perhaps the gunners do too, in their plus fours, with their Gaelic-speaking guides, if there are any around. I hear the soft voices of Joe MacLeod and Joe MacVinish.

Maps and census information

The difficulties with maps of the same place over history is that place names, and places named, change, generally as a reflection of changing human occupation and land use and simple demography.

They also change as Gaelic is interpreted. For example, Alexander
Bruce gave 'Glen Inan' in 1733, as he heard the phrase, and Necker
de Saussure in 1808 gave 'Glen Innen' (for Glenfinnan [Gleann
Fhionnain] in which the *fh* is silent); the (emphasised) svarabhaktic
vowel in Arnamwr*a*chan was written in 1633. Boundaries may not
always be correctly shown, but apparent errors are not always
errors. Rivers and streams can change their courses as the result of
floods. Then again, deviances of what may really be the truth, the
position of an early nineteenth-century bridge, for example, may
be best explained by emphasis on the map-drawer's major purposes
and emphases; often approximations and symbols suffice, indeed
are demanded for simplicity's sake in the making of more important
points. All we have for Cregag and Callop, that is even slightly
accurate, begins in the mid eighteenth century, when old fortune
for the Gael began to slip away. Earlier 'tis fancy or flourish.

William Roy's mid-eighteenth-century maps, and the Taylor and
Skinner Scottish road maps of 1776 show no road between
Maryburgh/Fort William and Àrasaig. The National Archives of
Scotland holds correspondence and other material pertaining to the
improving of the new road from Lochy Ferry to Glenfinnan and
beyond to Àrasaig/Loch-na-Gaul, dating the start of that serious
improving work to 1804 – there was trouble with the first earlier
contractor on the Loch-na-Gaul/Àrasaig to Glenfinnan section and
there was already a road of sorts from the Lochy as far as Kinloch
Eil. Between those termini, from Glenfinnan to Kinloch Eil, in the
Langlands' map of 1801, a dotted line is given. There is a record for
the completion of the first butcher's cleaver version of what is now
the famous Glenfinnan monument by a latter-day, young, amiable
but rakish, Alexander MacDonald of Glenalladle in 1815. (The real
Mac Iain Òig led the famous emigration to St John's Island/Prince
Edward Island in 1771–2 and never returned from gentler and
much more fertile slopes where Clanranald's radically commercial
rule did not run – Ranald of Clanranald's granting of 'a tack of the
said [Clanranald] estate' (GD201/1/273) to David Bruce, the
surveyor chosen by the barons of exchequer to survey several of
the forfeited estates, perhaps show the chief's early and little-
known change of heart.[34])

There are in particular two pre-Ordnance Survey maps of the whole area, held in the map collection of the National Library, to which I will refer, which are informative in their different ways. The first is 'This map of Argyllshire', dedicated to 'John Duke of Argyll' by 'George Langlands & Son, Land Surveyors' of 'Cambeltown'. It was published on 1 August 1801. The other is a map of southern Inverness-shire, the part that was surveyed in 1820 by William Johnston, land surveyor (fl.1806–1840) for John Thomson's (1770–*c*. 1840) *Atlas of Scotland* (1832).

The Langlands map of 1801 marks the northern boundary of Argyllshire along the Callop River from Loch Shiel east for a mile, then has it cut north along the eastern border of Cregag to Drimsallie and then continuing north-westwards to just past Lochan na Càrnaich behind Cregag, then north to include the watersheds of the Dubh is Fionn Lighe rivers, finally following the Loy River to the Lochy and south. In other words, it includes in the shire of Argyll a large mountain area of the Cameron of Lochiel estate that drains into salt water. It also clearly excludes the Cregag farm, which, with one exception, doesn't.[35] That feature aside, the map's purpose was to deal with the demography and the travel of the powerful. That purpose was generally expressed symbolically, for the shire and for its abutting country. Gentlemen's seats are clearly defined in the legend, often with owners' names given on the map; slate-roofed houses are also defined, and so are farm buildings, in the legend – all, one assumes were the permanent or long-lasting buildings; the farm buildings may represent tacksmen's or main tenants' homes. The Langlands map also marked roads and prospective roads. There is a road, for example, along the north shore of Loch Eil; it is fairly straight and ends at Drumsallie. There it becomes the dotted line referred to above (the symbol signifying a prospective road) which runs to a farmhouse at 'Glenfinan' – the name 'Douglach' looks to be associated with the 'Glenfinan' farm building, 'Douglach' being printed across the land at the head of Loch Shiel – but this was the Dubh Ghlaic [Black Hollow (or valley)] mentioned above and below (however one interprets *glac* as hollow or valley, the existence of a name for what is part of a spectacular march between 'countries' is not insignificant).

This dotted line part shows no reflection of the twists the later road took, it is a symbol. The straight-line depiction of the road from Drumsallie east to the Lochy, the important old drove road along the north shore of Loch Eil, likewise is simplified. However, the surveyor-mappers took care not to indicate a bridge over the one broad river, Allt an t-Sùileig [Little Willow Burn], at Fassifern. The road stops at one bank and takes up again opposite, and that the road is straight and near the shore makes sense as, there, at Allt an t-Sùileig, the river would have been easier for cattle to cross than inland to the north where the water was faster moving and the course narrower and rockier. With the cost of building safe, spate-proof stone bridges to consider, in and after 1803, the new road takes several kinks inland at the rivers to minimise span length.

The Langlands map shows no gentlemen's seats in the abutting part of Catholic Moidart (Inverness-shire) that is shown; there are two simple farm buildings, not even slated houses, straddling the Glenalladle river and there is only one farm marked at Glenfinnan.[36] At 'Calpa' there is one farm building, and Auldlaig and Drumfern are given as homes, south of the Dubh Lighe. There is another to the west of Corribeg, perhaps the one in front of which Keith MacPhee was photographed in 1920.

Thomson and Johnston's map of Inverness-shire, in four pages, does not locate, but ostentatiously commemorates, at Glenfinnan, the monument and its builder, 'Glenalladle'. On that old sheet there is only one building shown in what is now the little village of Glenfinnan and that is 'Strona guine' [Prisoner's Point?] near where the big house stands today, which presumably was the farm building in the Langlands map. The Slatach river on the 1820 surveyed map is 'Ault na Mia'. (William Roy's map will be considered later.) The map, however, also includes, in a wood above the road, 'Cregag', with no spot for a building, only rounded (deciduous) tree symbols – this perhaps signifies the absence of a stone house on the farm and a preference to place the name more faithfully to the farm than any non-permanent residence. Other significances of Thomson and Johnston's 1832 map will be discussed too but, reasonably assuming that Glenfinnan had a population continuously from 1745 to 1832, using the low and the high land, then these two men, like the Langlands, only marked on their map buildings that were substantial, probably of stone and built and occupied (or not) by property owners, wadsetters and long-term leasers (I think including more than the shire voters). There could be no estimating the number of local subtenants from such documents. Their important stories can only come now from the cities and the New World.

The greatest innovation of the 1841 census is that it names the people it counted. It also gives them by their physical homes at the time (by arbitrary census taker's number, his or her order of recording, one home at Craigag, one at Callop, thirteen at Corribeg, fifteen at Kinlocheil, for example). The census does a good enough job with minor place names although it does not give them all,[37] and it pays no heed to kinship relationships, although much is deducible about the latter. The terms 'independent', 'farmer', and 'Ag. Lab', while useful, do not allow any cadastral deductions. Where houses are concerned, however, there were hundreds of people in many homes in Clanranald, Cameron and MacLean (Ardgour) country, many of which, I presume, are gone, leaving nothing or almost nothing behind of an ancient subsistence agricultural world interwoven with kinship and often unwritten understandings, coexisting for a while, and proliferating into modern poverty, with the newer commercial world. The richer, controlling folk left buildings, some of which remain occupied and not greatly changed, some deserted, others that in time have become other homes with fashionably squared ends, chimneys and slated roofs instead of thatch, others again that have suffered the ignominy of having become byres (like the one I saw from the bus, roofless and forlorn somewhere near Kinlocheil) and unused byres, perhaps also pens like the one up the viaduct road in Glenfinnan, and dykes. The rest of the homes, the majority, have disappeared, leaving the suspicious pro-Highlander, living among the descendants of Highland emigrants, to suspect that those people really were often perceived as little more than temporary, unnecessary economic supernumeraries, ungatherable into context other than the modern commercial one. (When I visit from Nova Scotia I am aware of a keen knowledge of local historians of the richer, literate people and their doings, MacMillan's people, but an ignorance of the almost unrecorded majority, or so it appears.)

If these forgotten people had used stone for their unowned homes, or part of them, one must bear in mind the spread of stone walls (stane dykes) and sheepfolds (fanks) when the enclosings became a passion among landowners in Gaelic Scotland when improving bit deep in the late eighteenth century – there are still stane dykes to be seen up the Gleann Dubh Lighe where there was only one family of (Appin?) MacColls in 1841 and one of Olivers in 1946 (not to stay for much longer). (Between, there were Farquhar MacRae the shepherd and his family in 1861, and Alex MacDonald, the shepherd and his family in 1881, and probably others.) The Revd Donald M'Gillivray wrote in his entry in the New Statistical Account in May 1835 that the 'Fassifern' of the day, Sir Duncan, third of Fassifern (1775–1863), had a quarry at Fassifern from which he profited in the construction of the Caledonian Canal (1803–22) and the building of the Fort William esplanade (1830s I presume).[38] Quarrying was also a lucrative product of the need for sheep-farm enclosures (march dykes and other enclosures) and storage buildings (perhaps including woodland enclosures), and for the building of mills, new houses for the newly reorganised Highland society, sheep-farmers to landowners, and shepherds, within which group there was great mobility (as evidenced in the decennial censuses used, from genealogical work, and from land sales announcements), as well as for churches and glebe-houses. Quarriers are mentioned in the 1861 census, none in Glenfinnan, possibly indicating the itinerant nature of the job – two lived as lodgers at Cross in Àrasaig/Morar at that census taking.

Although, from Robert Adam's and Donaldson's photography, one cannot compare the vernacular stone dwellings in Glenfinnan over time (for roof and chimney details for example), if one takes in Gaelic Scotland from Mingulay to Glenfinnan, from 1905 to 1937, there is a discernible progression in vernacular building styles. It begins with old, sometimes deserted, round-ended, thatched, chimney-less homes that both people photographed, Adam in Mingulay and many other places, Donaldson in Skye, Morar and Ardnamurchan, and elsewhere, the inhabited ones (with or without added gable-end chimneys – Adam lived in John Mac-Lean's on Mingulay in 1905, in which the additional stone chimney is obvious), and the squared-ended, chimneyed homes,

like the (unidentified) 'wayside' home in Glenfinnan photographed
by Adam on 23 February 1937, which had a chimney at each gable
end. Some of the bothies of today were the shepherds' new stone
homes of the mid nineteenth century.

The tons of gravel required for the building of the improved
road from Lochy Ferry north of Fort William to Drumsallie, from
1804, by Dick and Readdie, were obtained locally although the
suppliers were not given in the sources to which I have had access.
There is no mention of Ewen Cameron, second of Fassifern's
profiting from this scheme, but it is not unfair to suggest that he
gained from his local quarry for this project as well. Many a local
family was thereby drawn, temporarily, into the southern money
economy.

Creagag and the last active Jacobites

During school time, on weekday mornings, I have long ago
forgotten the exact time of day or how we knew it (I don't
remember any clocks and battery radio reception was poor because
of all the mountains around Craigag), I used to leave the house, pass
the hurst of rhoddies, through the gate, then I took the newer lane
down its twists below a heathery and lightly treed hill to the right
(the lower, southern extension of the Craigag tongue) to *creagag*,
the big boulder. On top of the boulder I used to wait for Mrs
MacVarish's children and we'd walk the mile or so to Miss Fraser's
school in Glenfinnan together: a mile, or a mile and a half, on the
twisting little road through the tight woody gateway to Catholic
Moidart. Perhaps they knew they were Protestants. I didn't know I
was, and it turned out I wasn't.

The old Creagag boulder was smoothed. It sat deep in the
glaciated valley-bottom soil, probably loch depositional as well.
That a boy could easily climb it suggests that only the top and its
gentler slopes showed. If that were so then the whole thing must
have weighed many tons. The old road to Glenfinnan and on to
Mallaig naturally wended gently round it and the shoulder, to its
south.[39] Half a mile further on, with the knob of Torran Giuthais
crowding the river from the Sunart side, it also rounded, drama-

tically sharply, like a switchback, the barring outcrop just before where the Callop joined the loch, the most unforgettable and dramatic corner in my Highlands. And, though I didn't know as much till 2002, the old road had also been faithful to small hills, ultra-local features that could not be detected from even the 1:50,000 maps of the later twentieth century because the contour range was not small enough.[40] The road was built in an age when straightness didn't matter much, just gradient and breadth enough to accommodate a horse-drawn carriage, two horses, or four (and perhaps four young men abreast; the tariff in September 1873 for crossing Lochiel's Lochy suspension bridge was four shillings for a four-wheeler and two for a two-wheeler. Pedestrians crossed for a penny); the surface, sometimes to a depth of over a foot in the centre, was gravel. The one-lane tarred road with passing places that I remember, not including banks (that I can't remember) and ditches, may have been narrower than the Dick and Readdie gravel road (which was generally from thirteen to fifteen feet wide) and the twelve-foot-wide road built to accommodate the lead mines at Strontian [Sròn an t-Sidhein] and New York and Drimantorran [Druim an Torrain/Ridge of the Hillock] in Sunart to the south.

I don't know if passing places served the horse and buggy age – the (unidentified) McGregor who owned the Locheil Arms at Banavie in 1873 was responsible for the posting arrangements for the queen, which may mean he saw that the royal conveyance met no oncoming traffic to and from Glenfinnan.[41] The tarred road that we knew must have run roughly on the line of the old drove-road/ way for cattle heading for Fort William in eighteenth-century black cattle days. By the time of the tarred road most of the people had gone and the droving business to the Lowlands no longer existed.[42] The *creagag* I knew had white veins, and cracks. It was an erratic that had probably been broken off a jutting part of Beinn an Tuim, or perhaps from one of the Ardgour hills, in the age of ice. It had been ruthlessly ground down and rounded. Thinking about it sixty years on, the old boulder would have stood proud of the Callop floods. It was taking the modern weather well, but awaiting a violent end, one that I would have prohibited had I been the engineer. If moved at all, it should have just been nudged aside and an exposed side engraved with runes. Rest here and consider what passed.

Although he gives a list of 'well-known boulders' in *Bygone Lochaber,* MacMillan may not have known the Glenfinnan road well enough to know about this rock, but he does include a story which strikes me as describing it, at least indirectly, in August 1745, two centuries before we got there in David Orr's brown van. Neither does he include in his list, Clach mhic Bheathain [Mac-Vean's Rock], high up on Meall na h-Àiridh above Callop, nor the other Clach mhic Bheathain to the south of Drumfern on a much lower outcropping.[43]

Among MacMillan's sources was the diary of the Revd Dr Archibald Clerk of Kilmallie parish,[44] author of the lengthy Ardnamurchan parish entry in the NSA (1838) and who, in 1864 wrote down a story he had from an old man, Ewen MacLachlan of Corriebeg, a Lochiel farm holding about a mile west of Fassifern, near the head of Loch Eil.[45] Ewen had been employed by the second Fassifern, Sir Ewen Cameron, who had been about five at the time of the second Jacobite Rising against the house of Hanover in 1745. MacLachlan told Dr Clerk, from the story he'd heard, presumably in the Fassifern family, that when the Prince's standard was raised at Glenfinnan (19 August 1745) eight four-gallon casks of gold were loaded for carrying east toward An Gearasdan Mór [Fort William], on the great adventure that some people still scoff at.

> There was difficulty in carrying them owing to the roughness of the road across Stronchreagaig. They lashed them to poles with birch woodies and carried them on men's shoulders. When they came as far as Drimnasaille the carriers resolved to help themselves to some of the gold . . . (See *Bygone Lochaber,* p. 138)

Today the relevant place name 'Drimsallie' is mentioned four times on the Ordnance Survey maps. The first, Drimsallie Mill, lies up the Dubh Lighe [Black Water] on the east bank about half a mile before it takes a turn to the east to join Loch Eil, about three miles from Glenfinnan. The second is in the north–south hill ridge feature Druim na Saille [Willow Ridge], which lies to the east of the mill. The third is in Coille Druim na Saille [Willow Ridge Wood] through which the old road ran almost as far as the head of

Locheil (and on east to places like Corriebeg and Fassifern). The
fourth is the farm of Drimsallie, which is a good two miles to the
east of the mill, on flatland just about at the head of Loch Eil, five
miles from Glenfinnan. Clerk's term 'Stronchreagaig' may come
from *sròn a' chreagaig* [nose/spur of the little rock] or *sròn chreagach*
[rocky spur] – more correctly *sròn na creagaige* or *sròn creagaige*, since
all Gaelic diminutives ending in 'ag' are declared by the etymologist
to be feminine. Whichever, or whatever else, it is almost certainly
the *creagag* of the old Cregag, couched in a little Highland humour
– there was an old custom of competition in lifting big rocks,
although it would have taken *Finn* himself to have moved this one.
Perhaps Glooscap lobbed it over from Five Islands in the Bay of
Fundy.

    There are two possibilities for the *Sròn* part of Sròn a' chreagaig,
a couple of hundred yards apart. One is the shoulder just west of
where the old rock was, the other where the old Cregag farm was
on its height of land. Walking east from the Glenfinnan gathering
in August 1745, heading for the Lochy, before the Commission for
Highland Roads and Bridges-sponsored road was built (autumn
1804–*c.* 1812), the old footpath leaving Glenfinnan would have
crossed the Finnan where it was safely fordable, about where the
viaduct is today, then hugged the hills around the flatland at Ceann
Loch Sìl at an altitude of about twenty feet (above mean sea, not
loch level).[46] Then it certainly turned sharply back on itself round
the treed outcrop of ancient metamorphic rock to the left where
the Callop joined the loch (travelling east, the Catholic gateway to
Le Culte).[47] Without a road that headland would have been
difficult for gold carriers, but they would have avoided it, going
by boat. The old eighteenth-century track must then have wended
through the hardwoods on the wooded north bank of the mean-
dering Callop in the cleft between the steep mountains to the north
and encroaching ones from the south. It would have clung to the
hills to the north because the Callop irregularly flooded.[48] The
south bank of the river was not an option; in Argyllshire, at the
sharp turn from Loch Shiel was characterised by Lochan Port na
Creige, an extent of rushes, and the little knobby Torran Giuthais
[Piny Hillock], which is shown in Adam's flood photographs. Then
the south bank became not clearly discernible from the road in the

woods. It was slightly less elevated and generally swampier and bulrushier for about half a mile, from Torran Giuthais near the mouth of the Callop to about the deep pool at the curve. In that stretch lay Lochan Dubh Ghlaic (through which ran the Sunart–Kilmallie parish line; NB *Glac* (nominative masculine) has a nominative feminine variant *Glaic,* the form used here) and Lochan na Sròine Gairbhe [Lochan of the Rough Prominence]. At about where the deep pool in the Callop is, where the road presses near, Meall na h-Àiridh in Ardgour comes in from the south, marking about the end of the bulrushes and lochans. There was also the lochan on the north side of the river, Lochan na Crìche. Although I have no memory of it, the (1804?) road passed to the north-west of Lochan na Crìche, when the six-inch map was surveyed in the 1870s. The Glenaladale–Locheil Allt na Crìche line bisected this lochan. These four lochans and the distribution of cat's-tails afford some idea of the extent, and the frequency, of serious flooding by Loch Shiel.

The eighteenth-century track then must have emerged at what might be the *sròn chreagach/creagaige* of the story and immediately after, passed *creagag,* my old grey boulder. Then the track probably skirted the low, floodable pasture of the Cregag farm on the north (between the two driveways to the lodge) at whose east limit the land rose to the height of land about where another track branched to the original Cregag buildings, and beyond to the Callop farm (with a branch off to Dalriach farm, crossing the Allt Dubhaidh). This minor watershed height of land is the other possibility for *sròn chreagach/creagaige.*

All the positionings of those farms reflected the irregular flooding of the Callop. Without (or even with) a bridge over the Dubh Lighe, at or below the mill, and with peaty, boggy land to the south, the Jacobite army in August 1745 would have clung to the skirts of the hills to the north (of Blàr Creagach), just as the new road did *c.* 1800, and does to this day.

Obviously to me, the casks of Jacobite gold would have been carried by boat up the Callop and as far as the deep pool where the barrels would have been taken on land. One has to presume that the gold carriers trailed the main body of the army or else would have felt no temptation to steal. Probably the withy means of carrying occurred to the porters at the sharp river curve, where in my time there was ample woodland. Perhaps MacMillan's Stronchreagaig referred both the whole lower Cregag area including up over the big boulder place and up over the little height of land.

I can't remember if I have, or had and lost, a photograph of the boulder, but the missing photographs must have shown where the old Cregag was because it was almost in line with Callop from where I made the exposure. I don't think the old rock could have been in the two photographs taken of Callop and the hills behind. From up where the two approaches to the lodge met, near the yellowhammer's nest, the boulder was down and to the right a little and probably could not have been included. It was there in 1970 when M and I were there, but when Seumas and I were there in 2002 it was gone. Without it there was no ready reference point any more. And, sadly, more micro-topography than the old boulder had fallen prey to the improvers of the latter-day petrol people, the people of the recycled, computerised automobile, and the globe, the skies and the black of space. The old pasture had been replaced by a rank neglect. Marginal it may have been; now it was useless. (In case you doubt the big/little rock story, I had a letter in October 2005 from one of my nieces, the only one I know living in Great Britain. She told me that she and her father, my half-brother Tim in Victoria, New South Wales, had driven up to look around Glenfinnan about twenty years ago. As part of the holiday, Tim had planned to show her Craigag Lodge. She was driving and remembered going back and forth looking for the main identifying marker that her father had in his mind's eye for Craigag Lodge, the big old boulder at the road end.)

3

Getting away from Saxon Scotland, and early impressions

If it was in the late summer of 1945 that we went to Craigag, I'd have been only going on four, old enough to retain the few stray memories of Edinburgh in wartime that I still have (a frosty winter moon on the slate roofs of the tenements on Buccleuch Place, a baker's shop round the corner and the early morning aroma of rolls, a great broad stone fireplace in some old building, the forbidden public paddling pool behind the tenement in Buccleuch Place). But probably it was in late 1946 (I don't like to admit that an even shorter time was enough to trap me into endless fascinations and curiosities about Gaelic Scotland, and Gaelic Canada). If 1946, my father would have had time to adjust to peacetime a little, but more important, to have learned about Craigag Lodge at all. For him the marches between Locheil, Ardgour and Clanranald country probably seemed one of the most sequestered and almost inaccessible corners of a Scotland that he would doubtless have disliked to admit he knew nearly nothing about. He would have known about Wendy Wood in Moidart, perhaps also about Mary E.M. Donaldson (1876–1958, who lived at Sanna in western Ardnamurchan, north-west of Ardnamurchan Point, from 1927 to 1947) and George Scott Moncrieff (b. 1910). I am not aware that he or my mother knew anything about Gaelic Scotland – they were Edinburgh people and there never could be any changing the prism through which they saw their world, as far as I know. Craigag, Callop and Glenfinnan were probably sub-suburban for them. Later on, she sometimes told me of her surprise at the depth of my attachment to Glenfinnan. My mother never really supported nor fostered my awoken interest in Gaelic Scotland; to her it was a meaningless and useless subject. In retrospect, our paths diverged at Craigag. My father never realised the influence of Highland Scotland on his only son (and would have been surprised at his two Nova Scotian grandsons, one of whom does a neat step). All the time we lived there he worked in Edinburgh and only got to Craigag every second weekend, if that.

Whenever we got to Craigag, in fact through all the years I lived there, the big house by Loch Shiel side stood eerily empty, not old-looking like a worn-out, ruined castle, but modernly slightly grotesque, inflated, out of place, like the concrete railway viaduct. The house, a modern Glenalladale House, stood near where the *Slatach* (Ault na Mia) from the west joined the long, steep-sided loch that divided a little of north Sunart, from Glenalladale's Moidart. I heard about the strange blue light that sometimes shone from one of the top windows, though I need not have been warned off; there was nothing mysterious or attractive about the place.

I also remember the remains of some sort of makeshift building, rickety and temporary, on top of the little hill behind what I recollect as a little shop about in the middle of the stretch of road that ran from the corner where the Callop lazily joined the loch, by where the old quay at the north end of the loch was, to the old stone bridge over the Finnan. These tumbledown bits and pieces on the knoll were the relics of a film about Bonnie Prince Charlie, some scenes of which were made in Glenfinnan. By the roadside, tucked in snugly below the hill there was a little shop. My first thought was that the shop had been run by Janet MacCracken (*recte* Templeton; there were three Templeton sisters living in Glenfin-nan in my day – Janet, Judy who ran an excellent drama group, and Margaret who had married a MacCracken and who ran the Stagehouse Inn), but the trouble is that I also have one clear memory of Janet, behind her metal-rimmed glasses, in a little shop near John Monaghan's railway station. The little shop near the monument was run by Mary MacDonald, and I am sad that I have no memory left of her. Today where the little shop was has become a large, commercial visitor centre,[1] like a neon sign in the night. There was almost no traffic in my just-post-war days, at least not when we walked the road – I have no memory of a tour bus, but a penny was to be made in the summer from visitors to the modern version of Glenalladale's Jacobite monument (there were still halfpennies/hayp'nies, jenny-wren farthings, and silver threepenny bits (for Christmas suet puddings) in those days and a few people still worked for a few pounds a year). I never climbed the hill behind the shop to check the relics of the film industry although, like countless other people since, I later took photographs of Loch Shiel from that brackeny vantage point (Tor-a-Chant presumably). There is a framed black-and-white one within a yard of my right eye as I sit here in Judique, but not the earliest one I made though – the new-cut path near the water's edge on the Sunart side is like a raw scar; it was not there in 1951.

Where that old Bonnie Prince Charlie film is concerned I have assumed, for decades, that it was made in or near 1945 to commemorate the raising of the Jacobite standard on 19 August 1745, that, in some strangely embracing, vaguely nationalistic way, it was a film made to celebrate the end of the Second World War, which, where Britain was concerned, after all, was a Pyrrhic victory – Great Britain was beggared, saccharine in your tea, Madame, pickled egg perhaps? That date is about right. Alex Korda's *Bonnie Prince Charlie* was shown first in 1948. It was shot in Technicolor in marvellous Highland country, including a cloudless Glenfinnan and a cloudless Glencoe for which they must have patiently waited. I have no memories of any filming or film people in Glenfinnan.

Indeed, the only stray memory I have of strange-celebrity met near Glenfinnan was when I was maybe six, and I was standing with my father near the quay at the mouth of the Callop, where the steamboat *Clanranald* docked, on a warm summer day (in my thoughts) and there meeting a green tartan-swathed, bonneted, alien person called Wendy Wood. It is only the oddity that I remember; she was distant and intense and said nothing to me that I remember. Having read her books I know that she had emerged from her Highland home at Alt Ruadh (Allt Ruadh/Red Burn), in Moidart to be seen, and to encourage Scottish nationalism at an early Glenfinnan Highland games. I certainly never saw the star of *Bonnie Prince Charlie*, David Niven, and in his autobiography, *The Moon's a Balloon*, he left no record of Glenfinnan, or that picture – flops are to be forgotten. Clement Attlee's relative is another person I have all but forgotten.

Maybe here a less specific memory of a memory of a thought may be a truer avenue to introducing these curious explanations of why, for example, and among many things, I am in Catholic Judique, living, until March 2006, quite near Floraidh Ghòrach, one of the last little nub of Gaelic speakers, well over ninety, who milked cows, spun yarn, shat in an outhouse, never drove a car, and who loathed her alien neighbour and never ceased to spill out her vitriol on him to all and sundry. (At Glenfinnan I was always too young to sense any infighting and jealousies that I now know happen in all small communities, and above which many people rise, to their greater strength of character, but don't forget, for a while from the spring of 1945 there was euphoria and lots of drams, despite the rationing. Hitler's mad northern, Wagnerian-inspired supremacy dream had been destroyed by brave men and women. Soldiers from all over the world had romped and trudged the Glenfinnan hills and driven nails into the woodwork of Glenfinnan House. In the new normal, people were beginning to conceive new attitudes and visions at the end of the anti-Teuton war. My grandmother was a Victorian who had learned German folk songs at school – *Die Luft ist kühle und trübe* – and that had disappeared.)

I still remember thinking, in Glenfinnan, that there must be a hilly shortcut to Craigag from just about where Mary MacDonald's little shop stood on the edge of the valley flatland. All I had to do was climb up Tor-a-Chant, over where the annual Highland games hill-race circled, and on into the upper reaches of the hardwoods that clotted the Inverness-shire bank of the Callop Gap, over the bit of rough mountain skirt through which the railway tunnelled and I'd be home. That thought had occurred to a boy who had learned a Highland pride in hill-climbing manliness, an eighteenth-century notion. I suspect that I tried it but I know I never completed it, and that is why I know that Prince Charles's army, with eight casks of gold clad in copper sheathing, boated and then took the obvious old path, wherever it was, down by the Callop, emerging near the *sròn* and the big stone at my lane-end.

There were times when I tumbled down to the boulder not by the new lane but by the last tongue of Beinn Tuim, near where the gold carriers passed on their way to Drimsallie with the still-small Highland army (mainly of MacDonalds and Camerons). Even then

I was attracted to images of an older, roadless world and brave
Highlanders contending with, and masters of all heathery slopes
against all comers. I had not yet learned about Wade's roads and the
Highlanders' antipathy, in and from 1725, to anything wider than a
well-trodden track – for them their countries were small, integrated and threaded together, and within, by subtler travel traceries.
For those that didn't have horses (and horses were common along
Lochiel in 1745), they'd rather have died fording rivers in spate, it
seems, than have stone bridges that attracted the other, alien
Scotland and its language and laws, into their secretive kin-
countries and delicately balanced economies, land understandings
and politics.[2] Already, somehow, Highlanders to me in my innocence were a superior, stronger, healthier, more mannerly and
moral race of people than the English and the Lowlanders, and,
with my few images of them I identified more and more profoundly. It had nothing to do with religion either. I didn't know
religion or facetiousness or irony. Much of the old Highland
mannerliness still existed in rural north-eastern Nova Scotia in
1972, and still persists, often in a post-Gaelic world, the other side
of the *Floraidh Ghòrach* coin.

The only reason I remember going that rougher way from
Craigag Lodge to the boulder was that one day I came on the sickly
reek of bloated rotting flesh among the trees and hidden from the
road. I remember the bloat, the antlers and the glazed eyes, and the
bluebottles. Poachers, I learned, drove the old roads late at night,
shining a powerful light across the hillsides and shooting the deer
that stood trapped for that fatal moment. I don't remember ever
hearing shots, but my little room was in the north-west corner, the
coldest in Craigag Lodge. They could not always bring their illegal
quarry out of the hills and simply abandoned dead and dying
creatures where they fell. For these people, as far as now I know,
there was only Calum Lowrie, the gamekeeper at Callop. At the
time I had no idea if we were living on his territory, who employed
him, or how many poachers he caught. Shooting estates needed
gamekeepers. For long enough all I knew from my mother was that
Calum had a telescope with which he travelled at least some of the
hills in his thick grey-green, tweedy clothes – it wasn't until I had
been long in Canada that she mentioned that Calum had played the

fiddle. In the 1940s boys taking small trout, the occasional salmon parr, from the Callop or its tributaries, Calum let flourish beyond his mandate, kindly man. The Highland people I knew were all kindly and thoughtful of boys, whose little joys they happily remembered.

So it was probably 1946 when we travelled north and west away from Saxon Scotland and into the shadow of an older Gaelic heartland. I was much younger than David Balfour and, for a boy, the Highlands almost immediately became a land of magic and enchantment where a lad could fly like a buzzard high on the air over the crags, and bound down the bouncy heather, basket-hilt in hand, to cut down the hated alien redcoats. I think it was in the late summer or autumn that we arrived. An almost lost memory out of an undated mild mistiness tells me that I was driven there in David Orr's brown van – my father didn't own a car and didn't drive; my mother had owned a car at Thistle Lodge/Castlehaven[3] in the 1920s, a big American Buick, but no longer drove. Although we travelled north and south by the old West Highland Railway over the unforgettable Moor of Rannoch, by Loch Treig, that was later on. I can't summon a first memory of our first arriving at Craigag but I remember the van's being passed on its left side by one of its own wheels in the darkness, in the redolence of wet leaves on rough tarmac in the wilds somewhere near a bridge. That memory has refused to wither away but has never been confirmed.

In the very early days, possibly just before we got to Craigag itself, maybe before we even began looking for somewhere to live there, I remember that we stayed in a room or rooms on the ground floor of a building a little apart from an old house at Annat, about two miles west of Corpach, and one from Kilmallie church. Two Weir sisters lived there. The one I remember was very quiet, and gentle and kind, although I only have two slight memories of her, as well as splinters of memories of Annat from my brother Tim which strongly modify my own wispy, smoky reflections. I remember her being a little tentative and reserved and know it now to have been because she was dealing with the mother of two Dollar boys – she taught there. Tim's memory of Annat involved his stepping back into a wasps' nest while fishing and being stung again and again before getting clear of them. The river in my mind's eye flowed through old woods – perhaps I strayed there with him on a better day.

Annat may or may not be a name with pre–Christian religious significance but it is one of those Highland names which crops up in many places from Aberdeenshire to Argyllshire; besides the Loch Eil one, there is one south-west of Gaskan on Loch Shiel; there are also lots of Coire Buidhes [Golden Corries] and lots of *Moy*s, and Keppochs, and probably lots of Fraoch Bheinns just as there are uncounted 'Salmon rivers' in Nova Scotia and 'Maple Drives' in English Canada. This Annat, the buildings, lay between the inverted Y of two branches of a river that drained south off Druim Fada [Long Ridge], into the narrows that might be seen as separating Locheil and Loch Linnhe. Not a delta but a sizeable flatland extending inland, north, like a spearhead from the flat northern margin of Loch Eil. In 1841 there was Annat House and four other homes, but nearly a century earlier, in 1746, there had been eight families living there, and a single man; the whole place was a thriving collection of cattle farms under the leadership of an Allan Cameron, late land–officer of Locheil. If their claims for losses at the hands of Cumberland's soldiers between 1745 and 1747 are accurate, there were 86 cows (42 Allan Cameron's), 13 horses (9 Allan Cameron's) and an old mare, and 273 sheep and goats (95 Allan Cameron's). (In 1783 and 1784 the tacksman at Annat was Colin Campbell; he was also baron baillie, a man of local power.) I don't believe that any of Allan Cameron's and later people's old cattle world existed at Annat in 1946, or even a century earlier, and that is a story retold times over, although where Craigag and Callop are concerned the hints are much more hidden.

As with Craigag, for some reason I have no memory of going to school for the first time, or of my first visit to Callop. Still, those places are my home. I fit there somehow, even sixty years later when little is left of the fabric I knew. People know me whom I have not met since we left the Highlands in 1951. We seem all to have many jigsaws into which forgotten people and forgotten memories fit if only the circumstances are right.

4

Iseabal Friseal, Glenfinnan

Miss Fraser, plumpish, forty-ish, who looks at me a little sideways from an old photograph on the dusty piano top in Judique, is the one who taught me to read English and write it with a metal-nibbed dip pen. Not long ago, in 2007, I learned that she was from Cannich near Beauly in Fraser country, daughter of a victim of the Great War and sister of a victim of the second. I remember her as an enthusiast about the Jacobite Highlands who passed that simple, unrefined enthusiasm on without any obvious reserve. She had a sister who was a nun, suggesting that the family was Catholic, so my later curiosity about that fundamental Christianity had an easily explained bias. I certainly was touched by her thoughts. For me, those memories are profoundly evocative and pleasingly super-impose the one dark memory I have of her.

The Frasers generally were Jacobites in the 1745 war. Iseabal would have known about the arch-nationalist outlander and pro-Gael, Wendy Wood, near Glenuig in MacDonald Moidart, the Englishman Edward Compton MacKenzie (1883–1972) in Barra, the English-born Episcopalian, strongly Jacobite Englishwoman M.E.M. Donaldson (in Ardnamurchan), and Scott Moncrieff the Scottish Catholic novelist (in Eigg, 1945–51), and all may have concentrated her nostalgic Jacobitism. Whatever she told us about Jacobite times fell on my receptive ears, for it became part of a curiosity and a stimulus later to learn about a trans-Atlantic early Scottish people, the ones who spoke Gaelic. She taught in English, although I learned the words to a Gaelic song she taught us to sing for a Fort William *Mod*. A longer Glenfinnan memory than mine, Ronnie MacKellaig's (b *c.* 1932), recently told a relative newcomer, Eileen O'Rua who asked on my behalf, that he remembered the teacher and both her parents living upstairs in the old schoolhouse and that he didn't remember them speaking Gaelic. He associated the family with Fort Augustus in the Great Glen. Iseabal Fraser was completely pro-Highland.

Since I remember hearing some of the rote questions and answers, she taught the Roman Catholic catechism in the classroom. I learned from her that I was a Protestant and could not go into the (only) church in Glenfinnan. She was teaching a class of about a dozen, almost half of whom, I think, were Catholic Gaelic speakers. How much I might have learned had not a Victorian law demanded that Scottish schoolteachers teach only in English, forcing Gaelic to be a slightly secretive tongue. I don't remember hearing Gaelic spoken by my classmates outside the school, although in retrospect I know I sometimes sensed a distance from two school friends, walking together down the hill to the old low road, which later, looking back, I know and deeply regret that I misunderstood. Gaelic by then was on the way to becoming a secret home language, gateway to deeper personal truths, and views, and prospects, and aspects (for those who had not been touched by commercial thought and affectation), but not to the job market and not for sharing with outsiders, the people later called the white settlers.

Giuthasachan and connections to Cape Breton

It was in October 2002, sitting in the comfortable living room of a house in Kinlocheil (the house of one of Joe MacLeod's daughters and her husband), near the post office, above a north-running line of healthy young oak trees, that a completely forgotten memory of Miss Fraser and her field trips came to me. Somehow and sometimes memories may be condensed, rearranged, even invented, but some are curiously latent for long periods, undisturbed by what must be an ineffably large set of neural sparkings in the vicinity. When this one left my conscious memory I can't say, except that it was totally new then and conceivably had lain dormant since the year we left Craigag never to return, in 1951, I think. I would not have even recognised Pat Monaghan because I hadn't seen her since she was about fourteen, but something triggered a question. I asked her if Iseabal Fraser ever took us over the loch to see the deserted stone house over the loch at Giusachan.

We had been in Miss Fraser's school together, she lasting the full primary years I presume and then going on to Fort William. I can't remember getting into a boat (which we would have done near the big Glenaladale house). I can't remember crossing the loch – there was no other way to reach Giusachan on the Ardgour side. There was not even a track. You would have had to have crossed the Callop almost at Callop, and then scrambled through very hilly and rocky, and difficult country west by Torran Giuthais, then south-westwards along the loch-side along the western skirts of Meall na h-Àiridh [Hill of the Summer Pasture], Meall a' Bhainne [Hill of the Milk] and Sgorr nan Cearc [Crag of the Hens].

She told me that Iseabal Fraser had taken us. I thought she might have registered a hesitance and surprise, as though she too had forgotten that day. But maybe I had said the name wrongly. 'It was a damp old house,' she told us, describing the old inside walls of which I had no memory at all. Her memories of Glenfinnan were continuous, overwhelmingly mundane and non-childish and, much more often than not, taken for granted like the smells in one's home, and one's daily habitual shiftings. I keenly remember things, just a few things, particularly the aromas, that happened walking the Callop–Glenfinnan road. But I lived through no road-widenings, no changes, no adolescence there, as she had, and my memory was trapped like the ant in amber.

No one brought up the subject of any unstated but perhaps personal guiding principle for Miss Fraser in Glenfinnan, to revitalise local Roman Catholic Jacobite historical consciousness. School day trips may simply have been normal and preferable to classroom work – I remember almost none of the latter, except letters and numbers, snatches of catechism, and a word or two of a Gaelic song. I had little notion of what school was about at all.

Being endlessly fascinated by Old and New World links going back to pre-Victorian times, and there aren't many involving Glenfinnan, I launched into the story of a Presbyterian Cameron, Ailean mac Uisdein Bhàin, who emigrated from that Giuthasachan to settle in Mabou, Cape Breton in 1821, bilingual, literate and traditionally musical. Ailean converted to Catholicism in Mabou, for want of a Protestant church, and had a Gaelic-speaking descendant, Sandy Cameron, who, till he died on 31 May 2007, lived in Mabou on the old south-facing farm looking over the water to the pioneer graveyard. That Cameron presence in Ardgour and Sunart in Argyllshire from the seventeenth century (thinning at the end of the Napoleonic Wars), added to the Allan Cameron mentioned by Somerled MacMillan who was farming in Meoble in South Morar in 1803, had for years made me consider the possibility of almost-planned Cameron land expansion into Clanranald's South Morar country, as well as southward into old MacLean and MacDonald countries. The Cameron holdings in Sunart, at Glen Hurich, went back to the seventeenth century. The Glendessary Camerons had a strong leasing presence in Ardgour that was ended by Ewen, ninth MacLean of Ardgour in 1685 and litigation went on into the eighteenth century over Glendessary rights to the Innerscadell farm. Later Cameron expansion was more into Morvern by Cameron of Glendessary, with Cameron females marrying into the old Morvern MacLean families. The Cameron farming at Giuthasachan could have been indirectly influenced to some extent by Fassifern and other Cameron land accumulation in Ardgour,[1] and in Strontian before 1745, but much more likely began with the Dungallan Camerons extending northwards along Loch Shiel from their main holding near Polloch, at Glen Hurich.

However old was the traditional black cattle Highland Gaelic farming occupation at Giusachan, whoever lived there from 1740 to *c.* 1820, the nineteenth century saw first sheep-farming, then deer shooting and fishing, and then the disappearance of even one family living there by 1945. It is a case of typical nineteenth-century decline writ with lamentable clarity, a little very marginal acreage changing outsider hands until nothing of tradition remained except the carefully collected place names for the six-inch maps in the 1870s.

In the mid 1830s, Giusachan was a sheep-farm and business run by a Catholic, Dòmhnul Ruadh [Red Donald] Cameron. He did not own the property. The subject of his Catholicism is never explained, hardly proof of anything greater, but maybe. The later

1830s was a time when the Highland and Agricultural Society in
Edinburgh was awarding prizes for improving sheep breeding and
Glenfinnan was involved (see *The Scotsman*, 16 September 1837).
Red Donald Cameron's business dealings were with Corpach and
Fort William, whither he rode. The track down the south side of
Loch Shiel that is shown on the six-inch map, which was surveyed
in 1874, was obviously the same, or a widened version of the one
that Red Donald rode on horseback in the 1830s – there was no
such remains even of a track in the 1940s. If he crossed the Callop
River it would have probably been at the shingly ford I used.
Nothing is known of Red Donald's parentage or roots. For all that,
the Cameron who emigrated to Mabou, Cape Breton in 1821,
from Guesachan, was Allan, son of John Ban Uisdean, a Presbyterian (Ailean macIain Bhàin, 'ic Uisdein). The suggestions implicit, to me, in this emigration are of conversion of a mixed
Highland farm to a sheep-farming enterprise, and of the con-
commitant dispersal of the last non-Presbyterian folk. (Across Loch
Shiel, the Glenaladale estate was advertised to let in the *Inverness
Journal* of 16 September 1825). Once the old subsistence farming
people were gone (perhaps in 1821), the Giusachan farm followed
the same pattern as Morton's Callop and Cregag farms, only more
dramatically fizzling out.

It is a Presbyterian record that divulges that Red Donald the
shepherd at Giusachan, and his brother Paul, were Roman Catholics (and that both were married to Presbyterian women, sisters). An
Ardnamurchan-parish-born shepherd, Donald Cameron, who had
400 sheep on land in Ardnamurchan parish in 1851, is known to
the Cameron archives as Donald Cameron of Guesachan (in
Ardnamurchan parish). Two of his younger children were born
in the parish of Kilmallie, which abuts, to the east, suggesting that
he was at Guesachan [Giuthasachan] about 1834 and about 1836
and moved away.[2] Donald's Presbyterian, and fundamentalist, wife
Margaret is associated with a story of her (boating and?) walking to
the Free Church at Strontian from Guesachan which shows that
the family was still there in 1843 (Margaret was dead in 1851). It
seems from that that Guesachan had become a sheep-farm by 1834.
Red Donald was living at Garbhan [Garvan] on Loch Eil (in
Kilmallie parish in 1902) in 1869 according to the research of

Dr Robert S. Cameron, Australia. I've taken the Strontian story from an article by a Martin Stewart who walked the south shore of Loch Shiel in May 2004, publishing his observations and photographs, but not his sources, on the internet.

While the genealogy of the emigrant Ailean mac Iain Bhàin 'ic Uisdein Cameron is well known in Cape Breton, from *The Mabou Pioneers,* the history of the later Giusachan shepherding Cameron family in Sunart is harder to find. Hoping to save his name from oblivion among the large number of forgotten Scottish Free Church Gaelic-speaking ministers, an article was written (duplicated?) by M. Macaulay, called 'Hector Cameron of Lochs and Back [Lewis]'. Hector was born at 'Guiseachan, a lonely farmhouse on the south-side of Loch Shiel' in 1836 and raised a Roman Catholic in a Catholic family. His father was called 'Red Donald' Cameron and he was the Giusachan shepherd of the 1830s. His business interests, before the church disruption of 1843, took Red Donald to 'Corpach and Fort William' often riding a fine grey horse and on the way he grew into the habit of stopping at the schoolhouse at Corriebeg (by Kinlocheil) and arguing religion with the SSPCK teacher there, Neil MacLean (see the 1841 census). Red Donald was converted to the church that was to become the free church by MacLean in or by 1843, when his son Hector was seven. Red Donald's brother Paul was converted not long after. Alas for local history their grandparents and great grandparents are not named. They flourished in the first five improver decades after 1746 when records of the tenantry were rare, and seldom were the despised and feared Catholics mentioned (except occasionally as objects of later conversion).

A court case at Tobermory in 1854 adds to one's appreciation of the spread of sheep-farming northward up Loch Shiel from lower Sunart. Archibald MacDonald from Gaskan, near Glenaladale on the Moidart side, was accused of stealing cut and barked oak from the Riddell estate at Gortenmhoiran (Goirtean Mhorain/The Field of the Meadow Saxifrage).[3] The Gortenmhoiran farm on the lochside was leased by a James Milligan who kept a Dugald Cameron (50) as his shepherd. The theft was reported to Dugald by the 'parker' Colin Cameron (50) who lived at Camuschoirk (Camas Choirce/Bay of Oats?) where he was employed by the head

forester, McLaren. The other witnesses included Dugald's wife
Anne, and his nephew John (16) who gave his evidence in Gaelic.
In explaining the value of the oak MacDonald had taken, it was
recorded that it was used by its legal owner for boats, vinegar and
cabers for homes. The recording of the case may represent a
deviance from compliance with tradition by the outsider. No
ruins of houses at Goirtean Mhorain are shown on the Landranger
1:50,000 map of the area although they were seen by Martin
Stewart in the early twenty-first century.)

One way and another, Camerons in Lochaber at the time, are
presented to readers as preponderantly Protestant – often the
encouragement to assume as much is almost deviously placed –
but one of the chief's sons, Alexander, had been a Jesuit priest in
1745, and another, Charles (*c.* 1747–1776) who became chief in
1762, was an Episcopalian, and two daughters became nuns. In the
muster roll of active Jacobite Camerons in *No Quarter Given*, the
Cameron clergy are given in this order: Catholic, Episcopal and
Presbyterian. Catholic and Episcopalian numbers in Lochiel, until
and after the estate forfeiture, are not known and the record,
conveniently, is the victorious Presbyterians'. Generally uncon-
sidered is the fact that those writers considered the presence of non-
Presbyterians as overlookable, as advertising a failure of improvement. Clanranald to the west was Catholic. So were Glengarry and
Strathglass to the north. So was Keppoch to the east and the debate
about the religion in Glencoe, Episcopalian or Catholic long into
the eighteenth century is still lively enough to suggest resistance on
the part of the more numerous Cameron estate people to imposed
Lowland Presbyterianism[4] – an interesting isolated case of a
Presbyterian minister at Kilmallie is Duncan MacIntyre (1757–
1830), eleventh of Camus na h-Eirbhe (near Callart on Loch
Leven, part of the Lochiel estate); ordained in 1784, he held
Kilmallie from 1816 till 1830; his father, an Episcopalian, had
been wounded as a Jacobite at Falkirk in 1746; his mother was a
Glencoe Episcopalian; his appointment may reflect the flexibility of
transition from Episcopacy and Catholicism in Lochiel. In the
1790s and on into the nineteenth century, at the time of the
Cameron clearances, the Morar church records show a small
Cameron presence in North Morar which was Catholic, for

example. It may never be possible to deduce how much local revulsion at the imposure of Presbyterianism on the people of the Lochiel estate was involved in the emigrations from the estate in the long emigration period, but particularly in the early nineteenth century. There were MacMillan emigrants to Glengarry County, Upper Canada in 1802, among others, who were Catholics. It is appropriate to suggest that such a speculation has a strong tinge of plausibility, and that the older Christianities were deeply resented by the new controllers.[5]

If Iseabal Fraser knew the Red Donald Cameron, Giusachan, story in the 1940s, she either didn't tell it to us or my memory just cannot recall it. Sarah MacVarish and Donald Cameron at Callop, and Joe MacLeod, surely knew a great deal about the history of upper Ardgour, upper Sunart and Glenfinnan, but their knowledge went ungathered. Calum MacLean, who knew and interviewed Joe MacLeod *c.* 1950, was more intrigued by lore and story than local history. Mary Donaldson and Wendy Wood would have needed to spend time in Inverness County, Cape Breton, to have caught glimpses of the significance of the older Gaelic world and its bonds and consciousness of its place in kin history and small countries. The interests of neither one were shallow and both of the women chose to live Highland lives where old West Highland communities had once upon a time existed, but there was not prompt or comprehension enough by then to examine its overseas continuity and to put everything together. Calum Mac-Lean, who was a Gael, would have loved, and been lionised in, Gaelic Cape Breton – many pieces of what he had realised was an incomplete puzzle in Highland Scotland would have fallen eloquently and (I suspect) startlingly into place and what he certainly would have written would have been invaluable.

Guesachan was occupied in 1733, as shown on Alexander Bruce's 'Plan of Loch Sunart', only then it was called Glashaden. In the Langlands map of Argyll in 1801 there is only one farm building marked on the south side of Loch Shiel between Scamodale and the mouth of the Callop River and that is Glaschorin; whether this is Glas Choirean or Giuthasachan is undeterminable. However, in 1820 Guesachan is was called 'Glaschorren' (Glas Choirean/Blue Corries) by William Johnson (see Thomson, *The*

Atlas of Scotland, 1832). There is a mountain about three miles to the southward of 'Guesachan' on the modern map called Glas Choirean, which lies immediately west of Sgurr Ghiusachain [Piny Outcrop], from which rises the stream that exits into Loch Shiel where Giusachan is today. Someone may have transposed the names of the two mountains but more likely, Giusachan, in post-Gaelic life times, was considered a pendicle to Glas Choirean. The bathymetrical survey (in this case surveyed in 1902) shows five buildings at Glas Choirean and one main one with an outbuilding at Giusachan.

The rapid de-population/Gaelicisation of Giusachan, or greater 'Glaschorren' is roughly outlined in the records of *The Scotsman* newspaper. The issue of 4 September 1872 advertises the auction on Wednesday 9 October 1872 of,

> the beautiful HIGHLAND PROPERTY called GLASCHORN or GUISACHAN, on the south side of Loch Shiel, with SHOOT-INGS and FISHINGS extending westward from the Head of the Loch, with the Island of Glenfinnan, and containing about ten square miles of surface, situated in the Parish of Ardnamurchan, Argyllshire. The Sheep-farm is cheaply leased at £175, the lease expiring at Whitsunday 1878; and the annual burdens are about £25.

(In the 1880s sheep-farming quite quickly became unprofitable; hints of this decline were apparent a decade earlier and influenced Morton to build Craigag shooting lodge.)

The description added that the land had two fine red deer corries and was bounded by the Earl of Morton's deer forest of 'Corra Glen' and Sir Thomas Milles Riddell's lands of Scamsdale and Glenhurich (where the Cameron shepherd was in the 1850s). To the north the boundary was the Callop, beyond which lay Glenala-dale (as far to the east as Allt na Crìche) and 'Loch Eil's forest' (from Allt na Crìche to include a portion of west Cregag). There was only the farmer's home at Guesachan, presumably the building Iseabal Fraser took us to see in the 1940s. The advertisement of 1872 also noted that part of the place was well stocked with Scottish firs

[Giùthasan] and birches and that a good loch-side site might be selected for an appropriate home. Whether or not there was a quota on salmon, sea trout, and brown and yellow trout to be taken from Loch Shiel is not mentioned. The 'upset price' was £7,000 and applications were invited by a Perth firm of solicitors. The owner's name is not given but by September of 1873 it was the property of the Earl of Morton and it remains part of that estate. Whether or not Morton had at last re-established the boundaries of some early northern Ardgour is unknown.

A fisherman's report in *The Scotsman* on 26 July 1879 described the 'Deer Forest of Guisachan' as rising boldly above the small river that runs into the loch. All connections with indigenous Highland farming were gone, no word of sheep or cattle. In 2005 the Guesachan valley part of the old sheep and deer farm still belonged to the owner of the Cona Glen estate. The fisherman-writer of 1879 wrote of splendid examples of old Scotch firs, in groups and singly, which were growing on the property. He saw no road or track, although according to the six-inch map surveyed five years earlier, there was one. No house other than the one we saw that day many years ago, and a roofless rectangle of stone walls to the north nearby, exists on the one flat piece of river-mouth land at Guesachan these days. There is now a gravel road cutting a scar into the steep hillsides, from a new bridge at Callop all the way to Polloch and beyond, but no sheep bleat on Red Donald's old sheep farm these days. The Callop farm, although it followed the same course of development, from mixed Highland black cattle sub-sistence, to sheep, to sheep and deer, to just deer and whatever roamed, supported several people into the 1950s.

From the Upper Loch Shiel plate (53) of the bathymetrical survey (1902) in volume 4 of Murray's loch atlas (based on the six-inch OS surveys), there are glimpses from the namings, of the pre-invasive/commercial-agricultural world from Glas Choirean north to the Callop river. Glas Choirean itself lies below Coire an t-Searraich Bhuidhe [Corrie of the Golden Colt]. Two hill streams (including Allt Fearna/Alder Stream) to the north-east at Giubh-sachan are Sròn Laoigh [Prominence of the Calf], An Àiridh Mhór [The Big Shieling] and Tom nan Dearcan Fithich [Knoll of the Raven Berries (*Vaccinium myrtillus*, whortleberry)]. From the six-inch Ordnance Survey map itself, published by Major General John Cameron RE, nearer the Callop, between 56° 51′ 30″ and 56° 51′ 45″ north of the equator, south of Eilean Ghleann Fhionain there are Rudha nan Gamhna [Point of the Calves], Port nan Gamhna [Port/Ferry of the Calves], Glac nan Gamhna [Hollow of the Calves], and Ceum an aon Mhairt [Path of the one Fat Cow], all visible from Clach mhic Bheathain or very near it. This map also shows tellingly, a 'sheepfold' south of Lochan Port na Creige and north of Glac nan Gamhna, and two much larger sheepfolds, one abutting and the other a little north of the river at Guesachan, near Drochaid na Craoibhe Daraich [The Oak Tree Bridge]. Guesachan doubtless became an outlying sheep-farm, or pendicle, of Glas Choirean in the commercial farming days, but its habitation is remembered by the name Tom nam Fòidean [Hill of the Peats], lying just south of the farm.

Among those names, Port nan Gamhna and Lochan Port na Creige, show water transport of beasts over a short distance to avoid the swampy, bulrushy area running from Lochan Port na Creige along the Ardgour side of the river Callop as far as the big bend. Beasts would have been moved in that direction for Lochaber; cheaper than going south and using the Corran ferry. Among others, a prominent Loch Shiel-side drover for whom there are records for 1811 to 1817 was James MacDonald, Glenalladale. He was a drover and dealer in sheep and black cattle.[6] Presumably his animals were gathered from Moidart, for the greater part, but he may have assembled beasts from places like Glas Choirean and Giusachan across the water. More important than establishing his range of cattle sources is that MacDonald, if he took his beasts to the Callop, must have used boats to move cattle to the head of Loch Shiel from places like Glenalladale and Dalilea. It was not at all by accident that cartographers were given the old Gaelic names; neither are those names reproduced so faithfully by English-speaking cartographers by any accident.[7]

Not many Scots people are interested in a stray connection between Guisachan and Mabou. I doubt many Scots would be impressed even by a collation of names of emigrants from that or any other Gaelic area in the great emigration years, 1770–1840, for there is a blinkering power in national ethnocentricity that allows overlookings and inadequately based rationalisings. I might have mentioned the late-eighteenth-century MacFarlane presence on the Glenaladale property. The extended MacFarlane family that emigrated to Nova Scotia on the *Dove of Aberdeen* in 1801 claimed to have lived in and left Glenfinnan and it has always struck me as most likely that they moved to Glenfinnan from typical MacFarlane country in Argyllshire (Loch Sloy area) after the Captain John emigration to St John's Island in 1772. They were part of the filling of an almost demographic vacuum caused by Captain John's emigration. But few Scots want even to speculate about that – there is a similar lack of interest in the first removings from the Keppoch farms up Bohuntine. Of the MacFarlane family movements there is almost no record except family history in Cape Breton. There is a lonely Sloy Brook in Upper Margaree where one of the MacFarlane descendants had a mill (nearby lived Allachan Aonghuis Dhuibh MacFarlane, the piper-fiddler. One of these MacFarlanes married into the Scotus family.) It fits into almost nobody's concept of the old Gaelic Highlands today and even M.E.M. Donaldson's research in the written record did not uncover Sagairt Àrasaig's genealogical history of the Highland Scots of Antigonish county, which exposed the MacFarlane story, among others, in the last decade of the nineteenth century.

My memory of visiting this Giusachan only needed an intimate nudge to reappear and hints that much more remains locked away. A lot of information is easily forgotten.

Borrodale and two hiding places

Iseabal Fraser also took us to Borrodale House in the Àrasaig old forest where I saw the glassed-off piece of a wall in the old part of the house where the quasi-regal visitor in 1745 was said to have placed a hand – I didn't know that the original building had been torched after Culloden, but the false memory still has the power to enchant. She took us from there to one of 'Prince Charles's caves, down at the root of a long peninsula that struck out into Loch nan Uamh [Loch of the Caves] (more of a shelter from the rain than a useful hiding place; M.E.M. Donaldson found a more likely candidate inland) – standing outside on that tongue of land I remember the sudden ear-splitting clap of thunder overhead and the gathered grey-black clouds that day; it was elemental. She took us to the silver sands at Morar – I remember fuschias blooming with their red and purple bell flowers at the fringe of the sands.

She it was who told us, on our way to a Christmas party at the Cameron-Head mansion at Kinlochailort in a big black limousine, that in an old tree trunk at the bottom of a steep hillside that we couldn't see the prince had had to hide from the Hanoverian soldiery in 1746 after Culloden. Two trees are remembered by Jacobite romantics; the better known is a big one in South Morar somewhere, perhaps at Coille Allmha to the west of the Meoble river on the loch-side, wherefrom Simon Fraser of Lovat was winkled like a maggot by the Campbell and Hanoverian soldiery after Culloden; the other was the one Miss Fraser talked about. But it was a dark night when we were driven to the Kinlochailort party and for well over fifty years I had often wondered where that tree had been, and if it could still be there. A generous host told Seumas and me the same story, without a word of prompting, at a daylight hour in late 2002 as we were not far westward of Glenfinnan, and I learned that the steep slope down to the trees was actually the northern side of the *Slatach* glen just outside of Glenfinnan – so the bonnie prince, yet again, was not far from whatever Glenfinnan amounted to in those days.[8] I never saw the tree and I know no one who has scrambled down to look for it, but since Iseabal Fraser told us about it I have always imagined that it was still there.

I've always wished there had been many more excursions. I would have remembered for ever, with indelibly boyish frames of reference, Glenaladale, Dalilea, Eilean Fhionain, the old burying ground down the loch, Loch Beoraid in South Morar, the ruined house in Kinloch Morar, Meoble, Inverlochy Castle, Torr Castle, but for all that, the trips we did make left indelible imprints on my mind, like those early Highland games that (Kinlochailort House) Francis Cameron Head and his wife Lucretia Farrel started in 1945 at Glenfinnan. Those few were undoubtedly among the most important of my earliest memories for, as I've told many people since, when I found myself sitting, bored, in a history class in Edinburgh four or five years after leaving Glenfinnan, my thoughts were of Jacobite Gaelic Scotland. I resented being force-fed English history, not just because Scotland was of secondary significance to many French-speaking Normans, Turnip Townshend, Jethro Tull, the Tolpuddle martyrs, good King George, William Pitt and Benjamin Disraeli, but because there was nothing other than the most condescending, perfunctory and poor attention whatever paid to Gaelic Scotland, on the contorted images of which so many Lowland companies dined. Edinburgh was a foreign capital, profoundly disturbed that it was Saxon, using a stark, lunatic religion of the chosen to identify itself. I've proudly carried my 11 per cent in the third-year history class, rock bottom, although, along with that unshakeable reactionary pride went, for decades, the almost unshakeable idea that I could never do history, for which I hold Lowland Presbyterian Scotland and its rigorous education system responsible.

I had very few schoolteachers who were lastingly and particularly influential positively, but one was the strapping Iseabal Fraser. With one or two little memories of actual classroom work in Glenfinnan school to the side – like most folk I'd have taught myself those things soon enough – I learned a lot from her of late Victorian pro-Highlandness, however romantically and contrivedly offered it was. In cutting through the superficial imagery she lathered on, I came actually to learn something. Luckily there remained to me something of the widespread old Gaelic warmth and hospitality in Callop and Glenfinnan just after the war. That old spirit, with its faults and hypersensitivities, was still being gradually eroded by the enemy, from without and within until, by Queen Victoria's time, much less remained, of rural people and tradition north-east of *Eire*. That loss is what angers me. And, that it might not have been is shown by rural Gaelic Cape Breton, without which there would be only a shallower nostalgia.

The triumphirate in the high hollow

Iseabal Fraser's primary school is still there and lived in in Glenfinnan. It is a two-storey building, which, in my time, looked much like some of the homes at Achentore [Achadh an Todhair/Dung Field], in a sedate line, on the road into Fort William from Onich [Omhanaich] to the south.[9] Those nice grey-stone buildings, like the Grange in south Edinburgh, proclaim that the poor are somewhere else and that here the sedate and refined are left to pronounce Highland middle-class superiority. The Glenfinnan school is one of the larger grey, schisty buildings nestling in a little cluster of buildings on the right at the top of the steep hill up from the crossroads and the main bridge across the Finnan. Not including the church below the road, I remember two buildings, the school and what I thought to be the priest's house. Still not including the church, today there are three, one being a modern bungalow, the priest's new house, where once a kindly priest fed a lonely traveller kippers at some very early, quiet and dewy hour.

'So this is *home* for you,' the priest gently, understandingly said, when I had explained who I was. In 2002 the other old, two-storey, square-ended stone building was still there too only it fitted into almost no memory. Reason told me what it was just because it looked to be the oldest up there. It was derelict and neglected and its rusting corrugated iron roof was bleeding oxides on to the aged, squared igneous rocks. I learned that it was called 'the castle', a name that was new to me. It was almost clinging to the road, almost an undesirable obstacle to traffic. I stood thinking and just could not imagine it. Then I realised why: the new two-lane road had taken perhaps twenty feet of green from what I remember. The old building had lost its roadside grounds, grass and shrubbery and looked, not like a maturing old Victorian mystery, but like something that had been lucky to escape the wrecker's ball.

The church is marked on the six-inch map surveyed in 1875 but there is no other building, and 'the castle' was nothing if not a substantial, eminently recordable structure built of masonry and cement, the sort no self-respecting cartographer with the least interest in middle-class demography overlooked. I looked at its old weathered walls in October or November of 2002 and was unconvinced that it was never Father Patrick O'Regan's home, or storage perhaps, just after the war. The modern bungalow that is, or was, the priest's house, nearby, is probably old enough to have been there in 1951 (there is a priest living there but parish work continues to be done by Fr Roddy Johnstone of St John's, Caol). I just do not remember it. It has no second storey, and the verandah (I think) also excludes any use of a ladder. However the old stone building is still owned by the Roman Catholic diocese (of Argyll and the Isles) and, if permission is granted, may become used again, for broader community purposes.[10]

This third stone building, however, does appear on the 1902 one-inch map that was revised in 1895. The cartographic evidence also shows it to be the newest of the three stone buildings of the hill triumphirate, built probably by Fr Donald MacDonald, the builder of the church. If it were, he seems to have had two purposes in mind for it. The obvious one is that it was a glebe-house, but for the priests to come after him, whom he knew would not come from the privileged estate-owning Glenaladale family with a family mansion nearby. Fr Donald MacDonald [Ronald according to the 1861 census, where he is given as aged forty-six] was the priest-brother of Angus MacDonald of Glenaladale, and Fr Donald/Ronald died in 1895. So the 'castle' was built between 1875 and 1895.[11] Cardinal Newman died in 1890. According to Ronnie MacKellaig in March 2006, the other use of the building was as a coach-house. Was Fr Donald seeking to usurp another change-house, perhaps the Stagehouse Inn half a mile west along the road? Or, assuming the building that became the Stagehouse was not, or was no longer, in the horse-changing business, was he anticipating the greater use of the new high road to the isles over some place on the old low road by Glenaladale House, innocent of inside information about the coming iron horse? I believe that it was Fr O'Regan's glebe-house, or at least study space, some time between 1946 and 1951. Mr MacKellaig said that the living quarters were upstairs and that there was a little staircase to the upper floor on the school side of the building. I don't remember a stair but the upstairs was the living part. Mr MacKellaig also knew that an Angus MacDonald had lived in the old building.

What began as the new school still stands commandingly where the road turns quite sharply left, with a camber, to parallel the unseeable railway line hidden away in its deep gneissic slot a little to the north and higher up. Excepting the church, the two Victorian stone buildings stand in a south-ish-facing little hollow of a

southward projection or tongue of the hill pasture, *Tom na h-Aire*,
between the road and the railway line.

The little one-lane road we walked to school crossed the headlands
of the Finnan river almost in a straight line, but not quite. The
Callop river-mouth end of the flat is now wooded, as though in
craven atonement for the blasting of one of the Catholic Highlands' last guardians. You can still see outlines of the old rigs from
the Highland farming days;[12] the road was straight enough to start
with but kept to the hills. Then, at the shop below the hill, where
the track out to the monument near the loch edge began, the six-
inch map shows a deliberately straighter road to the main bridge. It
was at the shop in 1946 that the road deviated a few degrees from
the older way, cutting out half a mile of walking to the old crossing
point up the river. The new straight road crossed low-lying land,
and was built up gradually above the soggy flatlands from the shop
to the one-arched bridge. The monument stands, half-madly
defying the floods, almost at the loch-side with its feet nearly in
the mud as if 1813 to 1815 had been drier years – you could see the
little enclosed graveyard nearby with its one or two memorials
between the monument and the Finnan mouth, a soggy resting
place that for years I wished to enclose what's left of me. Acadians
would have considered building earthen dykes to save the land.
  Then there were the wooded riverbanks of the Finnan and the
stone bridge. When you crossed the bridge to the north bank of the
Finnan there was a crossroads – the old road ran westward from the
viaduct up the glen to the old Glenfinnan, near the Glenaladales'
big house (the modern Tigh na Slataiche). The new road from the
crossroads started up a steep wooded hill. On the left, seen through
the edging of trees, there was a pasture, the real glebe, sloping up
quite steeply from the low road – Fr O'Regan had the use of it for a
cow. Then still on the left, up the hill, the woods grew dense and
protective, completely hiding the little Glenalladale church – the
church, although high above the old Glenfinnan, and gazing
regally, so sadly down Loch Shiel, was visible from the pasture
and the loch to its south-west. To the right of the road the woods
were denser all the way up to the buildings. Just past the crossroads,
on the right there was a tall tree among the others I always wanted

to climb. The road had been carved from the hillside, to serve the stone triumphirate, and the wood to its right was dense on its steep slope with, I think, many tall pines. The ground under the pines and other trees was dark and brown, grassless, no spring primroses or wood anemones.

How the village had developed, and why, were subjects which only began to appeal to me much later on, and to which only recently have some answers begun to come. There is a record however, enough to allow some plausible deductions. It turns out that I was nowhere near the most unusual outsider in or near Glenfinnan – there was a shepherd living in Glenfinnan in 1861 from Kilbride, for example, but twenty years later, in 1881, there was an Allan MacDougall there, in the fifth home visited, an 'agricultural labourer' (a deliberately vague, perhaps derogatory designation forced on the information collectors). He, his wife Margaret and his first child (of those still living I presume), aged twelve, had all been born in Àrasaig; another son aged five had been born in Ardnamurchan parish (possibly in Glenfinnan or Glenaladale),[13] but there were two others sons, Donald (9), and John (7) who had been born in America. The children were all 'scholars'. The eighteen Glenfinnan 'scholars' are identified in the 1881 census.

Most of the school inspectors' reports for Glenfinnan primary school are available in the Scottish national archives in Edinburgh and run from 1877 to 1954. The owners of Miss Fraser's old school, now a rentable home, have written that it was built in 1876. Then it wasn't an addition to any little group of known and long-established buildings there in that little cup of shelter looking down a spectacular Highland loch. It was one element in part of a Catholic revivalism, but, sadly where Gaelic was concerned, a nail in the coffin. The church across the road was opened on 19 August 1873 (to the sound of the same two-drone, *lignum vitae* and ivory-mounted bagpipes that had been played up the hill at the raising of the Jacobite standard in 1745) by Fr Donald MacDonald (Borro-dale-Glenaladale's brother) aged sixty-seven from the 1881 census, and it had only been around mid-century that Angus MacDonald of Borrodale-Glenaladale had built the modern Glenaladale House, the empty mansion house with the blue light in the upper window

when I got to Glenfinnan after the war.[14] This little church and
school cluster, where religion was concerned, was built in reaction
to the feared spread of Protestantism, notably through a threat-
eningly efficient Protestant school and proselytising system that had
converted Red Donald the shepherd. (The school, the priest's
house and the church were built at Mingarry, at the other end of
Loch Shiel, in Moidart, in 1862, when Hope Scott owned that
estate. See, 'High Mingarry' by John Dye for Comann Eachdraidh
Mhùideirt.) These stone buildings all bear the stamp of acceptable
middle class and mark the last detaching of the old Gaelic world
from the new English one.

I have not read the school inspectors' reports, and the admission
registers (1877–1981) have a seventy-five-year hold before dis-
closure to the public, but I have had indirect access to the school's
log books (1877–1983) for which the waiting period is only half a
century, that and three of the nineteenth-century censuses, 1841,
1861 and 1881. My first school opened on 6 February 1877 and the
first teacher was a Margaret Cameron, who lasted nine years until
1886 – in the 1881 census she was given as born in Kiltarlity (Fraser
country) and aged twenty-five, unmarried; among her pupils were
the two American-born MacDougalls. Between September 1935
and 26 December 1938 the teacher was a Miss Sarah Kennedy, and
she was replaced by an interim appointment, Alexander Grant.
Then, with her first entry in the school's third log-book, dated 18
April 1939 . . .

Took up duty in this school today – I. Fraser

. . . we first meet Miss Iseabal Fraser.

My mother came home once in Edinburgh to tell me that she
had met Miss Fraser on Lothian Road. I can't remember annoyance
at her not having told me how to get to meet her myself; perhaps I
had not been gone from Glenfinnan long enough although, almost
without exception, schoolteachers to me have always been un-
befriendable.

In my day the little turn in to the school from the twist in the
road was unpaved and stony. To the north, there was a short

steep grassy slope up to a thin, gapped line of bushes where a fence enclosed part of the Tom na h-Aire hill pasture that must have ended, over a little summit, at the railway line, hidden in its cutting. Beyond the line lay mountains like those behind Craigag, ages ago scoured by ice, now heathery, brackeny, rocky and scraped, often hidden in eastbound clouds. For me, those mountains were the enfolding arms of another consciousness in which a primary school played almost no part, officially. Children from anywhere coming to live there are touched forever by those rugged mountains.

The hill pasture north of the school may only have been a pasture for sheep in the late 1940s – I remember on one occasion plenty of sheep, and men, at the sheep dip on the hill side of the low road between the main road bridge and the Gillieses' house at the viaduct – but almost thirty years earlier, in 1920, one of Robert Adam's photographs shows that the Tom na h-Aire shoulder of Fraoch Bheinn was (or not long before, possibly, had been) arable land. The rigs stand out clearly from the 1920 Adam exposure. They are clear both above and, if I am right about a dark area of photograph being a railway cutting, below the railway – there are two cuttings just east of the station – above the school. The rigs follow the contours and may have been originally ploughed by man and horse rather than man and *cas chrom*. Adam took the photograph from above the railway line. The same photograph, which will be discussed for a different purpose below, does not show any part of the roof of the schoolhouse and one is struck by the denseness of what appear to have been pines hiding it. If they represented a plantation it is possible that they were seedlings around 1870. I don't remember such dense and extensive coniferous wood when I went to Glenfinnan school, although in 2002 there were still pines in the area, in front of the church, to the east of the school on the standard knoll, and down the hill by the road, and on the south-west side of the station lane, but of an age I did not assess. It was not primarily young pine foliage that hid the church in 1946. Down at the loch-side in 1947 all that was left of what had been a sawmill was a vaguely contained rectangle of wet, unbouncy sawdust. The last pine plantation had gone. Adam's 1920 photograph may point to old Highland subsistence farming,

and whatever Brinckman asked in reparation for his lost acres from
the railway company in 1898 is better explained in this light. I don't
know when Tom na h-Aire moved from arable to pasture,
although in 1920 there was little or no heather or bracken in
Adam's photograph.

I do not really know the depth of Gaelic thought and memory in
Glenfinnan just after the second German war, only that it existed.
The loss of people to emigration over nearly a century, the new
people, particularly estate leasers like Brinckman, English in the
school, the triumph of Victorianism, the road, the railway, all were
nonetheless regarded as absorbable by some folk, for I became a
Saxon Highlander there in a very short time. Joe MacLeod was a
source of lore for Soirle's brother Calum MacLean around 1950,
probably also for Somerled MacMillan and Robert Adam. Who
knows what John 'the post', the two Chirsties, Archie MacKellaig
and Archie Gillies (and at Callop, Sarah MacVarish, Donal Farrich
and Calum Lowrie) and people like them passed on to the next
generations? They all showed the tenacity of the older consciousness.

About fifty years earlier, in 1895, an anonymous letter to the
national newspaper, *The Scotsman* (10 September 1895, p. 7), told
of the memories of veterans of the 1745 Jacobite war for Bonnie
Prince Charlie, at only one remove. It told of the Gaelic bard Mary
MacKellar's having been raised by a grandfather who in turn had
been raised by a grandfather who had been an active Jacobite in the
Forty-five. The writer didn't doubt that some of his readers would
share his memory of a dignified old man from the Fort William area
who had been held, as a babe, by his godfather, 'the Piobair dhu',
the black piper of the Keppoch MacDonalds at Culloden. As
recently as 1892 there had died in Ardgour an old Cameron man
who had been raised by a grandfather who had been 'out'. Then, in
1894, a 100-year-old lady died in Ardgour who had known a
woman whose family had had to flee from its north-west Ardgour
farm (Cregag, Callop, Drumfearn or Garvan, perhaps) when Prince
Charles's army approached Kinlocheil in late August of 1745 – the
Ardgour MacLean chief was a minor in 1745 and the family in
general terms did not join the Jacobite cause and army, and some
tenants may have felt threatened by nearby Jacobite Camerons and

others. *The Scotsman* letter-writer's letter was of course in English and there can be no assessing how unusual, or commonplace, or simply romantic, in Gaelic Lochaber, such proudly retold reminiscences, were. The early nineteenth-century Inverness newspapers often mentioned 'the last veteran of Culloden' in their columns. However mad-cap Charles Edward's determination to put his father on the throne of north and south Britain appeared, clearly it did not seem quite so outrageous to all Highlanders, or to all Lowlanders, that summer of 1745 – not everyone went to war at the point of an officer's sword, and just as clearly a line of simple regret persisted here and there in Gaelic Scotland for a long time. A sizeable bit of the schizoid nature of the Scotland I knew comes from that lost cause.

The chaffinch in the window

Among my memories of Iseabal Fraser and Glenfinnan school is only one dark (and unerasable) one, one that a preference for innocence still keeps me from considering, but through which emerges a memory of Father O'Regan that has not yet been confirmed. One lunchtime one of Mrs MacVarish's children from Clydeside and I were strapped before the class for having rescued a chaffinch that had managed to become stuck between the upper and lower parts of one of the upper-floor windows in what for decades I have known to have been Father O'Regan's two-storey priest's house. We had decided the bird should be rescued and somehow we had found a ladder, put it against the wall, climbed up and into the room and freed the innocent. Doing that, we broke some rule that no one had told us about, breaking, entering and liberating a helpless creature fluttering for its needed freedom and sure to die if ignored. I am still embarrassed, and angry enough not to have asked anyone about it. I am left with a memory and only the surety that it has not been corrupted from outside. It is the only occasion that I recall Iseabal Fraser taking out and using her strap. I don't remember being aware till then that she even had such a thing. I don't believe she ever used it, before or after our punishing that day, for all the time up to my leaving for the sooty, mountain-

less Saxon lands in the year the Brabazon flew over Granton Road.
It was unfair, although had the chaffinch demanded the price I'd
have paid it without demur.

   Although this may be one of my deceptive memories, this one
involves the ladder to a second-storey window of the priest's old
stone glebe-house, an upper window at the Tom na h-Aire side of
the building. It was the priest's house, no one else's, which is why,
I've always assumed, we were beaten. The only building that
answers today is the old stone building in that high hollow next to
the school called 'the Castle'.

Half a century ago and more, in Miss Fraser's time, her classroom
was on the ground floor. I was never upstairs. There were
outdoor toilets to the back of the school, across a little al-
most-enclosed courtyard. To my surprise, I remember looking
from somewhere near the school to the sheltering piney crest,
and seeing a tall, dark-haired young Highland woman who was
Father O'Regan's housekeeper walking across the lush grass of
the little burn that divided the school from the priest's home (not
inconceivably the bungalow – I can't bring the thought into
focus). I have forgotten her name. She spoke English with a
fascinating, liltingly lovely Highland accent I can never forget.
She has always seemed unapproachably beautiful to me in my
thoughts. For some unexplained reason, another image of the site
of the schoolhouse stays with me.

   The Highland woman has become, somehow, one of Caraid
nan Gàidheal's characters in one of his conversations in Comh-
radh nan cnoc. When I first tried to read those religious
conversations, not understanding much, with the Cuairtear,
with Eòghan Brocair, with Lachann nan Ceist, with Fionnladh
Pìobaire agus a bhean Màiri, with am Maighstir Sgoile, and with
Iain Òg, one of the places that they immediately occupy in my
mind's eye was a little, thatched Highland stone home somewhere near Iseabal Fraser's school. It was nestled in the little
grassy and treed hollow, well sheltered from the winds on three
quarters, watching down Loch Shiel, knowing nothing of the
formal education that lay ahead.

Tha thusa 'an sin a Lachainn, mar bu mhiann leis na seann daoine, a' leigeadh do sgìos, air chùl gaoithe 's ri aodann gréine, a' leughadh mar a b'abhaist.

[It's you there, Lauchie, like the old folk were wont, resting from their work, on the back of a wind, to the face of the sun, reading as was the way.]

There was a strong redolence of the old Jacobite past just there, near 'the castle' in its tranquil, sunny hollow, caught in the mists and temporalities a boy knows and that I can't quite recover. Maybe it was just because it was Glenfinnan. Finlay the piper (one of MacLeod's characters), an old loyal Jacobite, was from Glendessary, probably the Morvern one. The moderate Presbyterian MacLeod from Morvern would have been pleased to think someone more than a century later would put his didactic, invented conversations into what was a really Jacobite corner of the world, Roman Catholic, MacDonald of Glenalladale's Glenfinnan in the north of Moidart, east of Àrasaig. Even in Gaelic there was the same need not to enquire deeply and to create phony dreams, only in Cape Breton there was little of that into the 1970s. I know that there was a world around me, a substantial part of which I could not enter. Nonetheless, I have always loved it and would have fought for its continuing against any ism or ish.

At school we used copybooks, copperplate, up light, down heavy, and 'A new broom sweeps clean', which I blotched. I remember beginning to learn decimals, after fractions, not long before I was taken away. I remember the sweets given out to us from someone living in Tanganyika who must have had ties with Glenfinnan. I have no recollection of the taking of the school photograph, although I am grateful to him or her. I am grateful to my mother for saving the positive for me. It reminds me of what Màiri Matheson looked like, and John Keenan, and Jimmie and Alasdair Gillies at the viaduct, Pat Monaghan and a few others, as well as Miss Fraser (who otherwise would have been just a leather tawse). The only discord I remember at Glenfinnan school was over a beautiful little shiny-feathered chaffinch. To everyone I was simply Johnnie Gibson, and that warms a heart that suffered later from social presumptions of no value at all. Perhaps to a certain extent it is in the absence of cruelty that lies my affection for the place, but I know too, just as surely, it was much more because of kindnesses shown and deeply subconsciously registered for my lifetime. Robert Louis Stevenson observed that among the signs of a successful life was being liked by children. Almost all of the Highland people that I met had that very important gift and it was not taught in anyone's school.

St Mary's and St Finnan's, the Glenalladale church, the 'colossal pile'

No one baptised me as a baby or a boy. I am almost as certain that I was never inside a church of any kind, by myself, or with either or both parents until my Glenfinnan days, and then not the church you would have expected. 'Protestant' children did not get into one of the lovelier Catholic churches in Scotland in those days. Not even a whiff of incense and powerful mystery, not a muttering of church Latin, neither a sip nor a crumb of the one true faith, all were denied us. For some it may have been that old hatreds and bigotries died very hard, but mostly it was just fear at anti-Catholic parental reaction. In Glenfinnan I think I felt only reaction to those things, with occasional strayings into unthought and rote spites on behalf of a splinter Christian variant that held as true some of the same scientific absurdities.

At least once, in fine weather, most of us in Miss Fraser's little primary school, Catholics and non-Catholics, went down to the site of the old sawmill at the loch-side below where the Finnan joined. Over the old new road we went, through the gate into the little magical, leafy chasm, like a maze for only a matter of yards, and then out, passing the northerly side of the church, then by the rhododendrons, down the (priest's) pasture, across the low road to the loch-side. We played in the wet, orangey-yellow sawdust, somewhere near where Dobbin Blythe's beloved child son was drowned not long after I was gone to Edinburgh. That once, I think, was in the flowering springtime because I remember the rhododendrons. Mine was a world of so-cleverly presented beau-

ties, of tininesses seen for the first time within the completeness of
high mountains and a powerful past.

I cannot remember if the front of the church was visible when
you turned the sharp switchback corner where the Callop joined
the loch, the magic inner doorway to Clanranald. I don't think it
was as you walked the road that crossed the old field land where the
monument and the little graveyard were. Thence, over the bridge
and up the hill to the school it was completely hidden in the trees. I
don't remember seeing it from the school, which cannot have been
more than a hundred yards away. To the roadside of it, at the top of
the hill, there was a thick brake of trees, with dense bushes and
undergrowth that completely hid the church (and its bell), like a
classy jewel setting. But from the sawdust pit and from much of the
lower road where the roadside line of trees were tall and straight
and wet enough to support ferns in some of their branch axils, the
church with its entrance was there for all to see, framed in minor
majesty against stepped, rugged mountains into the Highland sky. I
see it in the humid, sunny warmth of a summer's day. It had, as it
still has, on its slope down over the pasture field to the low road, its
thick bib of rhododendrons, which bloom in their Mediterranean
flourish of creamy white, red and pink flowers. There were also
pine trees almost guarding the church's main entrance – a few are
still there. Did a latter-day Glenaladale at Glenfinnan protect his
pines? Who owned and ran the sawmill down at the loch's edge?
Adam didn't photograph it; there was no building for me to
remember.

From that main door side of the Glenalladale church the view
down the upper reaches of Loch Shiel is as breathtaking as a view
down Loch Voil at Balquhidder in MacGregor country far south.
Both lochs slant to the south-west in almost poetic deference to the
great geological torment that caused both, and another fault in aged
rock (the Aspy) in northern Cape Breton where MacGregors,
Campbells, MacKinnons and MacDonalds settled. It was by the
loch that MacDonald of Glenalladale, Captain John's father Alexander, and others approached Glenfinnan with Prince Charles in
August 1745 to set the Jacobite war in motion to rid the kingdom
of its German dynasty, its almost tyrannically determined Whig-
gery, and, for Scotland (some must have hoped), domineering

Presbyterianism. If there were some substantial building standing where the big house now stands, presumably Strona guine [Tigh na Slataiche], now, perhaps, incorporated in the big house, then it is sure that Glenalladale's boat docked nearby. There appears not to have been alternative deep water. There was no 'road'. Had they landed at the mouth of the Callop, there was no bridge over the Finnan and the fording place would have been considerably up-stream in rainy weather. It would have been most convenient to land at the loch-side near the big house, or near the Slatach on its east bank.[15] The nearest high point for raising one's standard then would have been somewhere like the site of the present church, or even higher, at the rim of the hollow about a hundred yards further up as the fairly recently exposed carven rock face claims. It would have been visible to people coming via the Callop and via the Finnan from Kinlocharkaig (Cameron country, including the original Glendessary and Glen Pean whence men were antici-pated). It is worthy of note that when Wendy Wood and Mac arrived at Glenfinnan by train from Loch Ailort to the west on 18 August 1945 to celebrate the bicentenary of the raising of the Jacobite standard at Glenfinnan – assuming the monument to mark the spot – the steamboat *Clanranald* was docked by Glenfinnan House because there was a shortage of water at the (Callop) pier (*Mac's Croft,* p. 172). The best place to tie up then was at the Big House near the mouth of the Finnan. Presumably the local people were always well aware of fluctuations, which leaves one to wonder why in 181?–1815, before Waterloo, and when there was a new road not long opened, young Glenaladale built a monument so near the loch edge.

Time has isolated many of my little first-discovered beauties and blurred the edges. I have no idea where the little hedge over the little road from the school began and ended, leading to the twisty, leafy path to the church. I can only remember the thickness of the brake of woods and undergrowth hiding the church; I've forgotten the edges, except the one at the road. Any remembrance of the little gate in the hedge over the road from Fr O'Regan's 'castle' is enhanced (but in no way corrupted) by M.E.M. Donaldson's writing of her having gone through the same gate to get the church and the bell around 1922. This was the way that the priest and, I assume, some mass-goers slipped to go to church early on Sunday morning. There was no need for a car park in those days – I think that only Dobbin Blythe had a vehicle, a lorry, although the Stagehouse may have had another. (Dobbin lived in a new bungalow at the west end of the village beyond where the old low road joined the newer high road.) If the light in the church on early winter mornings were candlelight, it was magical, heaven only a chant away on a tendril of incense.

The narrow path with its leafy, hedgy sides, fell several feet after you slipped through the little gate. I don't remember its crossing the stream that flowed, mostly unnoticed, past the school but it might have. What Donaldson didn't note was an impression given only to a small person. The hedgy sides stood taller than me and in the summer sun it was warm, humid, sometimes almost dreamy, out of the breezes. It was even more enclosing and enchanting, and hiding, to me, than the dense and aged oak and beech hedges in Devonshire where the birds and butterflies thrived. I don't remember a path joining from the big house (as shown on the 1875 six-inch map) but it went beyond the church on the school side in order to find an easy place to cross the stream I've forgotten, and then doubled back.

The little secret path is grown over today and a lonely horizontal Glenaladale funerary slab hobnobs silently with support hawsers for a power pole where our little path used to open to the church. Most of the trees that once hid the church from the road are gone too, maybe all of them. Now there is proud exposure replacing an almost spiritual covertness, son of cruel and arrogant persecution, but you see, today the Gaels are almost gone that the Saxons so feared. The trees and maybe some of the old hedges have been cleared to make way for a small car park at the top of the hill and from there a new broad, straight, well-defined and electrically lit path takes you to the north side of the church. The church bell that was at the altar end of the outside of the church is now open to view – there never was a spire. I don't believe I knew the bell existed when we lived at Craigag. Seumas and I stood by the flat gravemarker just about where the little path used to join the church's plinth. It was from the start of that new path to the church that I looked at 'the castle'. It stood close to the road, as it never had before.

I have no memory of Fr O'Regan talking to me. I remember a distant, saturnine, black-haired character who was held in awe. His powerful status had touched his beautiful housekeeper with an urgency and an aloofness which I didn't understand. It hadn't occurred to me that he was Irish although surely I had heard that – not the sort of thing the impious anti-Catholics, like my agnostic parents, would have left out of conversation. I didn't know until much later that he had had an article published about the time we lived at Craigag in which he made the case for Saint Patrick's having been born in Banavie, near the Lochy Ferry. I had heard that he knew something about Saint Patrick but it wasn't until 1997 or 1998 that I read a copy of his work, in Guelph, Ontario. A descendant of Allan Glenpean' showed me the only copy I have ever seen. O'Regan's case is based on the similarity of the place name Banavie with one in a Patrician document of early provenance. Patrick must have been a Pict, using O'Regan's reasoning.

O'Regan's Gaelic-speaking housekeeper in Glenfinnan may have afforded the priest the opportunity to practise the Scotch Gaelic he must have learned in Benbecula. If he had a cow or two on the hill pasture allotted him, between the church and the old low road, perhaps she did the milking, in old Gaelic fashion (but where? I remember no cow shit on the road to and from school). The record of St Mary's Catholic church in Benbecula shows that a Fr Patrick O'Regan served the parish from 1931 to 1940 and this is the same priest. He must have learned Scotch Gaelic there, if he had not learned it even earlier; there were probably not a few unilingual Gaels in Benbecula in the 1930s. He may have said mass in English at Glenfinnan but, as in Glendale in Cape Breton in the 1970s in the days of Fr John Angus Rankin at St Mary of the Angels, he surely heard confessions in Gaelic from most of the older generation, and some of the younger.[16]

I think the first church I ever entered was a Free Church of Scotland and that was either somewhere near Corpach, in the parish of Kilmallie, or near Blaich in Ardgour. I think my mother was invited by Sarah MacVarish to attend, and I was taken as a matter of course. I don't know how we got wherever it was but Mrs MacVarish was the leader in that expedition. I have no memory of the service but I have recollections of my mother much later talking about the precenting of the psalms. She used to talk of there having been neither organ nor piano and of the starkness of the interior. Actually my only, very vague memory of that day long ago is the approach to the church; there was some sort of border running along the left side of some kind of treed avenue, at least there were trees and a wall on the left. It was summertime. I don't believe I knew anything about God or religion except what I had heard from Iseabal Fraser, not to overlook the curious references I picked up at home. The only Christian church that I ever began to join was, on the other hand, the Catholic one, and peculiar as it may seem, disregarding the inquisition, I am still less filled with distaste thinking of the irrationalities of that church – in Scotch Nova Scotia the deeper vein of cultural conservatism (including an unusual acceptance of eccentricity) is to be found in the Catholic communities, not that there was such a great deal of difference, it depended on the tyranny of the particular minister, or priest.

I learned in May 2007, from Pat MacBrayne, that after her old mother died, Iseabal Fraser married an old childhood sweetheart, then a widower with two children, and lived in Craiglockhart in Edinburgh. Perhaps that happened after we left Craiglockhart for Bruntsfield in 1958. I wonder, had I seen her on Colinton Road, if I'd have recognised my old teacher, or she me.

But there is another St Finnan's Catholic church, this one a cathedral in what was for generations the Gaelic New World. It was built in 1833 in Muileann an t-Sagairt [The Priest's Mill] (Alexandria) in Glengarry county, Upper Canada, forty years before St Mary's and St Finnan's was built high above Loch Shiel by Glenalladale. The land on which the New World St Finnan's was built, under the aegis of Maighstir Iain mac Iain 'ic Iain (Dòmhnullach) (1791–1845), had belonged initially to Spanish John MacDonell (Scotus) who died in 1810. Spanish John sold the land to Revd Alexander MacDonell, the bishop who founded Muileann an t-Sagairt, who in turn sold it to his nephew, Colonel Angus MacDonell. Finnan's influence was powerful on the Clanranald and the Glengarry MacDonalds.

5

John 'the post' MacDonell and others of the last generation of Gaels

It was walking home from school one day, down the hill to the low road and the bridge, that I asked John MacDonell, John 'the post', how you said yes and no in Gaelic. His answer took a few moments' thought and was not at all a simple one. All I remembered was *'tha'* and *'chan eil'* and a thoughtful explanation I didn't understand, and may not have believed. That memory is one of only two or three that I have of John MacDonell and it involved a delightfully pregnant pause, but it was formative and was one of those little things that eventually combined and forced me to look beyond the simple and distorting world of modern Jacobite and Teuchter images to truer things. With other seeds, it let me see more in Duncan MacRae than just a good comic actor based on one of Munro's *Para Handy* characters. From it, and other contacts like it, I also gradually came to understand civility as it was expressed by a folk who had not yet learned to subordinate all standards to mental acuity of an acquisitive sort.

When I remembered to an old friend recently old John standing by his tall, black bicycle near the main door at Craigag – he must have delivered some letter or parcel – all that I realised that I remember, gratefully, is an old gentle Highland man about whom I have learned only a little since. I suspect that the bike was some sign of his official status as letter carrier and he felt a need for it when visiting the Earl of Morton's shooting lodge, and its lonely woman occupant; I don't think anyone would have stolen the machine had he left it nearer the road, but had it been spotted, then what? I just accepted man and machine then as I do now.

In 1967 at a pricey restaurant high up in the top floor of a

Toronto high-rise building a young lady served me and an Edinburgh school acquaintance who had just arrived from the Lowlands. She had an unusual accent and he wondered where she was from (in the wide English-speaking world). I didn't say anything although I thought I recognised a *blas* and the next time she stopped at our table I asked her how she was in Gaelic, *Cia mar a tha* . . . ? Her face lit up immediately and the floodgates were opened! Gaelic and more Gaelic! If ever I felt guilty and inadequate at not having more Gaelic it was then. There felt I first my semi-Scottishness and the feeling hasn't left me.

Much later I came to associate John 'the post''s name with the last person living at Kinlochbeoraid [Ceann Loch Beoraid]. I can't remember who told me that, but it has been another of those important links with Inverness county in Cape Breton. Loch Beoraid lies in the rugged mountain country about eight miles to the north-west of Glenfinnan, beyond all roads. It lies in the old South Morar estate which, before 1782, slipped from the hands of the last two MacDonalds of Morar, Captain John and his eldest son Simon, and, with a minor proviso favouring the unfortunate MacDonalds, became the property of General Simon Fraser of Lovat (d. 1782).[1] Like Loch Eilt to its south, and Loch Morar to the north, Loch Beoraid runs east–west, however it drains (from its west end) northward via the broad Meoble river to Loch Morar. The Cape Breton story concerns an island tributary on a little mountain lochan to the north of Loch Beoraid, Lochan Tain 'ic Dhùghail [Lochan of Dougal's Cattle], and a curious event that happened there at some undetermined date before the last Mac-Donald tenants at Meoble emigrated to Cape Breton *c.* 1800. The story is the Cù Glas Mheoble [The Grey Dog of Meoble], an old, well-known Highland story put on paper at last, I think, by Dr John Shaw from Fr John Angus Rankin in Glendale in the 1960s, with confirmations and additions from Dougie 'the Gill' MacDo-nald of Low Point, Cape Breton, one of the last South Morar family sources. The story, for generations, had been alive in Inverness county oral tradition. The appearance of the *Cù Glas*, only in the South Morar MacDonald family, was a harbinger of death. Dougie the Gill claimed to have seen the animal running along the shoulder of the road near Creignish in Cape Breton and,

according to Glenfinnan lore, it was seen on the doorstep of No. 2
Gate House in 1952 just before John 'the post' died.

I asked Pat about John 'the post' and my thought that he had been
the last man living at Kinlochbeoraid was kindly denied – John and
his sister lived in the shepherd's house by Loch Beoraid in the 1930s
but there were people at Kinlochbeoraid into the 1950s. Pat told us
that she had many times crossed the hill, about four miles there and
back, to deliver mail from Glenfinnan to Kinlochbeoraid. (The track
over the hill begins at a cairn by the Allt Fèith a' Chatha burn near
'Leachavouie' about where the Mathesons lived not far west on the
road from Glenfinnan; the old track cut north steeply to a pass
between two mountains, and then come down to the house at
Kinloch Beoraid.) Pat pronounced Meoble, 'Mewble'.[2] The sadness
of South Morar with its empty places, Ard Ghlas and Inbhir Rosaidh
in Druim a' Chuirn, Coire Odhar (mór is beag), caught on old OS
maps in sheep and deer times, is even deeper than that of Kinlocheil-
to-Glenfinnan. Both places have been long empty of Highland folk
and longer detached from the old Highland cattle economy.

What must old John 'the post' have known about the latter-day
Camerons in Meoble, maybe about the music and dance rhythms
of that complex glen, of the *Cù Glas*! Father Patrick O'Regan may
have questioned him – who better to wheedle harmless old
memories than a confessor – but I know of no extant record of
any such effort. Maighstir Tearlach, Father Charles MacDonald, in
the 1870s and '80s must have had access to many older memories
but again nothing of the tale remains because, if his book is
anything to go by, he didn't delve or value the pre-commercial
economies and concepts of ordinary folk. Through him we have
easy access only to the echoes in Scotland of the main powers in the
area, including Scott-Hope and Lord Howard of Glossop, when
South Morar was disappearing as an old Gaelic estate, people like
Boisdale and Glenaladale, who struck hard bargains with John and
Simon MacDonald before Fraser got the whole thing. In the
Maritimes of Canada, PEI and Judique in Cape Breton, the name
Rhetland persists as a family descriptive, and there was Dougie the
Gill (b. 1900) who told me he was of the old Mac 'ic Dhùghaill line
itself, but much is gone and dissolved for ever, the real pith cast
away for want of a philosophical point of view on economies.

I assume that John 'the post' was a local man whose patrilineal pedigree went back, in the Knoydart and Glengarry to Moidart area, for at least twenty generations, to the Gaelo-Norse expansion of Somerled in the twelfth century, probably with marriage infusions from even older local genetic strains. It is partly the guessing of such a long association of family and country with an old man I knew in his last years that I find even more important and attractive now there are so few MacDonalds even in one of their homelands. ('*Mur an obraich sinn a-mach dòighean anns an aithghear-rachd taigheadar saor fhaighinn dha na daoine ionadail, le taic àiridh dhan fheadhainn aig a bheil a' Ghàidhlig, cha bhith againn ach suburb de Ghalltachd,' do sgriobh Aonghas Pàdraig.* No available, affordable homes for local people and it all becomes Lowland suburbia.)

John 'the post' MacDonell lived with his sister Chirstie at the Gatehouse (Donald MacLeod, the Glenaladale estate gardener's house) just below the road near the Stagehouse. They died within a day of each other in 1952. I met Chirstie at the door of that house, once, and for some reason retain the memory to this day. About two years ago, I was asked about the M.E.M. Donaldson photograph of the little girl Chirstie MacVarish standing on the little Bracara road, looking out over Loch Morar, a load of twisted heather roots over her shoulder, before the Great War, and if I had known the adult Chirstie – I didn't even know why I had been asked. I said no and perhaps I was right. It must be that there were two Chirsties living in the Gatehouse from 1947 to 1952 or *c.* 1952, Chirstie MacDonell, John 'the post' MacDonell's sister, and Chirstie (MacVarish) MacDonald, old neighbours on the Meoble estate. Chirstie MacVarish, b. 19 January 1898 at 4 Bracara, had had to leave her just-deceased husband Alasdair/Sandy MacDonald's keeper's house in Meoble in 1947 and had lived in Glenfinnan from then until 1952.[3] Chirstie's youngest daughter Teresa MacDonald, born in 1942, probably went to Glenfinnan school with me although I don't remember her. Chirstie (1898–1986) moved, at about the time John 'the post' and his sister died, to Corpach and is buried in Morar. Chirstie MacDonell in Glenfinnan story claimed descent from King Robert the Bruce.

That same curiosity about the last of the Gaels I met pushed me to find out about another Highland neighbour of ours at Craigag,

Peggy Oliver, known locally to Ronnie MacKellaig as 'Peggy the Mill'.[4]

One might have thought that emigrations to Canada were over a century in the past in 1945 but that, as you know, was not so. With a friend and my school geography I left for the Dominion, no hat, no gloves, on 27 January 1966 (two of fifteen thousand other North Britons that year). The great Gaelic emigrations to America and Canada began roughly in 1770 and in the case of Canada ran until about 1845 (although they never stopped completely). They were emigrations not just of multi-generational families, as they often were, but of varying proportions of entire communities. The 1802 emigration led by Archie Murlaggan and Allan Glenpean (MacMillans) that attracted the Callop MacMillan to go to Ontario, displaced most of the MacMillans from greater Kinlocharkaig on the Locheil estate; the Keppoch estate lost its essence with the almost mass emigration of MacDonalds and Campbells and Beatons and others, before and after Waterloo – most of the decreets are readable in Edinburgh. Those and many other Highland places were changed forever as the mighty unroaded empire was white-peopled. The main flood of Highlanders to North America was over by 1845, but Highland folk were emigrating to Canada in the 1880s and the 1920s, just not so much in communities, more as simple families or as single people.

The Olivers from Gleann Dubh Lighe [Aillidh?] emigrated to Ontario in the late 1940s leaving a little stone farmhouse high up in a wooded glen beyond Drumsallie Mill, above Drochaid Sgainneal. In Toronto I thought I had 'em. (Inasmuch as the little house was square-ended, chimneyed and stoned, as I recall it, it perhaps represented the march of sheep-farming in the Locheil holding and dated probably to the first half of the nineteenth century and about the time the dykes my brother remembers seeing at Lochan na Càrnach.)

I don't remember their going-away party at the Glenfinnan hall but heard about it from my mother. She had grown friendly with Peggy in those few years. They corresponded when Peggy was in Picton in Ontario and that name, and the postal address, RR2, stuck in my memory as though I knew I might need it some day far away. Peggy Oliver was a tall, strong, red-haired Highland woman.

Her walk with the milk from home up in Glen Dubh Lighe to Craigag was not easy, almost two miles as the crow flew, but I don't clearly remember her coming often to the house. She must have saved herself half an hour by walking the railway line from the bridge over the road. I do remember however once visiting the Olivers in their little isolated stone croft-house, Drumsallie Mill House. It was steep country but there was just enough pasture for a cow or two, doubtless part of George and Peggy's agreement with the employer. Only the haziest of images stays with me. I know too that I was told that there had been once upon a time, a home even further up the Dubh Lighe and at one of the homes there grew a fruitful old gean tree.[5] George, if he ever shepherded, must have had collies but I can't see one at the little house in my mind's eye. Calum Lowrie shot ours when it began to follow distemper's orders.

By the time that I left Scotland in January 1966 for Montreal, the Olivers had slipped far into my older, protected conscious-ness, never as forgotten as Giusachan, but when the story of Highland people became irresistible to me, in Toronto, a year or two later, I wondered if they were still living in Picton. I had to go to a map to find it, south of the still-unfinished 401 in eastern Ontario, near the Bay of Quinte. One summer M and I decided to drive to Picton and ask around. I saw no obvious imprint of the Native People of long ages; the land had been stolen by the British (and German) Loyalists whose roots were set down in and from 1783. It was not a big place, Picton, and mostly quite rural and farming. Somewhere I talked to a watery-eyed old, old man who was out about his white-shingled garage where he had a very old automobile. He told us that the Olivers had moved to Ottawa and it was there that we tracked them down, in a one-family home not far from the parliament buildings. I have a photograph of them tucked away in an old album. I would not have recognised them twenty years after they left Drumsallie, nor they me – they had known a boy. Now Peggy had white hair. She stood many inches taller than George. She knew more about me than I knew and was interested in my fascination with Highland affairs. She told me that a book I had, written by a Scottish solicitor, *Thoughts on the Origin and Descent of the Gael*,

1814, had been written by an ancestor of hers, James Grant, from Glen Urquhart (I believe it was).

Various Highland records show that Peggy Oliver was born Margaret McLennan (1904–1982), daughter of Donald McLennan, Glenluie [Gleann Laoigh?], Glengarry, and Margaret MacKay, Craigend, Glengarry, both Presbyterians. George Stewart Oliver (1907–1975) was born in Glasgow. They were married in 1938 by Fr Angus MacQueen in Àrasaig and both of their home addresses were 'Mill House, Drumsallie, Kinlochiel'. George in 1938 was a 'railway surfaceman', in 1975 a labourer, and in Peggy's death notice in 1982, a carpenter. If he did any shepherding at all he must have picked up the knowledge from his wife. Peggy Oliver's Highland background is the interesting one, the one that fits the modern, Victorian Highland estate mould. Her father Donald (b.*c.* 1856) was given as a shepherd when he married in 1887. When Peggy was born the record shows him as a 'deer forester'. His father, Murdoch McLennan was described as a 'fox hunter (deceased)' in 1887.

It was from Peggy that I got news of Sarah MacVarish at Carn Dearg. You see, some time not long after M and I were in Scotland around 1970, the Olivers decided to go back home and they settled at last in or near Fort William. Now it was my turn to correspond and Peggy and I did, a few times, over their last years. I have at least two letters from her, from Caol, both written on small sheets of writing paper over a faint but recognisable blue outline covering the top third of each page of the Glenfinnan monument, Loch Shiel, and its steep mountainsides, reaching away to heartland Moidart and Sunart and Ardnamurchan. It was from Peggy that I learned when Sarah MacVarish died. I forget who told me that George Oliver had died not long after they got back to Gaelic Scotland. His home at the time was No. 1 Gatehouse, Glenfinnan, my Angie 'the bar' MacDonald's home – George Oliver's last days were with friends in Glenfinnan. Angie 'the bar' by then had become Angie 'the gate'. I don't remember Angie's aunt Peigi from South Uist but have it on excellent local authority that when she came to live in Glenfinnan, and to work for Archie Ruadh MacKellaig, she spoke not a word of English. As Archie's son told Tearlach MacFarlane, that didn't matter since Glenfinnan was all Gaelic-speaking in those days. Chirstie and her brother John 'the post' MacDonell lived at No.2 Gatehouse.

A quaint, dark story attaches to George Oliver at Mill House, date unknown but maybe before Calum Lowrie was at Callop in the middle 1940s. The gamekeeper at Callop at the time, or one of them, was Johnnie Ruadh MacDonald (from Drumfearn). Staying with John for a while was a Billy Murdoch, later or then serving in the Seaforth Highlanders, and Billy was invited to the Drumsallie Mill House by George Oliver for an evening of friendship and to play cards. When they were settling George reached under the bed and pulled out a coffin and proceeded to deal the cards on it.[6]

Two Gaels living in Glenfinnan when we lived at Craigag, Archie Gillies and Archie Ruadh MacKellaig, were also at the heart of what I remember as left of Gaelic, though in slightly different ways. I seldom met or spoke to them but when our paths crossed it was obvious that they lived in a world different from mine and that distinctiveness is what stays with me. I knew four of their sons though, two Gillieses, that I knew were Gaelic speakers who may now know my regret at not having been able to talk to them properly. Both of Archie MacKellaig's sons, older, were also Gaelic speakers. An unchecked recollection tells me that both fathers had some connection with the Glenfinnan and/or the Glenaladale estate and were sheep-farmers – I remember going to watch a sheep-dipping at the *fang* on the north side of the low road to the Gillies's viaduct house and I think Archie Gillies was involved. Jimmie and Alasdair Gillies are caught in my old school photo on the piano. They lived in the viaduct railway house, which was gone in 2002.

Gillies is an old North Morar Catholic name, and one that was found in South Morar in the late eighteenth century, and far, far beyond as well, but I don't know their history in Glenfinnan beyond that the only Glenfinnan Gillies family was untouched by the religious reformation.[7] A one-time deputy prime minister of Canada, Allan J. MacEachen, a Cape Bretoner, Gaelic speaker and now retired Canadian senator, claimed distant cousinship with these Gillieses.

MacKellaig is an old Catholic Àrasaig name. In *Beloved Morar* Paul Galbraith mentioned two MacKellaig priests from Àrasaig, a few miles to the west of Glenfinnan earlier in the twentieth century – I know of none of the name in Gaelic Nova Scotia. Archie Ruadh MacKellaig lived in a house near the big house. It stood, as it still stands, tucked into the hill just above the low road, in trees in the old village, and in other hands. I think the house was two storeys high. I think I remember a protruding front porch. It was the home of the stuffed twenty-eight pound Loch Shiel salmon that Archie had caught with the fly. Archie is remembered as a great Highland dancer and a great local character, the man who rescued the Glenalladale bagpipes from destruction when the big house was being cleaned out. With Alasdair and Jimmie Gillies gone from Glenfinnan, there cannot be many more people living there today except Archie MacKellaig's son Ronald who have Gaelic as their mother tongue. I took Seumas to meet Ronnie MacKellaig in 2002, duly primed to realise that Ronnie spoke English the way I remembered the older people speaking in 1950 (before Glasgow and other Lowland accents weaseled overconfidently into the furthest nook, as I saw it). Ronnie, like them, spoke with a discretion, a measure, and a Scottish accent that I seldom heard in the Lowlands. By 2002 he had long held the Order of the British Empire for his part in the running of the Glenfinnan Highland Games. I thought my son's meeting people like him in Glenfinnan as important as his earlier meeting Seonaidh Aonghuis/Johnnie Williams, Neil Aonghuis and Albert Johnnie Angus in Melford, Cape Breton. Something they were is almost gone, and not just the language they spoke.

In 1970 when M met Ronnie MacKellaig at the National Trust building that had been built to inform and perchance take a little money off the tourists going over to inspect the monument that the rakish Alexander of Glenaladale had erected just after the road went through, he had been surprised. His first reaction was that I was my oldest brother – they were about the same age. Charlie, he remembered as having been 'wild', a compliment in the old Highland world, and Willie as we called him at home, was nothing if not wild. But Ronnie remembered me in a moment. What I retain of our conversation was his explaining the back 'l' sound in

Gaelic. Not having yet been anywhere near Nova Scotia, and probably not even knowing where Cape Breton was, it was strange. Many years later, between 1974 and 1978, Archie Gillies's wife was on holiday in Glendale, Cape Breton, and I met her at the Glendale glebe-house. I asked her if she heard any unusual sounds in local Gaelic and she told me that it was exactly the same as hers.

An old daydream of mine used to be to get Johnnie Williams and a few others of the old Highland folk in Inverness county to South Uist, not for Johnnie's or their benefit but for the Hebrideans'. Luckily Gaels who had the older Cape Breton music and dance tradition have visited South Uist now, many times, and there is an awareness of what had slipped away in the old country. Going the other way, I should have had pleasure in watching Archie Ruadh's face if old Willie Fraser or Alex Graham put a few real Highland steps together to the playing of Màiri Alasdair Raonuil or Aonghas Iagain Raonuil (and Dòmhagan), or Raonul Mór, to tunes Archie would have known but would have been surprised to hear so phrased and played. He would have heard how bitingly, eloquently, old Highland folk phrased their reactions to Mr Cope. (Màiri Alasdair Raonuil was an Inverness county Tulloch Mac-Donald (the Tulloch not far from Loch Treig) who married a Beaton (Keppoch) and whose version of Johnnie Cope is a standard musical flyting. She could also dance. I am very pleased I was persistent enough to find and visit her a couple of times in Cape Breton before she died.)

6

Sarah MacVarish, the old Cameron man and Calum Lowrie at Callop

A few years ago I found out from a friendly Fort William minister that Mrs Sarah MacVarish had had a sister Euphemia, whom I think I met at Treslaig in northern Ardgour opposite Fort William on a day outing with Sarah MacVarish from Callop. We visited a house somewhere near the old Loch Linnhe anchorage of Camusnagael (Bay of the Gael) although I have no idea how we got there or back. (It may have been the same day, a Sunday, I remember going to the Presbyterian church service, with Sarah MacVarish – there was a little one-storey kirk not far from Treslaig but I don't know if this was the one we visited or the one on the Corpach side.) Until 8 November 2005 I didn't even know (or had forgotten) what Mrs MacVarish's maiden name was and only recently (September 2006) have I discovered exactly who she was, and where she was from.[1]

In Cape Breton MacVarish is a Clanranald name and is almost invariably Catholic with roots in Clanranald's Moidart. The church we attended with Sarah MacVarish, as my mother recollected it, presented a stern, musical-instrument-less service and psalm pre-centing which is in the Free Church tradition; it was a written appeal to a local Free Church minister that resulted in my learning of Euphemia and only then did I realise why I had been at Treslaig. I remember the door to a little stone house, and a few words passing between Sarah MacVarish and another woman, perhaps a short visit. The minister's indications were strongly that the sisters were from (mostly Presbyterian) Ardgour, and that is now confirmed. What her MacVarish husband's religion was, if he had any, I don't know.

Even in my days in Craigag and Glenfinnan there were no other MacVarishes around but once upon a time the name was not uncommon in lower Moidart, and elsewhere there. To people who didn't stop to think, they had melted away on the whims of time just as had the Chisholms in Strathglass, many of the Gillises and the MacLellans in North Morar, the MacGillivrays in Mamaidh and the MacEachens from nearby (in Àrasaig). Nobody in Glenfinnan has told me anything about Sarah, let alone mention Euphemia. An early, facile explanation was that the old local knowledge, so persistent in rural just-post-Gaelic Cape Breton, was getting threadbare even in the 1940s in Glenfinnan. In some quarters this may have been true, but the answer is more complicated, and, looking back, in what is the most obvious way. First, and in defence of the simple idea that local knowledge of who everyone was *was* disappearing, in August 2006, armed with the record of her marriage in 1902 and her death in 1976, it is true that Sarah MacVarish, and her sister, were from a different 'country', one with an emphatically different religion from most Clanranald folks. They lived in the by and large non-1745-Jacobite world of an Ardgour which has no Catholic identity that I have found. To an outsider, a non-Gael, on its surface, the divide was as deep and as obvious as was the one I thought I detected in 1976 between Catholic Glendale and Presbyterian/United River Denys in Inverness county, Cape Breton. But, reading the 1881 census record for Achaphubuil with care, and assuming its information to have been correct on a legally important point, it is clear that Sarah's mother was Catherine MacPherson, living with her MacPherson parents, with her baby Sarah, and this sort of information, taken one way, eminently gossipable, knew few intra-linguistic divides.

At 4 Carn Dearg *c.*1970, Sarah MacVarish was almost emphatic in telling us that her wedding had been a good one – I am unsure of the context – but, having been offered the conversational opening, instead of being flattered at a confidence, I allowed a stray subjective thought to stop me from asking her about it. That thought of mine was the more foolish because I was meeting an old lady of nearly ninety, for the last time to say thank you with an implicit goodbye. It did not occur to me that she might still be proud of having made a socially acceptable marriage to a fellow Gael, of having avoided migration or emigration, and had an interesting reason to mention as much. I missed the chance to learn about her

MacVarish husband and any family they might have had at that last meeting.

My unshakeable memory of Sarah MacVarish, and my conviction about her as an important, kind influence in my lonely boyhood at Craigag has always been strongly held. I choose not to entertain cynicism. Howsoever simply it may be given, there is nothing above kindness, and just a few solitary, unexpected instances have lasted me a lifetime. My feelings about Sarah MacVarish also now include a sympathy, welded sometimes to a sadness about a Christian society which often so readily forsakes its central tenet, or, at best, often only manages to cloak its short-comings with practiced expedient treatment of innocent outcasts by formula-living social workers or their equivalents. Handfasting was an example of an older wisdom. Under the new dictates the poor and defenceless suffer most.

On 8 November 2005 I opened an electronic mail from a man in Blaich who had been asked by the people at the Treslaig Hall if he would reply to my query about Euphemia in Treslaig, sister of Sarah MacVarish in Callop in the 1940s. He wrote that the two were sisters, Hendersons, one first married to a Boyd, the other, Sarah, to a MacVarish.

Henderson is a Glencoe and Appin[2] name as far as many Highland people are concerned, and in Glencoe non-Presbyterian for long centuries. They were among the sufferers in the 1692 Williamite winter massacre and I am tempted to link movement of Hendersons away from Glencoe to that event. There may have been some post-Culloden sympathy in Ardgour also,[3] although how much is unclear to me. I have traced the movement of no Hendersons from Glencoe or Appin to Ardgour, but there is at least one in Ardgour from the parish of Ballachulish-Corran. Ardgour is separated by only one or two saltwater narrows. In the early nineteenth century any attraction to northern Ardgour was the spate of road and canal building with Alexander MacLean's add-on crofter plan, a mix of sympathy and modernity. After 1841, probably before, the crofter population declined.

The records of the MacLeans of Ardgour give an early modern glimpse of one of the Hendersons. Although the lands of Inverscadale and Dalindrein, in Ardgour, were given in tack on 23 February 1810 by their owner at the time, Ewen Cameron of Fassifern, to an Allan Cameron,[4] these lands had been till then let to Alexander MacDonald of Glencoe.[5] A Patrick Henderson was MacLean of Ardgour's factor (see above) in 1829–30 but, not having access to sufficient records, what follows about the Ardgour (and Ardnamurchan) Hendersons is incomplete and is little more than a skeleton representation culled from the censuses of 1841, 1861 and 1881, and parish records, with Sarah MacVarish, her sister Euphemia (*recte* Sophia) and her people as the attention-point.[6]

First, treating the northern Ardgour Hendersons. In 1841, there were four family heads, Colin the weaver at Achaphubuil, a Ewan at Treslaig, a Ewan at Achaphubuil and a Duncan at Blaich. The Duncan Henderson at Blaich in 1841, aged '40', was the same Duncan Henderson, aged 56 at Achaphubuil in the 1861 census, in which latter record his place of birth was given as Ardnamurchan parish.[7] (There is as yet no indication if and how these four Hendersons were related but, with the name Sarah in mind, the 1861 census records the widow of the Ewan at Achaphubuil as a sixty-year-old crofter whose birthplace was 'BALLACHULISH-CO[rran, *(quoad sacra)* parish]'. Her oldest offspring at home was Sarah (29) who was born in Kilmallie parish *c.* 1832.) Duncan Henderson [Donnchadh mac Ailein] at Blaich, however, is the man from whom Sarah MacVarish descended.[8]

At that point in my enquiry the most important female Henderson appears in the 1881 census for Achaphubuil where, in the home of Ardnamurchan parish-born Martin MacPherson (70), a 'pauper',[9] and his wife Sophia, and an unmarried daughter Catherine (27), there is listed a granddaughter Sarah Henderson (0), born before the census-taker knocked at the door.[10] She would have been sixty-five in 1946 and eighty-nine in 1970, and it was a very old lady that I remember at Carn Dearg in 1970. Her sister was on one occasion represented to me, by someone in Fort William who knew her as Sophia (and her marriage certificate confirms this[11]).

It took me years to get round to finding someone who remembered Sarah and her sister Sophia. My informant had been boarded in Blaich, from Edinburgh, in 1945 when he was ten years old.

There followed from him the following mail, in response to more questions:

> Yes, there have been lots of changes in the past fifty years; none of the old landmarks exist anymore, new roads etc. – still lives in Caol with his wife – who was in school with me. I made a point of meeting them in Caol the other day – hadn't seen any of them for nigh on thirty years – he remembered you OK. The old Cameron man at Callop was a retired keeper from Conaglen; he was known as Dolfarrich – most people were known by nicknames hence the confusion in tracing them.
>
> I can remember Sarah Angus MacVarish when they ran the old folks' home at Stronaba near Spean, seems a long time ago. I myself have been a friend of the MacLeod family at Kinlocheil since I was a young man, attracted there no doubt by all these bonnie lassies, but especially by the lovely baking and teas given to us by Mrs ———— herself. My eldest son married Eilidh, one of Flo's daughters, so we still keep close contact with the family. They were telling me that they visited you in Canada.

From this memory, Sarah Henderson appears to have been married to, or otherwise associated with, an Angus, or an Angus MacVarish, before she moved to Callop farm, at the latest in 1945 (it was in the autumn, not winter when we reached Annat and the first school I went to was Glenfinnan, and I turned five, and was thus schoolable, on 3 December 1946), they had both run an old folks' home at Stronaba.[12] I remember no man living in Mrs MacVarish's little house in Callop when we got to Craigag either in 1945 or 1946. She was a kindly old widow probably in her sixties, who had taken on a heavy burden making a home for four young people from the Lowlands, giving six in all a home at the end of the war. She wasn't the only local, Ardgour person to get involved but she took on a big burden.[13]

The official record however shows that Sarah (Henderson) MacVarish was married to a Duncan MacVarish (and no record cited below gives him as Angus Duncan, Angus D. or just Angus).[14] The marriage was conducted, after the publication of banns in the Presbyterian church, on 25 March 1902 by the Revd John

MacLeod. Duncan MacVarish, a bachelor, gave his age as forty-five and his occupation as gamekeeper at Glenalladale at the time. He was son of the late Hugh MacVarish (shepherd) and the late Mary Kennedy. His death record, which was registered by his son Ewen MacVarish, 'Drimfern', presents some variant data. It gives Duncan's date of death (from arteriosclerosis) as 16 August 1931 when he was seventy-eight. He was son of Ewen MacVarish (deceased shepherd) and Marjory Kennedy (deceased) and was a retired deer stalker.[15] He was fourteen years dead when my informant knew Sarah – the 'they' in 'when they ran the old folks' home' did not refer to her first and only husband. I was unaware of Ewen MacVarish, Sarah MacVarish's son, when we lived at Craigag, but the record shows that she had one son. The record of his family continues to show nicely the mobility in many Highland families of the time of sheep and deer.[16]

Sarah Henderson, 'General Domestic Servant', gave her age as twenty-five at her marriage in 1902, when she was, according to her death record, twenty-one years and fifteen days. Her home was at Blaich where she was the daughter of Allan Henderson, crofter,[17] and Catherine MacPherson. The 1881 census shows one Allan Henderson, principal occupier in the twentieth home in Blaich; he was given as forty, and a locally born crofter with a son Duncan (10),[18] and two daughters, Mary (8) and Annie (5). He was also a widower. Sarah was recorded in the home in Achaphubuil of her maternal grandfather, Martin MacPherson and his wife Sophia McMillan. The deaths in Kilmallie for 1883[19] show that Martin McPherson died on 26 June 1883 at Achaphubuil, aged seventy-six, happy perhaps in one thing; his daughter Catherine MacPherson, pushing thirty, had married the widower Allan Henderson, at Achaphubuil on 20 April 1882. (Sarah Henderson's younger sister, Sophia Henderson, was born to Allan and Catherine on 5 March 1886 making it a family of five children at least. In 1928 Sophia Henderson married Alexander Boyd, Garvan.[20])

Simply because of Sarah MacVarish's kindness to me I am delighted to piece together something of who she was, because, in two main ways, her life illuminates much about the old declining Highland world of Ardgour and Callop, in her own Henderson and MacPherson, and MacVarish families. The little field with its hand-stacked stooks of scythed hay that I remember at Callop was something not to be seen much longer after I left. That is all the sort of information that is being rendered unattractive through literacy and commerce, in English, both of which were taking hold in the 1850s. Sarah Henderson's mother Catherine was described as a scholar in the 1861 census, and probably was bilingual. Sarah MacVarish, luckily for me, was one of the last Gaelic speakers in Callop.

There were three young Allan Hendersons in north Ardgour in 1841 and Sarah's, and Sophie's, father was the five-year-old Allan son of Duncan Henderson and Ann (Kennedy). The family lived in the thirty-second of forty-seven homes enumerated in the crofter community at Blaich, south-side Locheil. Duncan was still head of the family in the same village in 1861 but in 1881 Allan Henderson is the head of his new family and probably already a widower raising his children.

It is through Sarah MacVarish's grandfathers Duncan Henderson and Martin MacPherson[21] that I offer my speculative glimpse of what I believe to have been the kindliness of Alexander MacLean, thirteenth Ardgour, in the times when there was malicious social pressure on many families of ordinary folk from Campbell and particularly post-Campbell estate owners in Ardnamurchan and Morvern, when estates became commodities and genteel retreats from the batterings of commercial and professional life far away. They may not have been cleared but both were born in the large parish of Ardnamurchan and moved. Given exact leaving dates one might cast aspersions, but those dates are only guessable. Duncan Henderson (Donnchadh mac Ailein) (1795 or 1796–1868), probably came to Ardgour from Ardnamurchan parish in or before 1831 (when he married a Kilmallie parish woman at Kilmallie).[22] Martin MacPherson, the younger of the two (b. 1806 or 1807), appears to have moved to Ardgour around 1840. Both men lived in Blaich in 1861 and two homes up from Martin MacPherson there was a nineteen-year-old unmarried Sarah MacPherson working as a domestic servant. She had been born in Ardnamurchan and probably was Martin's daughter (her mother had been born in Morvern parish and lived there during the years of Caraid nan Gàidheal, Revd Norman MacLeod). MacLean's Blaich is beginning to look like a crash pad. Martin MacPherson did not live long enough to have been a direct source for Sarah Henderson's and her sister's stories.

Who knows what those stories might have been? The Mac-Phersons from Badenoch and the Hendersons from Glencoe and Appin were Jacobites in the Forty-five and suffered the hardships and the long reprisals. If Sarah MacVarish's grandparents were descended from people displaced after that war then they had a great deal to be grateful for, including Ardgour's tutor's/tutors' sage decision not to risk all on 19 August 1745. Her mother Catherine (b. *c.* 1842) lived with her parents till she was almost thirty before taking on Allan Henderson and his motherless weans. To some extent the woman who seems to have been Catherine's grand-mother, Catherine MacPherson,[23] must have heard of a world that must have included modern British memories of Waterloo, roads, the Caledonian Canal, steam boats, the death of Alasdair Fiadhaich, the emigrations, the Indian Mutiny, and the Crimean War, the railway fever, perhaps, and going back much further, to wisps of thought about the great American Revolution. More pertinently, Sarah's mother would have known intimately from her father about the movement of folk to Ardgour when Alexander Mac-Lean, and perhaps his father, still owned Cona Glen, the early nineteenth-century crofting experiment, and the emigrations to Australia. I had been much wiser had I known more when M and I bade Sarah MacVarish farewell.

My knowledge of Sarah (Henderson) MacVarish's husband Dun-can MacVarish in Glenalladale either as stalker or gamekeeper, or of his father Ewen MacVarish the shepherd is incomplete also, but, from the work of Tearlach MacFarlane, it appears that he was Duncan, son of Ewen, son of Donald (a sheep manager).[24] Fitting Donald MacVarish into what appears to have been the one other prominent Moidart-Glenfinnan MacVarish line, *c.* 1800, associated with Gaskan and area (including Annat, Drumloy and Langal), and latterly with Corryhully near Glenfinnan (John MacVarish's home), is not possible although there are first names common to both strains. We seem to be still at some distance from anything more than plausible speculation about the Moidart MacVarishes as a people, and their dispersal, a situation made more difficult by the fact that many of the name chose to become MacDonalds (apparently not including those living in North Morar and Àrasaig).[25]

What is clear is that for that adjustment period from *c.*1770 to 1800 there are gaps in knowledge of genealogies, which may not be adequately supplied from the New World or the Old, yet. Also, through any study of the available data on the Moidart Mac-Varishes, to me there is a sad forsakenness that blends with a stubbornness in this old strand of Clanranald tenantry which had to adapt to estate sales and resales, and to changing exigencies from about 1770. Tentatively, it appears that from about 1790 they were subject to forces which broke older land ties; some went to North Morar, others to Àrasaig,[26] not to overlook to the New World,[27] and as the Clanranald estate was sold off in job lots, (often) to local major tacksmen, then to non-Gaels, the last of the local people had to adapt to a market concept which included non-traditional mobility and the straitjacket of economist-inspired life and work. There may also have been a break for some of the MacVarishes from Roman Catholicism.

Reconstruction of the MacVarish story in Clanranald's Moidart still involves the guesswork alluded to above, including the possible kin link between Donald MacVarish and John MacVarish (Corryhully). For example, the census of 1881 shows a Duncan MacVarish living in the third home at Callop; his age was twenty-six; he was a bachelor, living with his widow mother, Isabella (58) and sister Mary MacVarish (20). This Duncan had been born in Appin and his mother and sister in Kilmonivaig parish. He was not the Duncan MacVarish who married Sarah Henderson. This Duncan MacVarish in Callop in 1881 was a son of Angus MacVarish and Isabella McIntosh.[28] However the occurrence of the names Duncan and Ewen MacVarish, sons of Angus and Isabella (McIntosh) MacVarish (see MacFarlane genealogy), suggests that these brothers were related in some degree of cousinage to Sarah Henderson's husband, the Duncan MacVarish son of Ewen the shepherd, son of Donald (sheep manager). Also, and despite the mobility of the shepherd and the new estate employee, there are geographical considerations to be added.

Sarah MacVarish's father-in-law, Ewen/Hugh MacVarish, (whom she may never have known) appears to have been a Catholic, almost certainly indicating roots in Catholic Clanranald – his marriage to Marcella/Marjory Kennedy in 1844 is recorded in the St Mary's Roman Catholic church in Fort William on 12 June 1844.[29] Although no home-places were included in the marriage record for Ewen MacVarish and Marcella/Marjory Kennedy in 1844, the same church record shows a daughter Flora, born in March 1849, at Muic on Loch Arkaig on the Cameron of Lochiel estate (left and cleared almost half a century earlier); that record gives Ewen MacVarish as a shepherd.[30] He was not there in the 1851 census and was not recorded in Kilmallie parish that year.

If Duncan MacVarish's census age is right he was forty-seven getting married to Sarah Henderson (the official marriage record gives forty-five, and the squeeze on time was from both directions). Sarah's post-war move to Callop then was a move to near where her husband had a namesake cousin living in 1881. Her Duncan MacVarish also represents what were almost the last Gaelic days in the area, son of a shepherd, himself a deer-stalker. His and Sarah MacVarish's only known son, Ewen, followed in his father's occupational footsteps, moving to where the work was. Duncan's widow Sarah knew the last hunting and shooting years in Moidart, although as the wife of someone who had had to relocate for work (assuming Glenaladale to be just that valley, then there was no continuity of MacVarishes there for example). She had grown up inured to the poverties, and riches, of crofting in northern Ardgour in the tenure of various earls of Morton, leaving Callop not long after we left Craigag. As a boy I knew nothing about her perspective. To me she was simply one of the last of the Gaels at Callop.

From the Cona Glen estate sale it seems reasonable to assume that Sarah MacVarish moved with those of her depending family, John and Jean Cameron, Jimmie Chambers and Tommie Borden, at least – Evelyn and May I am not sure about – from Callop to Torlundy in 1953. For almost sixty years I have known that John and Jean Cameron were twins. They were past school age of fourteen when we lived at Craigag. At Carn Dearg Jean described having been in service somewhere – at the Stagehouse in Glenfinnan I think – and earning twelve pounds a year. They were living with old Sarah in Claggan in *c.* 1970 and obviously were caring for her then. Later I got a glimpse of John from Peigi Oliver. Singlehandedly, Sarah MacVarish supported six children in the hardest of times.

Sarah MacVarish died in Glencoe hospital, Ballachulish, in the arms of tall mountains and myriad memories, how sad I cannot say.

As to the quiet, dignified old Cameron man, Dolfarrich, who lives mistily on the edge of my memory, he was Dòmhnul Fairrich Cameron. Of two possibilities the likelier translation is 'watching/keeping Donal' (*fairich, a' faireachadh*). He was a retired gamekeeper from Conaglen who was considerately treated by the Earl of Morton. Donald Cameron might have been born between 1870 and 1880. His local knowledge of Conaglen geography and people would have been valuable. If he had had typical Highland parents and grandparents, people who knew their relatives and neighbours, he would have been one of the last links, in the 1940s and 1950s, with the Locheil emigration years just after the Napoleonic Wars, and the Ardgour ones later to Australia. He might have been able to explain when and how the MacVeans came there and how long they were established at Callop and elsewhere, and by whom – I found them first in the Cameron archives by Dr Robert Cameron (Australia) in association with the Camerons at Giusachan and the source citation must be Patrick Henderson's intromission of 1829–30 cited above. Donald Farrich would also have known about Joe MacVinish, the man who worked the line with Joe MacLeod (but then so too would Sarah MacVarish). For me, the MacVinishes have melted away.

Though I have searched, I have not yet found a death record in Edinburgh for the Donald Cameron who was shepherd or gamekeeper in Conaglen, Ardgour. All I remember of him are two memories that my mother shared, the bigger of them having been of an unsolicited kindness shown her of sandy potatoes brought over from Callop by an old Highland man.

I have no memory of Calum Lowrie as a prepossessing or dominating person – he was kindly to boys and in my family he is still remembered as having enjoyed a dram, and playing the fiddle – but he was the prime occupant of Callop in the 1940s as shown by NAS GD253/129/19, 20 and 21. The *c.* 1913 photograph holding at the NMS, of a gamekeeper at Callop confirms that Callop was first a deer-stalker/gamekeeper's home. He was a tweedy, plus-foured, bachelor Highlander who took a telescope to the hill. There is a 'Màm Lourie' and a 'Duil Lourie' on the east side of the Fionn Lighe near Wauchan marked on the six-inch OS map but Calum Lowrie came to Callop from Achaphubuil. He was a Ballachulish Lawrie and played the pipes as well as the fiddle.[31] There is no local death record for a 'Calum Lowrie'. Johnnie Ruadh MacDonald (formerly of Drumfearn) told Tearlach Mac-Farlane that Calum had died at Callop in the late 1950s.[32]

My sadness at loss, early, early on, turned by-times to anger as the extent of what had happened fell into sharper focus. Many modern Scots people, for whom the extent of the loss of another language and another consciousness is not understood very well, may occasionally wonder. Those glens and river courses, like Callop, weren't just lived in by the literate bilingual. They were the home to a people who had a way of looking at the world, whether or not they were literate, if they were unilingual, or bilingual, or trilingual, whose significance often became nothing before waves of cash quantification, profit motives, improvement, sheep, deer-stalking, tourism, from long before the railway days. Adapt or emigrate or die. Almost all of the old and traditionally minded bilingual Gaelic middle class was co-opted or gone. The government will even pay your passage out. Doubly sad in many places, in the convenience of retrospect, was the involvement of Highland 'gentlemen' in the dissolution of that old society. Typically South Morar dissolved in the second half of the eighteenth century. Moidart began to suffer the inroads of gentlemanly capitalism even before Captain John left. Clanranald's mini-kingdom had begun to crash into Boisdalian reform and improvement long before the kelp failure, and, if you believe Somerled MacMillan, the Camerons of Locheil partially dismembered what remained of their old society from about 1803 with evictions. The nineteenth century, especially from the cattle price drops after 1815, the return to a skeleton standing army, was the end for thousands of the last free-spirited

Gaels in Highland Scotland. The wonder I discover is that there was anything left of Gaelic consciousness in Callop and Glenfinnan as late as 1946, but there was.

Where Glenfinnan is concerned, the bilingual Catholic gentleman who owned the Glenaladale estate, Captain John, who led Gaels to St John's Island in the early 1770s, was a man of old-fashioned decency and honour and considerateness, compared to many, although his imperious Catholic nature is hard to understand today. He knew the lie of the land in Gaelic Scotland, particularly Clanranald's detachment from the old consciousness. The giving of an extensive tack on 30 August 1776, by Clanranald to the Revd Malcolm McCaskill, minister of the Small Isles, when Glenaladale heard about it overseas, can not have come as a surprise.[33] Captain John knew all of those people who chose to live on the land he leased to them, and most of them as well as many of those who shifted but stayed on the Island, did well.[34] Their farms today are of great value. Glenaladale had no one, that I knew of, living in its main glen down Loch Shiel when I lived at Craigag, but probably there were sheep, to baa at the stags. Rhetland isn't even on the latest Landranger map and neither are extant ruins all marked showing where folk lived for generations. Accurate historical demographic maps of Gaelic Scotland would trace the fall.

Were one to suggest that in many areas of Gaelic Scotland, the majority of the old Highland folk emigrated to the New World, then the service given the world Gaelic community by people like John L. MacDougall (b. *c.* 1851–1928) (*History of Inverness County*), Fr Allan MacMillan (*To the Hill of Boisdale, et al*), Fr Alexander D. MacDonald (1907–1956) (*The Mabou Pioneers*), Stephen R. Mac-Neil (*All Call Iona Home*), John Colin 'Big John' and Mildred MacDonald (*Fair is the Place*), and Maighstir Ronald MacGillivray (*History of Antigonish County*), among very many others in north-eastern Nova Scotia, is the more essentially valuable. Among those who remained in places like Ardgour and northern Sunart were shepherds, gamekeepers, a few masons and woodsmen, people like Donald Cameron at Guesachan in the 1830s, Donald Cameron the shepherd at the Field of the Meadow Saxifrage (also given Gortan Mhoran/Gortenvorran) in 1854, Colin Cameron the woodsman at

Polloch under head forester Mr McLaren, on the estate owned by Sir James Milles Milligan, various MacVarishes, and Dòmhnul Fairrich Cameron at Conaglen. Those occupations were the ones required by the new estate owners, the people who took the common pastures away from the old folk and hemmed them into allotments with not enough potential. The great sheep-farming experiment had stripped many bottomlands of the subsistence people and their voice is only heard from New World family historians such as MacDougall and MacGillivray. The last Gaels, the shepherds and gamekeepers and woodsmen did not compile any comparable record that has been published, and there can never be enough interpretation of what the New World people wrote.

7

The road from the Lochy Ferry to Àrasaig (1796–1812)

Were one to begin with a question on the subject, concentrating on the Cameron–Clanranald marches on either side of Allt na Crìche burn in the Callop Gap, mine would be: when was the bridge built over the River Finnan, the one I crossed and which is still there? The main road bridge we used bears no date. Cartographic evidence from John MacCulloch's map almost proves that the bridge was in its present position in 1840, but MacCulloch's accuracy is questionable from a poor representation of a nearby feature. The only answer seems to be between 1804 and 1812,[1] just before the Gillespie's Glenaladale monument was built, before Waterloo.

National Archives records suggest that by late 1799 there was a new road of some sort from the Lochy to Keppoch in Àrasaig, but one that was in its most rudimentary stage in that old borderland between the Dubh Lighe and the Finnan. MacDonald of Borrodale and Cameron of Locheil were modernising commercial men, the latter readying to clear hundreds. Clanranald was under the management of alien men of business. The French war demanded no less than national planning. But for the fact that the James Kirkwood and Sons maps of Scotland in 1804 and 1810 give a completely incorrect representation of the direction of the road from Glenfinnan to Keppoch in Àrasaig, one should be tempted to conclude that there was no road from Kinlocheil to Glenfinnan at all; that area is shown by a dotted line marking 'proposed canal' (there was a road from Lochy Ferry to Kinlocheil). The 'proposed canal' stretch had no road because construction there posed the greatest problems, possibly as late as 1810, although the Kirkwoods'

A view over Kinlochiel to the north-west Ardgour hills with snow-capped Moidart peaks beyond.
In the right foreground is Joe MacLeod's house. Callop farm is hidden behind a small, almost
imperceptible knoll (Cùl a' chnaip – Back o' the Hill). Robert Moyes Adam, 3 April 1938.
(Courtesy of the University of St Andrews Library)

Old stone-walled, thatched buildings at Garbhan, south of Kinlochiel, in Ardgour. Robert Moyes Adam, 8 April 1933. (Courtesy of the University of St Andrews Library)

Amhuinn Dubh Lighe at Drumnasallie on the old Lochiel estate near the old mill, thirteen miles west of Fort William. Robert Moyes Adam, 3 October 1936. (Courtesy of the University of St Andrews Library)

Am Bàrd Aosda, taken from the 1904 edition of MacKenzie's *Sar-Obair nam Bàrd Gaelach*.

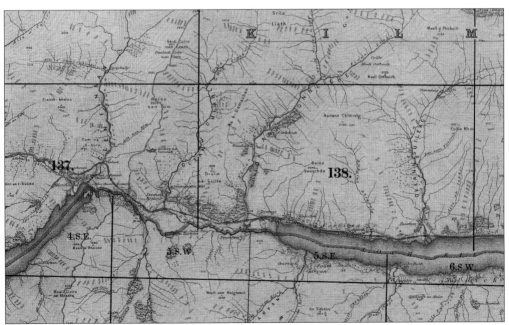

From the 1" Ordnance Survey map showing the south-west corner, including the Lochiel-Loch Shiel area; this was surveyed between 1868 and 1872, revised in 1895 and published in 1902. The boundary separating Cregag and Clanranald country is the same one that marks the western edge of Kilmallie parish, to wit Allt na Crìche.

An Adam exposure made from high above the school-house in Glenfinnan, Inverness-shire, on 21 September 1920, looking over dense coniferous woods and upper Loch Shiel to Sgurr Ghiubhsachan and to its left, steep-sided Meall a' Bhainne, in Upper Sunart. Robert Moyes Adam. (Courtesy of the University of St Andrews Library)

Ploughing at Ach' a' Phubuil, one of Alexander MacLean of Ardgour's crofter townships on the south shore of Lochiel in northern Ardgour. Robert Moyes Adam, 18 April 1933. (Courtesy of the University of St Andrews Library)

The Callop in flood. Near the mouth of the river, really a ribbon of Loch Shiel, this exposure was made from the Clanranald, Inverness-shire side of the wooded Callop Gap, looking over to a piny hillock in northern Sunart and beyond to the Glenaladale hills in Moidart. Lochan nan Sleubhach lies hidden between the two hills on the right of the photograph. Robert Moyes Adam, 3 April 1938. (Courtesy of the University of St Andrews Library)

MacDonald of Glenalladale's monument to the men who rose against all the odds on 19 August 1745. Adam's exposure shows the old one-lane road and clearly where it deviates from the older track that hugged the hills up what is the Finnan glen. Perhaps the small exposed area of rock at that point was a quarry for either or both, the monument complex and the bridge over the Finnan (not shown). The high-land rigs in the foreground silently emphasise the major use of the flat-land at the head of the loch, cattle pasture. Robert Moyes Adam, 21 September 1920. (Courtesy of the University of St Andrews Library)

The recently exposed carved granite rock high up in the bracken and heather above the Finnan on which the claim is made most eloquently and reasonably that here it was that the standard of King James was raised on 19th August 1745. The site is commanding, elevating and laden with sadness. It is not commonly visited, an auld, sad song seldom well sung; Boineid ghorm, ite dhearg, deis' an airm ' rinn mo leòn★. Author's photograph, October–November 2002. Tearlach MacFarlane took me to this inscription that he found.

★ Blue bonnet, crimson feather, garb of the host that caused my pain (from the chorus of a Jacobite song I first heard from the remarkable singing of Johnnie *Iagan mac Aonghais* Williams, Melford, Cape Breton)

The mountains at the head of Loch Arkaig at whose foot a 'barracks' was set up in 1746/47 by the conquering Hanoverians. This one-time homeland of many MacMillans and MacPhees and Camerons is still remembered as the place of the two main old holdings of Glendessary and Glenpean, guardians of the tracks to the Morars. Since the 1802 MacMillan-led emigration to Upper Canada, this once well-peopled corner has been almost empty of folk. Adam's photograph was taken from near Rubha Ghiubhais. Robert Moyes Adam, 13 July 1937. (Courtesy of the University of St Andrews Library)

A sunset on Loch Arkaig. Robert Moyes Adam, 12 July 1937.
(Courtesy of the St University of St Andrews Library)

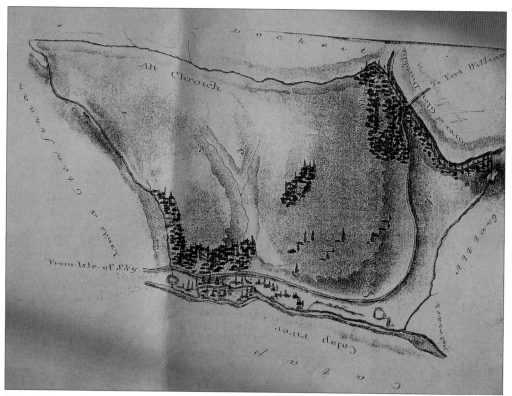

The old Cregag farm.1815 when it had long been part of the Ardgour estate. From the privately-held estate records of the present MacLean of Ardgour (whose wife, Fiona MacLean, kindly granted me permission to use the document).

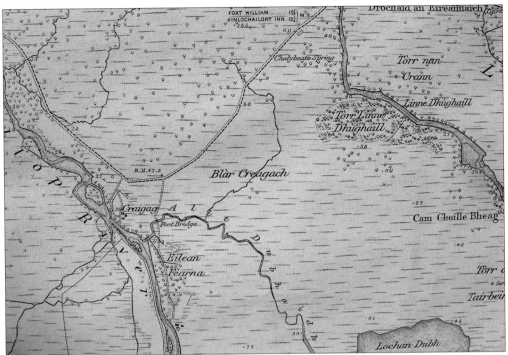

Cregag farm by the Callop river (also Cùl cnaip/Behind a knoll) and surroundings, from the OS 6" map drafted just before the modern lodge was built (*c.*1876). (Courtesy of the Trustees of the National Library of Scotland)

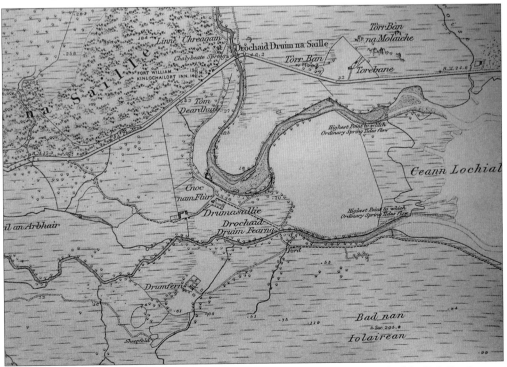

Drumnasallie and Kinlochiel from the OS 6" map. NB Linne [a' ?] Chreagain/Pool of the little Rock – cross-reference 'Eoghan a' Chreagan' in the text – running through Meall a' Bhainne.
(Courtesy of the Trustees of the National Library of Scotland)

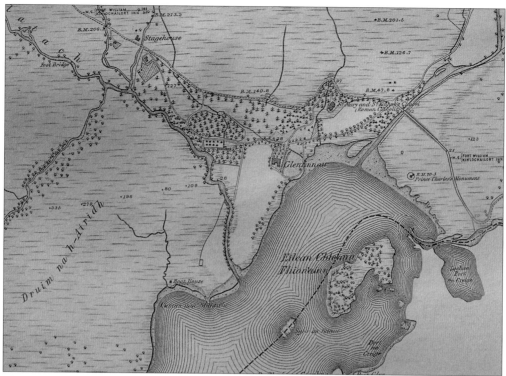

The village of Glenfinnan showing the new, high road, passing north of the new church. OS, 6" map, 1875. (Courtesy of the Trustees of the National Library of Scotland)

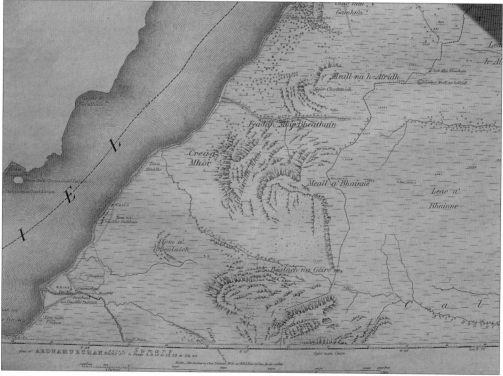

OS 6" representation of Upper Sunart and Western Ardgour (Callop farm and Cona Glen) showing the water-shed boundary. (Courtesy of the Trustees of the National Library of Scotland)

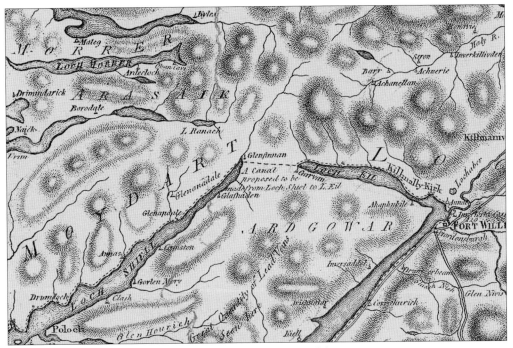

From John Ainslie's map of Scotland, 1789, a fairly accurate map of the area.
(Courtesy of the Trustees of the National Library of Scotland)

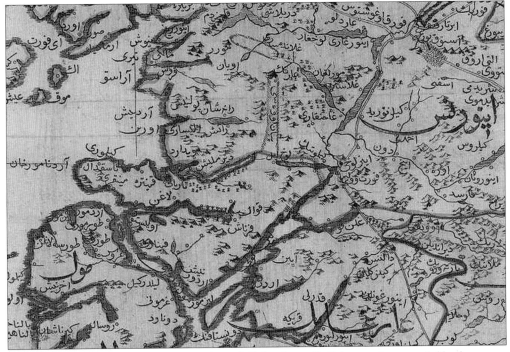

From the map of Scotland, 1803–04, by Mahmoud Abdurrahman Raif. Among the recognisable place-names are Inverness and Argyle and Mull (in large script), and Ardnamurchan, Tiree, Loch Eil, Loch Shiel, Kylerhea, Arash–[du?], Oban [in South Morar], Fort William, and Innerlochy (in small). I am grateful to Kurdish scholar and lecturer Jaffer Sheyholislami at Carleton University in Ottawa for the readings (he read the word/s running north-south directly above the Callop gap as 'Pian o wessie').
(Courtesy of the Trustees of the National Library of Scotland)

Iseabal Fraser and her class of *c*.1948, including the author (sockless and fringed), at the Glenfinnan School. Among the people I remember are James Gillies (far left) and his brother Alasdair (far right), Pat Monaghan (fourth from the right), Màiri Matheson (next to Iseabal Fraser), a Keenan and a MacPherson on either side of me in the front row. The two tallest boys in the standing row are Tommy Borden (at Sarah MacVarish's, Callop) and Jimmy Chambers (also at Sarah MacVarish's).

Maggie MacEachern, Hillsdale, Inverness County, Cape Breton, Duncan Peter Campbell's wife. Photograph taken by the author *c*.1978 at Duncan Peter's and Maggie's home in Glencoe, Inverness County. Maggie reminds me of Sarah MacVarish, Callop, of whom I have no photograph.

research was obviously inadequate. The Finnan bridge is a longish, one-span bridge which seems to be about two centuries old.

On 6 October 1799 a John MacPherson from Kenmore, Breadalbane, was approached by Clanranald's tutors and curators 'to make, repair and complete the present line of road from Keppoch in Àrasaig to the end of the new road at Glenfinnan.' MacPherson offered to undertake the bridge building for £6 per rood of mason work and the contract binding him dates to 10 and 15 April 1800, hinting that the big stone Finnan bridge was not yet built.[2] The end of the road could have been where the Finnan was most easily forded, or simply bridged, near where the viaduct is today. MacPherson's work displeased John MacDonald, the Clanranald tacksman at Borrodale, and he was forced to resign in 1800. Clanranald's powerful factor, Robert Brown, tendered his report explaining MacPherson's unsatisfactory work, and his (the latter's) resignation – Ranald George (b. 1788) was a minor not living on the property.

On 6 March 1802, Clanranald's business people opened negotiations with a John Livingston, road-maker from Ardnaclach [Ard nan Clach?] in Appin, to work on the same Clanranald stretch, from Keppoch in Àrasaig to Glenfinnan. The whole first road, from the Lochy Ferry to Àrasaig, was not finished to a satisfactory high standard by 1804, although by then Livingston had been working on the western, Clanranald portion, for three years, and easily meeting the approbation of John MacDonald of Borrodale[3] having reportedly done good work. By then, however, pressures to complete the whole road from Fort William to Àrasaig had grown because it was now obvious, by the employment of Dumfries man Thomas Telford on 1 July 1802 to present a report on the prospects for a canal through the Great Glen from Fort William to Inverness, that there would be a major, national transportation project nearby. No penny ante road would do. The bullet that no one seems to have yet bitten to that point was the building of the road through the Callop Gap from the old Cregag farm to the River Finnan. The Revd Alexander Fraser (b. 1728), minister at Kilmalie, had written in his parish report for Sinclair's Old Statistical Account (1792 or shortly after) that a canal joining lochs Eil and Shiel would be a great local advantage. Fraser, son of an Inverness baker, thought first about water potential.

Telford, not surprisingly, was also to research a possible canal
linking lochs Eil and Shiel but roads and bridges were really the
heart of the matter.[4] Telford rejected the canal idea in 1803 and
none was ever tried. Where the whole road, bridge and canal
scheme was concerned, according to a letter from James Donaldson
(surveyor of the old military roads, who died in 1806) to Sir James
Grant on 3 August 1802, Telford was instructed to make a survey
of the Highlands and report on measures for improvement in hopes
of stopping the emigration.[5] Telford well knew that his deeply
gravelled roads would serve thousands more sheep and cows than
Highlanders.[6] (From the same bundle, Telford, in a letter of 19
August 1802, to Sir James Grant, wrote of the need to prevent the
most useful inhabitants from leaving the country, perhaps meaning
the gentlemen-tacksmen, the folk who maintained local populations, perhaps just meaning the fathers of potential soldiers, men
who would welcome paid construction employment.) The great
MacMillan three-vessel (ship *Jane* and brigs *Helen* and *Friends*)
emigration had sailed from Fort William for Canada in July
(perhaps earlier) 1802.[7] In 1803 the stir to emigrate was strong
in Gairloch, and people left for North America; in 1804 Major
Simon Fraser the emigration agent was enticing Gaels to the New
World. All was driven by knowledge of economic change in
Highland estate policy from old to new dictates, and the seemingly
·endless French war which had seen and saw vigorous recruiting all
over Gaelic Scotland for old regiments and new, including fen-
cibles and militia – James Kirkwood and sons' two maps were
dedicated appropriately to Brigadier General Dirom of Mount
Annan in Dumfriesshire, deputy quartermaster general for Scotland
(1804) and to the same man as major-general (1810).

There were also very soon to be clearings by Cameron of
Locheil. Telford knew that about 3,000 Highlanders had emigrated
in 1802 and more would follow. Conveniently he may not have
bothered to look beyond government restraining policy as described in the Passenger Act of 1803 (in force, I believe, until 1827),
which sought to keep young Gaels of fighting age home.[8]

The Caledonian Canal project elevated the importance of the
Fort William to Àrasaig road in many powerful minds. Had fords
over the main rivers been acceptable earlier, by September 1803

things had changed. In March 1803 Telford presented his positive report on the Great Glen canal project. On 10 September 1803 he had obviously either travelled the Àrasaig road or talked to its builders, or both, and made proposals to alter the Fort William to Loch-na Gaul (Àrasaig) road. (As of 15 September 1803 John MacDonald of Borrodale was aware that Telford had suggested the altering of only one of the bridges on the Àrasaig–Glenfinnan road but which bridge is not specified.) In August 1804 the Perth mason firm of (James) Dick and (Thomas) Readdie was given a contract by the Commissioners for Highland Roads and Bridges for the road from Àrasaig to the ferry at the Lochy 'and building the bridges thereon.'[9] In 1804 the same National Archives record shows copies of the survey and report for the whole gravel road, ditches, drains open and covered, breastworks and parapets, and specifications for bridges, including inclines (later MacAdam roads, before tar, were also gravel on stone foundation).

John MacPherson had been ready to build bridges on the Loch-na-Gaul to Glenfinnan section, and may have done so, but he didn't last long. Livingston, whatever his skills, had longer on the job and produced a road, and presumably bridges as well, over the almost twenty miles, including some through some of the loveliest Àrasaig woods near Borrodale. However his standards did not reach Thomas Telford's for Dick and Readdie. Presumably MacPherson and Livingston enlarged whatever droving path existed from the west to Glenfinnan, leaving some difficult gradients, natural obstacles, perhaps even some customary fording points. The 1804 professional improvements on the portion east from Loch-na-Gaul to the Water of Finnan outlined for the Commission for Highland Roads and bridges demanded 'blowing off' of rocky outcrops that narrowed the road, plenty gravelling and re-gravelling and rebuilding where there were 'severe pulls'. Livingston, however, had laboured under financial limitations that changed with Telford's plans and the government's £20,000 for Highland roads and bridges. Although it is nowhere mentioned, Livingston may have been responsible for any rudimentary track expansion and any stream crossings from the Water of Finnan to the eastern bound of the Cregag farm at Allt na Crìche (where Clanranald's estate ended), but he, like MacPherson, must have known from local people that the Callop and Loch Shiel often overflowed their banks and that harder work would be needed to obviate recurring problems of wash-out. If either or both of them actually took the road, across the Finnan, to the Clanranald–Cameron of Lochiel line at Allt na Crìche (which was Clanranald's obligation, he paying for half of the cost of the road in his country after Telford became involved) they did not make sufficient accommodation since these floodings, of loch and river, were specifically mentioned in James Donaldson's report and survey in 1804 and were included in the Dick and Readdie contract. It is much more likely that from the Water of Finnan to Drumsallie was nearly virgin road territory when Dick and Readdie took on the job.[10]

The flood-prone areas included the head of the loch and a distance of about three-quarters of a mile up the Callop, along the route we walked to Miss Fraser's school from Callop. The pre-road rudimentary track there surely followed the old cattle track from Àrasaig Inn. It would have approached Glenfinnan down the valley of the Slatach, passed Glenaladale's mid eighteenth-century building, 'Strona guine' (Taynaslatich/Tigh na Slataiche) on the lowland near where the Slatach joins the loch. From there, probably, it would have continued on the north side of the Finnan until it came to a safe fording point for man and beast. This, I presume, was near where the railway viaduct is today, and where a bridge was marked on the 1872 six-inch OS map. This, I think, was where Livingston stopped his road *c.* 1803. There was no great flooding challenge in taking it that far.[11] I am unaware of any archaeology that has shown where, up the Finnan glen, there were homes *c.* 1800, although there probably were Moidart MacVarishes at Coire Thollaidh at the time as shepherds in the new régime – the stone house is probably coeval to the Olivers' up Gleann Dubh Lighe. Perhaps there were also homes on the edge of the fertile valley-bottom land that was beyond the reaches of a flooding loch about where the viaduct is today. The flat must also have included a large drove stance.

Approaching from the Lochy, the Langlands map of 1801 shows a dotted line from the Dubh Lighe to the Finnan River, but nothing may be read into its general-ness so one must assume that work stopped on one or other side of the Dubh Lighe, probably the east side. Robert Brown wasn't daft and it is no surprise that the actual Clanranald–Lochiel boundary at Allt na Crìche was not acknowledged in Donaldson's survey. Livingston must have known that forty-foot single-arched masonry bridges were feasible, if not always immediately reliable under Highland river spate conditions but felt no compunction about leaving that toil to another.[12] Whatever old Highland track there had been before MacPherson took on Clanranald's tutors' road plans in 1799, certainly it was sited, wherever possible, above flood water mark. If Glenfinnan was a cattle rest in droving days I suspect that the old, upper crossing was retained and used long after the new bridge, being more safely beyond any vagrant water's reaches. Indeed, along the entire line from Glenfinnan to the Lochy ferry, the little road I knew followed the foothills and made northerly kinks inland at Drumsallie, Corriebeg and Allt an t-Sùileig in Fassifern. The latest, late twentieth-century modern bridge at Fassifern completely cuts out this loop but in Glenfinnan the old road on the north of the river is still used, both east and west of the main road bridge and there is a bridge near the viaduct (which, as of 3 March 2006, leads to the estate manager's house). I was unaware of even the remnant of a track from the viaduct to Mary MacDonald's shop but I suspect there was one.

Coming from the magical switchback corner where the Callop entered Loch Shiel flat, the old road I walked to the Finnan bridge hugged about a twenty foot contour, and rough hillside, by the old rigs, to a point where Mary MacDonald's shop was. At Mary's little shop there began about a hundred yards of determinedly straight road to the main one-arch bridge. It never occurred to me to wade the broad Finnan there; only the brave and hardy would have tried it in times of spate. This straight hundred yards of road crosses almost marshy, floodable low, unrigged land and has a banked approach to the bridge which I clearly remember; we had to scramble down it to get to the Highland games. The road here reflected a different surface material, or was just drier, in Adam's exposure of 1920 but notwithstanding, it is shown on the six-inch map of the 1870s and there it looks more geometrically planned, straight, and at only a few degrees off what was the rough line set for it by the old track from the Callop corner to Mary MacDonald's shop. I think that this straight portion is where the Dick and Readdie road was placed between 1804 and 1812 and its placing had the primary purpose of keeping the expensive bridge high and clear of destructive river erosion – I remember big rounded boulders below the surface of quite deep water. Its other main purpose was to contend with the less destructive loch floodings and to afford greater protection to the drove stance – the point of divergence in 1875 was twenty-one feet above sea level and about ten above normal loch high point.

Although there is no written evidence that any older 'modern' track expansion by MacPherson or Livingston, pre-August 1804, clung to the hill-foot contours from the Callop round to where the concrete viaduct and little bridge over the Finnan are today, I am sure there once was one. Glenfinnan was the best cattle stance and beasts would not have been forced to cross the Finnan any lower down. The 1875 OS map still shows the little bridge near where Archie Gillies's house stood, almost below MacAlpine's viaduct. The 1875 sheet shows an arc of rough-ground shading linking the old road from Mary MacDonald's shop (at the end of the track to the monument which was cut to keep the queen's shoes dry in September 1873) to the upper bridge, but it is not as distinct even as the track marked down to Giusachan. However Robert M. Adam's 1920 *View from a knoll* Glenfinnan photograph shows a narrow path beginning where the shop later was placed, continuing from the old road from the Callop turn, running, clinging to the hill foot in the direction of the viaduct. In 1920 there was no shop yet, but there appears there to be an anomalously rectangular grey shape, possibly of exposed rock near it – the quarrying place perhaps.

The Lochy Ferry to Àrasaig road provided a short northern land link between the Atlantic and, via Telford's Caledonian Canal, the German Sea. Its significance was related to the need for ease of movement of potential Highland soldiery for the Napoleonic War, for the movement of bestiary and goods in times of the worst known war in which Britain had been involved since 1066. The year 1803 was a time of temporary peace and military regrouping for Britain and France, and the war still must have appeared as potentially nearly endless (no British naval victory yet, and only one infantry one, a radically important one in the Nile Delta in

1801 where Abercromby died and where the son of the old Campbell governor of Fort William in 1746 fought, and John Gillis from Kinloch Morar, Alasdair MacIonmhuinn, from Morar, and many others). For those who did not, or did not have to fight, the local road and canal building, from 1803 till 1822, was a golden age for many families in Lochiel and northern Ardgour. An unbroken road from Àrasaig to Kinlocheil clearly was chosen over any loch-and-canal or road-canal combination (by the Shiel river and across the moss from the Callop to Loch Eil, the *tairbeart* of Lochan Dubh Tòrr an Tairbeirt). From the military and improver point of view such a road was of easily defended need for the moving of troops, troop food and goods for later economic growth and development. From the point of view of many poor, and not-so-poor local Gaels, the scheme was a twenty-year source of wages, and for many who were reluctant to look beyond traditional subsistence living, a deceptive deterrent to emigration. There are no work records that I've seen so how the great work scheme touched Callop and Cregag is unknown.

However, the opening of the country, and the absorption of Gaelic society into the improving economic world by means of the armed forces, and semi-industrial schemes like road and canal building, by more insidious manipulations of the bilingual and still-powerful local tacksmen (some better thought of as chieftains, like Fassifern and post-Captain John Glenaladales, people like Borrodale, Glendessary and Dungallan) meant an end not just to some simple and precarious subsistence farming using apparently unproductive means, but to a complex system of kin relationships, promises and understandings and agricultural, fishing and forestry methods in a marginal land which, in retrospect, embodied ecological value and other potentials now ignored at our peril. Napoleon's threat was so great that it would not be ridiculous to suggest an imagined war function for Glenaladale's structure at the head of the loch. Alexander MacLean of Ardgour, a man of status and business, nonetheless tried to allow improvement on his Ardgour estate to permit an element of the old Gaelic world to persist, particularly in the crofting communities he set up (at Clovullin, Blaich and later at Garvan in 1810)). The most promi-nent of the opponents of the massive canal development was

Alexander MacDonald of Glengarry, champion of tradition as he perceived it and mocked as a wild man in his cognomen, Alasdair Fiadhaich. Who knows how a flooding callop River, and its removal as a geographical obstacle were conceived by folk living in the Catholic beyond of Moidart and Àrasaig? Without roads, Moidart must have only felt vulnerable from the ocean, and for long enough Gaelic Ireland, Gaelo-Norse shipbuilding technology, and a lack of charts, had stood guard over a very old and sophisticated civilisation.

If 1946 were anything to go by (which it may not be), most of the people lived in the lower part of Glenfinnan, to the south-west, and were served by the low road. I am aware of no evidence of home occupation in the last quarter of the Victorian century along the modern high road from the Finnan to where the Stagehouse was and still is. The new road bypassed the village. The people appear to have lived on the edges of the lower land, presumably by Strona guine, by the Slatach, and probably up the Finnan river, along the old road and up to Coire Thollaidh. Locating homes was doubtless the prerogative of the landowner and, despite the school and the railway, there was not enough growth in population to demand building on the higher land. New home building after we left Glenfinnan has been near the low road, where the little post office is and where Ronnie MacKellaig, the postmaster, has his new home; the last of the Gaelic speakers that I remember still living in Glenfinnan.

The six-inch map surveyed in 1875 shows a path wending across the pasture by which most Glenfinnan people got to the new church (1873) from Glenaladale House and other homes at the loch-side. It ran north-easterly to a point in the trees behind the church, not much below the schoolhouse. There it doubled back, tracing what was later surely the last little hedgy stretch to the church that we followed from Miss Fraser's school. The little stream that flowed between the school and glebe-house, under the new road and down to the north-west of the church, hidden in the trees, to the loch, is unnamed on the large-scale map but the crossing of it dictated the double-back. The 1875 map shows both the Finnan bridge and the new high road. The road was almost certainly built at about the same time as the new Glenaladale church, in 1873, seventy-three or- four years before I first walked it. The only source of temptation then to imagine that the bridge was built later than the Dick and Readdie period, during the Napoleonic Wars, is that it fits so well with the new road to the school, castle and church. If it was a Dick and Readdie creation then, leading to a right-angle junction with what I know as the low road (viaduct to big house) in around 1812 (or whenever it was opened), it was the end of the Lochy to Glenfinnan half of the new road. The exclamation point was the cleaver-shaped monument, like half of the front of Armadale Castle, guarding the Callop Gap.

The reporting of Queen Victoria's visit to Glenfinnan in September 1873 leaves the reader to deduce that the new church on its knoll, and Glenaladale's house not far to the west, were visible from the flatlands (after rounding switchback corner). There is no mention of the road or the bridge, although the royal personage, who loved the Highlands and its people (but said and did nothing about the clearances) lunched on a little eminence near Glenfinnan House, where John A. MacDonald of Glenaladale was introduced to her and showed her the old bagpipes and other 1745 Jacobite artefacts held in his family. The likeliest candidate for knollship with the view is just above where the school was built in 1876. The reporter noted that the Argyll side of the loch, with its mountains rising almost perpendicularly out of the water, including the highest, Scour Guisachan, was owned by the Earl of Morton. Her Majesty sat and sketched.[13] The great granite carven *creagag* commemorating the raising of the Jacobite standard, that Tearlach discovered in the late twentieth century, remained buried in heather and bracken or HM would have written about it.[14] Adam's 1920 photograph shows quite dense pine or other coniferous woods clinging to Meall na h-Àiridh and Meall a' Bhainne from the loch on the Sunart-Ardgour side.

Concerning the distribution of local people, even in 1946–51, excluding the new school-church-'castle' cluster, there was only one (non-stone) home on the high road, between the crossroads and the Stagehouse Hotel, and today even that is gone. (It was a poor, little tar-papery building set into the north side of the high road for the roadman I remember fondly, John Ford.[15] Excepting that newish stone complex, from the Stagehouse to Drochaid

Sgainnir there was only John Ford's bothy, the house under the viaduct, the stone Coire Thollaidh 'bothy',[16] Mary's little wood-frame shop under the hill on the flat, and Craigag Lodge on the north side of the road.) I don't know when the two-chimneyed Corryhully [Coire Thollaidh] bothy was built and, in my time, I don't remember anyone living there, up the glen of the Finnan; there was only the Gillies family living up by the viaduct. Archie's sons were the only people to leave me and Mrs MacVarish's children at the crossroads going a little east of north on the low road at the end of the school day. The new road and buildings must have seemed grandiose in their early years.

The old road that was there in 1799 winding west past Strona guine/Taynaslatich house, then climbing a gentler slope to the east of Amhainn Shlatach up and toward Loch Eilt is still there, lined by hardwood trees along its flat reach by the Finnan. The Thomson and Johnston map of 1820/1832 shows only one road through Glenfinnan, not accurately portrayed. Then there is the geological map made by John MacCulloch (1773–1835) published in 1840 in which, when the Glenfinnan–Àrasaig road crosses the Finnan river, it is shown, dramatically, immediately turning to the left. Where buildings are concerned, only the Glenfinnan Inn[17] is marked, above the road, correctly. However MacCulloch's map, while it also includes the island at the head of the loch, is inconsistent and does not include the unforgettable near-switchback turn in the road where the Callop River joins Loch Shiel.

About a quarter of a century after the church, school and high road were built, the West Highland Railway branch line from Fort William to Mallaig was opened in 1901 – the twenty-one arch viaduct had been finished in October 1898, probably within living memory of people like John 'the post' MacDonell, and integral to the memories of people like Archie Gillies and Archie MacKellaig all living in Glenfinnan when we were at Craigag. Sarah MacVarish at Callop was almost an adult when it was built and the tunnel drilled. Today there are pines on the (royal?) knoll, above and to the east of the hollow protecting the school house, 'the Castle', and the priest's modern house and from where there is an excellent vantage of the head of the loch, the lower reaches of the Finnan, the viaduct, and the now conifer-clad lower slopes of the west side of Beinn an Tuim/nan Tom. These pines and other woods are not shown on the upper side of the road on the 1875 six-inch map, although it is tempting to imagine local timber having been used in the building of St Mary's and St Finnan's Church, and the school and glebe-house in the 1870s. (It is there on that vantage shoulder, near modern pines behind the priest's modern house, that the commemorative stone with its datable chipping in Latin, lies exposed at last. The strangely accepted barrier to any acceptance of its authenticity, the monument, bears the claim that Scott accepted that there, by the water, the flag was unfurled etc. *Victoria scripturae*. If no one thought to tell HM in 1873, no one is known to have told the makers of David Niven's film in 1948 that another plausible place was some distance north of the hill behind the monument, north of the Finnan river – local lore had perhaps withered away; in fact by 1948 there had been an ongoing debate about the exact spot with various theories and defences.)

When and if local people forgot about this is not known but it was a heather and bracken fire in the late twentieth century that exposed the stone. Red deer grazed almost unseen in the tall brown brackens as, in late 2002, we wondered about long ago.

The road from Lochy Ferry to Loch nan Ceall on the Atlantic certainly did nothing to control or to discourage the modern commercial interests of people like Clanranald's advisors, and the chief's subordinates, men like Borodale, Glenaladale and Rhetland. In a desperate time of war it must also have had a calculated value to the landowners in Presbyterian Skye, and through there to the Hebridean droving business, as well as the Morar-owning Frasers of Lovat. There is also, however, a signal and salutary notice implicit in this road to the coast: it was the first durable intrusion into a Roman Catholic Gaelic MacDonald country. Ardgour and Morvern, Fort William itself, being on salt water, may have needed roads much less pressingly, but the facts remain that the pattern of roads that are shown on the Admiralty Charts 1426 (Loch Eil leading to the Caledonian Canal, 1841 survey) and 2155 (Sound of Mull, 1851) is a broken one. Howsoever unaware of local history – Jacobite romanticism lay ahead –

many of the wartime proponents of such a road might have been, the temptation to drive access through a very old and thorny anti-Presbyterian country would not have gone unnoticed in official Scotland.

8

Cregag/Craigag and Calap in a deeper historical perspective

The early period

Craigag and Calap/Callop have to be put together to gain any understanding of each place, although the fact that the former is in Inverness-shire, and the latter in (Ardgour in) Argyllshire, presents a gerrymander that might be explored – the Ardgour estate sketches of 1815 show Callop and Craigag in the Callop–Loch Shiel watershed, with one exception.[1] In terms of Highland land boundary concepts, however, since June 1633, the notion of isthmus *(doirlinn* and *tairbeart)* has dominated here the notion of watershed – perhaps it always had. The earlier history of the sheriffdom of old Inverness-shire, from the little published material to which I have had access, could however conceivably point to a watershed interpretation for the boundary of the Callop property, but with a farm to the north and another to the south of the river (Cregag north, Callop south).

My main source for this period, the promulgated *Acts of the Lords of the Isles 1336–1493,* refers to a very complex pre-Reformation time, but one which is characterised by the drawn out, intra-Catholic war between the Lowland Norman-Saxon (Stewart) kingship of Scotland (not yet clearly defined) with what appears to have been a prominent Gaelic fifth columnist, and the Gaelic/Gaelo-Norse lordship of Clan Donald of the Isles. Long Norman-English warring with France (intermittently from 1337 to 1453), and perhaps a lesser impact in Gaeldom than in England of the bubonic plague in the mid four-teenth century, prompted the Lordship's aggressiveness and readiness to experiment with a broader concept of country, for itself. That the

Gaels (the dominant element) involved could not re-establish the lordship or make any such declaration about renascent Gaelic power in western and northern Scotland, was in large part due to the politico-military actions of the Gael or Gael-manipulator Archibald Campbell, second Earl of Argyll, and his line – any general West Highland Gaelic regalist anti-Argyll sentiment had the Argyll actions of this period, among other things, as potential to re-open any resentment.[2] Archibald who succeeded his father in 1493, and was killed at Flodden in 1513 in Norman-Scottish service, had obtained Clan Donald land in Knapdale in 1481 and a royal commission as lieutenant over the Lordship of the Isles in 1499.[3] Coercive Campbell of Argyll action against the MacLeans of Duart in Mull (vitiated by a sour marriage between Lachlan MacLean of Duart and the daughter of Archibald, second Earl of Argyll) began just after Flodden in 1513 and continued until 1681. The path of coercion of the Cameron family by royalist politics and force is very incompletely recorded but the clan's, or part of the clan's, fighting in 1431 at Inverlochy against the Lord of the Isles's representative Donald Ballach MacDonald strongly sustains any argument that – like many other Norman-descended Scottish leaders (clan and otherwise), Cameron was *de Cambron* (Flanders) and not a Gael – intruded on the Gael with a view to rent-gathering and exploitation of potential military manpower.

The *Acts* referred to may not be complete and the efficacity of those charters that the Munros published in their book may not have precisely reflected the political power on the ground. At the simplest though, what emerges from the available documents is a changing balance of family/clan power and control over about 200 years of, among others, and for my purposes particularly, the lands along the north shore of Loch Eil and west, including Callop and (I suspect) Cregag (perhaps as far as what is now remembered as Clanranald country beginning at Allt na Crìche, although I have found no boundaries known for the early period) – Gaelic Ardgour should be seen as the meat in a Norman/pro-Norman sandwich. The Lords of the Isles used written descriptions of many land grants and among the earliest Gaelic families to see the value of such charter recording, at much the same time, were the pro-Norman-Saxon Scotland Campbell earls of Argyll. That classic divide between Gael and Norman-Saxon (even when the latter were

Gaelic-speaking) has haunted Scotland, and a great deal that has been construed by the literate victors as mindless, often greedy, vengeance, and simple inter-clan savagery, has profound origins, particularly lying in the Norman takeover of the north of Britain, and a hazed emergence of a separate northern Norman-Saxon country from feudal subordination to England.

The first document that mentions Cregag, given as Jean and R.W. Munro transcribed it, without their interpolations, is dated 10 October 1461.

> Charter of John of Yle Earl of Ross and Lord of the Isles etc in favour of his beloved cousin John McEan Mcgilleon of Lochbogg of the following lands lying in the granters Lordship of Lochabra in the Sheriffdom of Invernys, namely the lands of Banvy, MyKannick, Fyelyn, Creglwing, Corpych, Innernat, Achydo, Kilmailze, Achymoleag, Drumfarmollach, Faneworwill, Fassfarna, Stronsouleak, Conebeg, Achitolldow, Kanloch, Drumnafalze, Culinap, Nahohacho, Clerechaik, Mischerolene, Crou, Dalachan, Drondaim Lyndaly with pertinents, to be held in fee and heritage forever for the homage and service of the foresaid John McGilleon his heirs and assignees to Us and our heirs and successors Lords of the Isles in war and peace in accordance with the custom of the Isles with warrandice clause by the Granter promising to defend the Grantee and his heirs forever against all men. In witness of which . . . on the 10th October 1461.[4]

After 'Kanloch' the next four place names that appear are 'Drumnafalze, Culinap, Nahohacho, Clerechaik' and three of these seem to have lain to the west of Kinlocheil. The odd man out is Nahohacho which, from contemporary corroborating evidence from the *Acts,* the Munros explain as Wauchan [*na h-oachan*], up the Fionn Lighe burn, north of Kanloch.[5] Of the others, the first of the four is obviously Drumnasallie. It seems to me (as it seemed to Somerled MacMillan) that Culinap was an Anglicisation of an early equivalent of Cùl a' Chnaip and was an early descriptive of Callop farm, which is hidden from Loch Eil by that watershed height of land which holds Lochan Dubh Tòrr an Tairbeirt.[6] From other evidence in the *Acts,* the Munros explain Clerechaik as 'Clachak, still unidentified'[7] but there was only one other main farm holding west of Drumsallie to be considered and that is Cregag north of the river and at least Clachak [Clachag/Little Stone] is a fair synonym.

Six salient points emerge plausibly from this document. First, presumably neither Culinap nor Clerechaik had belonged to the Lord of the Isles's supporter, MacLean of Ardgour. Second, while the Lordship of the Isles was primarily a saltwater lordship, it ventured here, at least on paper, aggressively to commit a number of non-saltwater farms to a new possessor. Third, these holdings from Banvy (and others) on the river Lochy, along the north shore of salty Loch Eil, to inland Culinap and Clerechaik, were officially granted to 'John McEan Mcgilleon of Lochbogg' (Lochboyy?) who presumably had taken possession earlier than the charter date of 1461. Fourth, the likeliest condition was that MacLean had been rewarded for his support of Donald Balloch MacDonald's Mac-Donald of the Isles army in his successful battle at Inverlochy in 1431 against the army of Lowland, Norman and Breton-descended (Stewart) King James I. The fifth point is that the grant surely was aimed to contain possible Cameron expansion (if not to dispossess them) – the Camerons had fought against Donald Balloch. The sixth consideration concerns the document itself; the 1461 charter cited (from John of the Isles to John MacLean of Lochbogg) was taken from an abstract made by Niall, tenth Duke of Argyll from an original held at Inverary, now missing. That a Campbell chief should create and hold such a document is simple to understand, but when the original was acquired, and by whom, remains as unknown as its contents. Whatever deviousness one might think may or may not have been involved, I know no reason to think that the names of the farms concerned were altered, except perhaps by the accident of changed orthography – there were nineteen farms named in the 1492 document and twenty-four in the earlier one.

The same extent of land, including 'Clerechaik' was confirmed as granted to the same person, by royal charter dated 22 March 1493/4[8] – date of forfeiture of the Lordship to the Crown is uncertain but between 6 December 1492 and 29 August 1493. Then on 26 August 1492 *'Alexander de Insulis de Lochalch ac de*

Lochheil' (Alexander of the Isles[,] of Lochalsh[,] and of Locheil) gave by charter to

> *consanguineo nostro Eugenio Alani Donaldi capitaneo de Clancamroun'*
> *'totas et integras nostras triginta mercarum de Lochheil videlicet Cray*
> *Salachan Banwe Corpoch Kilmalzhe Achedo Anat Aychetilay Drumfer-*
> *malach Fanmoyrmell Fassfarne Corbeg Owechan Aychetioldown Chan-*
> *laycheil Kowilknap Drumnasall Clachak Clachfyne in Lochheil et . . .'*[9]

> [Our kinsman Eugene of Alan of Donald, captain of Clancameron . . . Kinlocheil, Culknap, Drumnasall, Clachag, Clachfyne in Locheil and . . .]

That the Lordship of the Isles inevitably collided with the Stewart kings (and that later on James VI instituted the Statutes of Iona in 1609) leave ironies and speculative deductions about the later Jacobite Risings of Gaels and many Gaelicised, but also there are complications and ironies implicit in the notion of a greater-Gaelic Lordship that began in the early fourteenth century. Amalgamating 'countries' in the greater Gaelic world tended to be temporary. The Lordship had roots in a Gaelic understanding of Norman, and Norse, power but also knew of older national Gaelo-Pictish power over what became Scotland. The acceptance became for some the threat of a Norman-organised and -ruled North Britain, which must have been widely obvious at all levels of the old Gaelic society nearest Ireland. Like many Gaelic Scots' eighteenth- and early nineteenth-century efforts to break into the improver/*meliateur* commercial world, the Gaelic Lordship failed and left in its wake dangerous intra-Gaelic aspirations and imbalances, and potential for outside manipulations.

It seems that at least 141 years pass (including the violent Protestant then Presbyterian Reformation, particularly involving the Covenanting movement) before the little Craigag appendix plays a recorded part, anonymously, in Highland history in 1633, and this one is impossible to verify (thereby, as lore, lending it credence in my mind).

The cattle raid and Lochiel's loss of Cregag

The next brush Craigag has with written history is alluded to in two reported stories dealing with the history of the Cregag farm: Donald Cameron of Lochiel's report given to a committee of the House of Lords in March 1889, and Somerled MacMillan's more complicated and contradictory one published in *Bygone Lochaber* in 1971. Cameron of Lochiel, locally resident chief from 1858 to 1905, championing the planned Glasgow-to-Àrasaig railway before a House of Lords committee in March 1889, made light of the Earl of Morton's opposition to the project (Morton was a Lowlander who was a distant cousin to Campbell of Argyll[10]). Among other things, Lochiel, much more nearly Campbell-related than Morton, although at lower power levels, described that portion of the earl's (Cona Glen, Ardgour) estate to be affected by the railway as a triangle of land (Craigag) of only about 320 acres' extent. Getting into his stride, Lochiel then told the committee that the land in question,

> Geographically ought to belong to him (Lochiel) or a neighbouring proprietor, Mr Macdonald of Glenalladale. A curious legend existed in that country as to the manner in which that land was acquired. The story went that a murder was committed on the bit of ground; and in those days, seeing the Chiefs and landowners were made responsible for what happened on their property, both proprietors – that was to say, his (Lochiel's) ancestors and the ancestors of Mr Macdonald of Glenalladale – refused to admit any liability, and had said the land was not theirs. Mr McLean, the other neighbouring owner, being a strong-minded gentleman, thought he would risk it. (Laughter.) So he took responsibility for the murder, and thus became owner of the land, which had been purchased from his successors by Lord Morton.
>
> (*The Scotsman*, 27 March 1889, p. 7)[11]

Lochiel readily accepted the isthmus idea over the watershed one but showed carefulness about the Cameron–Clanranald boundary. The landowner's responsibility for such a crime is not found in Erskine's *Principles of the Law of Scotland* (11th edition, 1820); therein however the crime of 'stouthrief' or robbery with violence, legally defined in 1515, was punishable by death.

Somerled MacMillan's tale is much less straightforward. It appears not to involve a homicide, but still, unfortunately, is amenable to historical speculation from the written record of two periods. The later period involves what was written of the area, by an English outsider, John Hill, in the 1690s. Unfortunately MacMillan gave no source for the following story about the land on which Craigag stands, but it is the sort of story that must have been grand *céilidh* material, in story and song, while there was a Gaelic community to perpetuate it. Unfortunately also, MacMillan associated the loss of this small piece of important march land between Clanranald and Cameron of Locheil with two Cameron chiefs rather than one, Allan the fourth of Locheil, and to Sir Ewen Dubh, his grandson, the fifth.

> We have good reason to believe that it was Allan, 4th of Lochiel, who got a band of MacMillans to seize a large *creach* (spoil) of stolen cattle, and, just as they were on their way back to Lochaber they were caught red-handed between Callop and Craigag. The wily Lochiel, rather than admit that the stolen beasts were on his land, he preferred to forego this strip of ground instead of paying a heavy fine imposed for such an offence. The place where the MacMillans were caught is now known as *'Drochaid Sgainneal'* ('Scandal Bridge').
>
> (MacMillan, *Bygone Lochaber,* p. 117)

In his appended explanation of the place names in his book, MacMillan wrote that it was at the bidding of Sir Ewen Cameron (Eoghann Dubh) that the MacMillans were driving the stolen cattle toward Locheil. In either case, the MacMillans seem to have become to some extent pawns in the Cameron affairs before the Reformation of the Scottish Christian Church. MacMillan, simply, did not want to tar men of his name with murder. Allan Cameron, fourth of Locheil (by MacMillan's numbering), succeeded to that local power in 1565. Inasmuch as he was succeeded by his grandson Ewen, fifth of Locheil, in 1647, Allan had an almost implausibly long career, but it was one which included some infamous rapine.

Cregag farm, whatever its extent and boundaries (see below), in the legal terms of the dominant power, at some time ceased to belong to the Lochiel estate, and for an undetermined length of time. Under local Gaelic legal perceptions and usages even, the only hint at the length of no-owner time involved is Donald Cameron's claim that it happened when MacLean of Ardgour was a 'strong-minded gentleman'. Three associated thoughts which impart a finality to this case: there is no evidence that Lochiel's superior, Argyll, contested the loss of Cregag; never, as far as I know, did Clanranald claim the land that after all was contiguous to his holding of Glenfinnan; and, there is no court case extant.

It was in the body of his text that Somerled MacMillan wrote that the Lochiel involved in the cattle theft was Allan, the fourth of Lochiel (*reg.* 1565–1647), but it was in an appendix dealing with place names, that the author stated that the MacMillans were driving their stolen beasts for Eoghainn Dubh (b. 1629 and *reg.* 1647–1719), Allan's grandson and successor as the fifth Cameron of Locheil. Allan was accused to the Scottish Privy Council in 1598 of a serious act of theft and brigandage in which women and children were violently molested. If this is true, there is no known record of the Cregag heist in that time and Allan Cameron would have ceded nothing since there was no outside power that might have coerced him. What's more, the chances of a place name's having survived so long are not good. Eoghann Dubh, better known to MacMillan as Righ nam Meàirleach [King of the Thieves], is a more plausible candidate for several reasons, least of which is the title MacMillan gave him, without explanation.

Allowing that the first bridge over Allt/Abhainn Dubh Lighe was built no earlier than 1796 then the terms Drochaid Sgainneal and Drochaid Sgainnir are partly misleading, and the confusion half explained. Accepting that there can be no proof that Allan was involved, what then are the chances that this cattle theft was a latter-day instance of the old Gaelic quasi-ritual event involved in choosing a future leader of the Camerons, Eòghann Dubh or someone nearer the present? The answer is very short. Drochaid Sgainneal [Scandal Bridge] refers to humiliation, pointing to an associated, unreported, possibly not indictable, latter-day murder, perhaps in some general way inconsistent with a long-accepted Highland practice.

If one were to suppose official involvement, in two periods of Eoghann Dubh, fifth of Locheil's time, from 1647 until 1719, such a force may have existed at Innerlochy/Fort William. Cromwell's General George Monck (commander-in-chief of the forces in Scotland and a Devonshire man) had his old Roundhead colonel, John Hill, build a fort for 250 professional soldiers of the New Model Army at Inverlochy in 1654 and set him up as governor there from 1656 until 1660, when Lochiel took over the fort for the king. In 1690, in revolutionary Jacobite times (many Highland chiefs feared a foreign king and the power of the established church), Monck's fort was greatly strengthened with twenty-foot high walls and barracks for 1,000 men, built by Presbyterian Gael Hugh MacKay of Scourie at what was late that year called Fort William. If royalist Lochiel were not threatened by 250 of Monck's men, under Colonel John Hill, between 1654 and 1660 (a party of whom he had ably defeated once), then the greater Williamite force under the same leader, Colonel John Hill, might even have been in a position to overawe a large part of Locheil's clan army and to have caught the MacMillan thieves, and threatened legal action against Cameron himself in the 1690s.

Noteworthy is the fact that Lochiel was not so charged and that no place name I know along Lochiel commemorates the well-known, sanguine events of the Monck–Lochiel period. If the Drochaid Sgainneal story dates to the 1690s there is a better chance of a place name's having survived into Ordnance Survey times. First, however, Righ nam Meàirleach – Ewen Dubh Cameron of Lochiel – in the context Somerled MacMillan wrote about him, might be imagined as little more than a consummate cattle thief. The simple secondary-source record to which anyone may have access, however, points to a powerful, sophisticated and economically modern, Jamesian man with an army of Gaels, rather than a cattle thief. He was raised in Campbell country and there is at least a reasonable temptation to suggest that he was part of a concept that involved occupation of post-Lordship MacLean territory north of Mull (which Argyll got in 1681). If Ewen Dubh was a thief, in a sense, of anything important, it was of other people's land and potential soldiers. Overseas he acquired land in the West Indies and North America. At home he headed a powerful family which included three first cousins, John, 'Eun' and Hugh Cameron who laid the foundation for the strong Cameron presence in Morvern, Sunart and Ardnamurchan, all achieved through a loan extended to the Earl of Argyll. John Cameron, son of Ewen Dubh's tutor/ brother Donald, was the first Cameron of Glendessary (to the west of Kinlocharkaig) and he was also a land-leasing presence in Ardgour in the early 1680s. According to an Ardgour family historian, the leases held by Glendessary Camerons in Ardgour were ended by Ewen MacLean, ninth of Ardgour in 1685[12] and, adding recorded precision, Inverscaddle, in Ardgour, was a subject of court of session legal debate between Allan Cameron, second of Glendessary (d. 1721) and Hector MacLean of Torloisk into the eighteenth century,[13] a case which extended one way or another to a 'decree and abbreviate of adjudication' declaring Kinlochmoidart to be owner of Innerscadell, dated 17 June 1740.[14] (The Dungallon Camerons were an offshoot of the Glendessaries.)

Ardgour reasoning for staying out of the 1745 Jacobite Rising was keenly self-protective of the minor chief-to-be (as was Fassifern's and other Camerons'), and the estate controllers must have rejoiced at the thoroughness with which most major Cameron land dealings were ended, officially fixed, and their (MacLean) hope of consolidating the old MacLean estate writ fairly clear at the forfeitures. They must have foreseen a hard relationship with the great Camerons of Lochiel if the Jamesian line had been restored in the Rising.

If the cattle raid happened under the order of Ewen Dubh of Lochiel, then who were the MacMillan lifters robbing of their cattle, how did they set out to effect the theft, and how could someone as locally powerful as Cameron of Locheil be implicated, harbouring stolen cattle deep in his own territory, and perhaps forced into demeaningly evasive legal tactics? If the Glendessary leases in Ardgour had been summarily stopped in 1685 there is a case to be made that Ewen Dubh might have greedily eyed the cows grazing at Callop, Cregag, Dalriach, Altlaig in north-western Ardgour, with some idea of retribution, but how many beasts might there actually have been? Fifty perhaps? And who could have enforced the law? Hill?

No lore exists of a major theft by Lochiel of Moidart, Arisaig or Morar cattle but that may not be absence of evidence enough. On the unlikely assumption that this was a local job, the Callop-centred farms were the furthest away from the Ardgour chiefly seat and most north-westerly of the Ardgour holdings (assuming they were not leased by the Glendessary Camerons or MacMillans). They both lay snugly out of sight from Loch Eil. Accepting that the nab was made at what is now Drochaid Sgainneal, only a mile away from Callop and on the 500-acre farm of Cregag, and, looking then first at the supposition that only official intervention could have incurred the loss of land to Ewen Dubh, in other words that the cattle thieves were caught by men with weapons, then the un-likelier and un-Gaelic thought must be considered first, that news reached Fort William extremely fast. The only official force was at Fort William. Access there was easy enough from Lochaber and Ardgour.

Were one to disregard all the evidence that is today easily available in abstract form at least, as I think Somerled MacMillan may have done in times when documentation was hard to find (if it were even known about), the most circuitous reasoning could claim that Locheil himself set up the pesky, independent-minded MacMillans whose reputation as reivers and independents living on the fringe of Locheil territory even Somerled MacMillan acknowledged. Hill at Fort William perceived Eòghann Dubh as cunning enough, and there was cattle thieving going on in the 1690s right enough, but Cameron control of the MacMillans surely did not require such perfidy. (Glendessary is near Kinlo-charkaig and there is no tale of Cameron–MacMillan internal conflict there.)

Nonetheless written claims such as MacMillan's need addressing. The quickest means of getting armed men from Fort William to Drochaid Sgainneal would have been by water, preferably with an east wind, to Kinlocheil. Prebble wrote that in December 1690, Hill had tried and failed to have the Privy Council provide him with a twenty-ton boat that could have mounted a culverin (long cannon) and convey a platoon of men, as well as smaller vessels for carrying fuel wood, but that by June 1691 Hill had a small frigate carrying eight guns for loch patrols. In that year also Hill wrote that he sent out 400-man parties twice or three times a week, both up and down the country. The Cregag cattle raid, if at this time, is not at all easy to understand in view of the risks. The prize surely would have to have been large.

In *Bygone Lochaber* the author mentions no ownership of the stolen cattle and nothing about the route taken by the thieves. At a very simple level, assuming that vainglorious, independent and unruly thieves only stole the Callop and probably the Dalriach beasts and assuming too that they chose to use the greatest surprise in their raid, then their best approach would simply have been via Gleann Camgharaidh south from Locharkaig and on over the watershed and down the Dubh Lighe at night, and then escape the same way they had come. A little more complicated route would have been via Allt a' Chaoruinn from Kinlocharkaig and over a height to the Dubh Lighe.

The most roundabout approach, and by far the most unlikely way to have handled this, would have been from the Catholic Clanranald west. Had they chosen to begin at or near Glenfinnan, however they assembled there (the main concentration of Mac-Millans was at the west end of Loch Arkaig whence Glenfinnan is accessible via Gleann/Allt a' Chaoruinn [Glen/Burn of the Ro-wans] and Gleann Fhionnain), but they risked observation by one of the Glenaladales. Then, if they had had to avoid going through the Callop Gap, there were two passes available to them through northern Sunart to Callop, access to which had to have been by boat. Between Meall na h-Àiridh and Meall a' Bhainne, using the six-inch map that was surveyed in 1872, there was what in the 1870s was called Feadan Mhic Bheathainn [MacVean's Crevice/ Stream/Chanter], a rough and high pass up Allt Feadan Mhic Bheathainn, which gave on to Allt na h-Àiridh to the west of Callop.[15] The southern pass, Bealach na Géire, lies between Meall a' Bhainne and Sgorr nan Cearc, running from the west up Allt na h-Innse Buidhe and then descending along Allt an Fhaing (Win-gate's map of 'Calap' in 1815 gives 'Alt n' Beallach n' gerridh') approaching Callop from the south-south-west.[16]

The quickest, most direct way was the best, there and back. It was a large *creach*, we are told, and the thieves would only be exposed to possible interceptors from Fort William for the time the animals were crossing Cregag farm and into the Gleann Dubh Lighe woods, and even then, with the woods at the bridge dense enough, to an even shorter distance and time. If the interception was achieved at night this all but guarantees foreknowledge on the part of any authorities involved.

The case for 1697, or within a few years, as the date for the Drochaid Sgainneal cattle raid is as strong as it is only because of the large garrisons of Williamite Scottish troops stationed at the garrison near Inverlochy in the decade 1689–1700. The MacMillans, according to Somerled MacMillan, had a record of reiving in Skye, Kintail and Glenelg, to all of which places they would have gained access by a northerly route or routes, from their west Loch Arkaig base.[17] The situation in Gaelic Scotland in early 1689, however, was, typically, complicated along clan, local identity, Gaelic 'country' rivalries, religious and other lines, little of which were of any interest to those caught up in, and reporting, national affairs. For some chiefs like the Duart MacLeans, the Keppoch MacDonalds and the MacIntoshes, the political horizons were of necessity fairly close at hand and involved balances of power within the *Gàidhealtachd*. Other, more powerful Highlanders tramped a wider yardage, the MacKays from the north, for example, Williamite military agents *par excellence*, and the Argyll Campbells for whom national political and personal affairs blended in clever, often acquisitive ways, at the time specifically aimed at depriving the southern MacLeans of their traditional Gaelic patrimony in Mull. To blame folk with national political vision and ambition, like Viscount Dundee and Campbell of Argyll, with their chief operatives, men like Hugh MacKay of Scourie and Colonel John Hill, for manipulating apparently small-horizon Highland chiefs and people living in what was another reality, is to overlook the ability of those people to be ready to take advantage of national and royalist thinking to assert their localisms – it is quite valid to consider Gaelic Scots, however fractious, as still considering themselves part of a broader, and to them, superior, Gaelic nexus, often very hostile to a Lowland-imposed national Presbyterianism, law and politics.

Meteorologically it is still accepted that the 1690s were years of hard weather and poor harvests in all of Scotland – I have not checked palinology or dendrology but accept the general statement, although not as a prime causative. From the point of view of Gaelic cow-stealing ritual, the Cregag heist could have fallen into this category but that is unlikely, given the power of Lochiel. This, overall, and growing power developed in the face of Monck and Hill, would not have at all encouraged Ewen Dubh to lure any feisty MacMillans into any devious, set-up trap (although he may have been angered at recent successful MacMillan pressure on him, in the late seventeenth century, to allow them to capture and dispose of a number of Macgillonie Cameron murderers).[18] That the MacMillans had longer roots in Kilmallie/Cill Maolain(?), the probably ancient religious base near Corpach, meant nothing to a man of Ewen Dubh's thinking and power.

Whatever his plans for the MacLeans, Eoghann Dubh, through his second, and most important marriage in *c.* 1663, to MacLean of Duart's daughter Isabel MacLean, had given evidence of attitudes to extending his power over MacLean lands south of Lochiel. The rift his grandfather Allan had earlier opened or exacerbated with the MacLeans was of no importance now. Ewen Dubh fathered seven children by Isabel MacLean, the second of his wives. Then his relations with the MacLeans of Ardgour were warmed with the marriage of his daughter Anne Cameron to Allan MacLean of Ardgour – she was born *c.* 1671 so the marriage probably dates to the 1690s. This was a time of expansion abroad and expansion at home for Cameron of Locheil.

The bloodless Williamite coup, in England, the 'Glorious Revolution', had begun with the Dutchman's landing in Devon in November 1688 to commandeer the British throne from Charles II's brother, James II. The Camerons, although, land-wise, subordinates to (pro-William) Campbell of Argyll, were staunch Jamesian royalists, against religious extremism and looking for greater independence and control in the area. Inevitably Ewen Dubh was appealed to by the Episcopalian Lowland Jacobite Dundonian, John Grahame of Claverhouse, and became thoroughly implicated in the war for King James. Somerled MacMillan's opinion is that clan Cameron contained or bordered an apparently unmastered, slightly anarchic Gaelic element in the MacMillans of Murlaggan on Loch Arkaig.

Apart from the remarkable victory of Dundee over MacKay at Killiecrankie in Perthshire (27 July 1689), the revolution was in no way glorious for either Gaelic Scotland or Ireland. In Scotland, while the forces involved were not large on either side, the war was a civil and religious one, both nationally and within Gaelic Scotland – Locheil had a son in the Scotch Brigade (in Holland) fighting with the government forces.[19] Resentment was buried deep at Inveraray and (after 1692) at Glencoe, and, where the un-Presbyterian people were concerned, on no trivial grounds at all. All or nothing religio-political conflicts conducted by nationally powerful people were without conscience, then as now, in their treatment of minority people like the Erse.

Something of the tenor of the 1690s for eastern Lochaber appears in another old cattle reiving story told and retold over at least three generations, and then committed to English print in the *Inverness Courier* of 17 August 1847, and copied by Robert Chambers in his *Domestic Annals* (1861). Whatever subtlety the original Gaelic story had, whoever the principals, whatever the adjectives and inflections, whatever the humour and irony, all that has come down the ages has to be construed in light of the force of possibly neutering print, and Gaelic Highland history is only vaguely and one-sidedly served. However it is from the uncertainty of war that big cattle raids happened and there are only two such periods examinable, the first being in the 1690s.

A twelve-year-old cattle-herd, William Bane MacPherson (1677–1777), tending beasts at 'Biallid' near Dalwhinnie in the autumn of 1689 remembered 120 stolen black cattle being driven by him by a dozen Lochaber men.[20] They told him that the cattle had been taken from Aberdeen(shire) and were being driven along Loch Erricht heading for a stop at 'Dalunchart' in what was then the forest of Alder south of Loch Laggan, in Badenoch. Shortly after the cattle and their thieves had left the Dalwhinnie area for the north bank of the loch, intending to head north thence for inland mountain recesses, MacPherson was interviewed (language used unknown) by the leader of about fifty horsemen, all armed gentlemen, who were trailing the thieves. With them they had horses laden with meal and shoes intended as the purchase price of the stolen cattle.[21] MacPherson tagged along out of curiosity and appears to have witnessed the defeat of the greatly outnumbered Lochaber thieves and the regaining of the herd. The Lowland gentlemen flew a flag of truce at Dalunchart and offered to pay the price. The robbers, sensing weakness, concentrated their cattle haul and spurned the offer. Action followed in which the gentlemen from Aberdeenshire easily prevailed.

The story in English suggests the remarkable bravery of even such a large and well-armed posse of Aberdeen gentlemen, venturing perhaps into a Lochaber noose, although they caught up with the robbers a day's walk from the latter's armed and safe haven of Lochaber. If not read with a wider knowledge, this isolated story ignores the endemic cattle thievery in non-Gaelic Scotland. The Lochaber thieves emerge as foolish, proud and inept cattle thieves and pathetic fighting men, much as do the MacMillans in the Drochaid Sgainneal story, but nevertheless both stories are worth examination and placing into a wider perspective.

As late as 1718 there were no roads from Aberdeen in Marr westwards through Badenoch and into the eastern part of Lochaber. Indeed the first road was constructed in order to allow early attempts to control Highland cattle raiding and whisky smuggling. The road map made in 1718 by Herman Moll shows a track or road from Innerlochy and Fort William, via the east of the Great Glen lochs to Inverness. The map was not reliable, and while a road is shown extending westward from Fort William to the ocean, it is obvious that the cartographer had no idea whatever of the Atlantic coastline, of interior lochs, rivers or mountains, and had invented almost everything about this route.[22] For all of the inaccuracy of the 1718 map, 'Loch Eyrachta' is shown, although at a strange orientation, almost north–south, with the northern third in Badenoch and the southern two-thirds in 'Broad Albyn'. The bathymetrical survey of Loch Erricht, which was surveyed in 1900, shows a track running from near Dalwhinnie in the north-east, down the north bank of the loch to about half way, passing through Dail na Longairt [Ship Harbour Dale] (recte, Dail an Long-phuirt or Dail Long-phuirt), before petering out in hard mountain country. At Dail na Longairt two rivers meet and empty into the loch (at 1,153 feet above sea level) and for some reason, in 1900, there was a well marked in the area, and Lochericht Lodge. The only route inland from Dail na Longairt in 1900 cut north heading for Kinloch Lagan/Ceann Loch Lagain, at the eastern end of Loch Lagan, still in Badenoch but just Lagan's length from the marches of Keppoch Lochaber and safety.

In all, in 1689, Lochaber cattle rustlers had good hopes of success on an eastward raid, and if the old man's story is correct, were probably a not unexpected feature of Aberdeenshire farm life, much as visits from Rob Roy's men were dreaded in the Lowland farms of Stirlingshire to the south within a lifetime later when conditions were different but still tricky for Gaelic North Britain under a German monarch.[23]

Somerled MacMillan, in outlining the MacMillans' prowess as cattle thieves, wrote that John MacMillan, sixth of Murlaggan, at Lochiel's behest, robbed MacIntosh of cattle in 1684, and claimed that he, Murlaggan, could take cattle from any people in Lochaber. John, according to Somerled MacMillan, apparently could operate outwith Lochiel's control inasmuch as he, John, would not support Lochiel against MacIntosh at about that time. MacMillan, however, also wrote that John's son Eoghann Òg mac Iain MacMillan, seventh of Murlaggan, fought with Locheil at Killiecrankie, but could only suppose that Archibald (eighth Murlaggan), Eoghann Òg's son, fought there with his father. Archibald, however, had a cattle-rustling brother, Dòmhnul Bàn Fiadhaich, mac Eoghainn Òg, who ranged from Skye to Kintail and Glenelg on his cattle missions. This man is the prime suspect in the Drochaid Sgainneal case, if it happened in the 1690s. He apparently conducted the last MacMillan cattle raid on Skye in the late 1690s, possibly dating the Craigag heist as a little later.

Staying with the 1690s, archival evidence offers one plausible source (NAS GD112/39/176/1) for the Drochaid Sgainneal cattle raid in the 1690s. This is a letter from 'Colonel John Hill, Fort William' to Sir John Campbell of Breadalbane, 12 November 1697, which reports that some of Breadalbane's tenants, with some of Hill's soldiers (at Fort William), had tracked and found stolen cows; the bearers of the letter were those same Breadalbane tenants. The thieves had got away but Hill intended to apprehend them,

> & then will send them where they may be hang'd, for the northerne district will hang none.

Hill did not accuse but implicated Locheil in the crime by writing to Breadalbane that Locheil claimed illness and could not appear (before Hill at the fort). Hill, who seems to some, from the deliberately (at times) not abundant written record, generally, not to have been bloodthirsty, but to have found himself in a reactionary, foreign environment, at the head of a Scottish regiment that contained several Highland officers,[24] and hemmed in with what he wished others to think were legal restrictions, and expressed his frustration freely about the lower, pilfering class,

> Ime sure wee'l never be quiet till hanging come more in fashon.

He also reported to Breadalbane that a party under 'Captain Meinyes' had, at Lord Atholl's desire, set out against 'the Frazers' with a commission of fire and sword, adding cryptically that

> Locheil shall rise earlier then ordinary if his polliticks outreach me in the bussines of these murderers.

Hill is crediting Lochiel with shrewdness. Letters at the time often appear cryptic, and were, simply because the bearer had been instructed to impart the greater message and details by word of mouth. Hill's letters to Breadalbane were neither complete nor at all ingenuous.[25]

A later letter to Breadalbane, dated 4 December 1697, explained that Locheil had been storm-stayed and could not get to visit Hill at the fort to answer Breadalbane's expectations (of Hill's interrogation) concerning the thieves and murderers. Hill is quoted,

> I am faine (where I find any stollen goods) to force sattisfaction without waiting for decreits from the justice courts, whose way of proceedure I cannot readily comply with, they'l hang noe theifes, nor examine any witnesses (in case of the parties non compeirance) aither as to the number of vallue, which (people perceivinge) make large claimes since they know they shall have (without more aode/ [adoe?]) all thats lybelled. (176/9)

Clearly the Scottish outrage, real and hypocritical, at the cold-blooded murdering of Mac Iain and nearly forty of his Glencoe people in February 1692 by Campbell of Glenlyon's company, had not disposed the local courts to prosecute Gaels for exercising their custom of stealing each others', and Lowlanders', cattle. Gaels in their treatment of cattle theft acknowledged older Gaelic legal convention and conceived of Gaeldom as a different polity. But, as Haldane observed, rustling was a national pastime so the distinction was blurred, except for Hill.

Bearing in mind the broad anti-Union feeling in Saxon and Gaelic Scotland in 1708, and even indecision on the part of some minor Campbells in the early just-post-Jacobite years, Hill's written attitude to people like Lochiel had to be couched in careful terms. Otherwise Hill was acutely aware of some of the politics in which he found himself, even if he disdained them. He did not write down the names of the suspects in the cattle raid case. Prebble discovered a sympathetic old man in Hill, despite his oblique order to the unidentified Scot James Hamilton to do the Glencoe massacre.

What emerges through the finicking confusion that many leading Scots people thought to be base, immoral rabbling easily controllable with appropriate might, is a minor Scottish civil war in which Highland Catholic society and other elements of that ancient Gaelic society, cattle-based, simply arranged into 'countries' occupied and still being struggled and married over, without the might of the MacDonalds united, separated from its mother Ireland at long last, in the maturing stages of the Anglicisation of its Gaelic and Gaelically oriented chiefs (which often involved extra-Gaelic marriages), was vulnerable to and being manipulated by a more powerful, clerically systematised legal system of landownership. Militarally, Gaelic techniques, when combined with fervent bravery, still allowed defiance and defeat of the slightly more lumberingly organised Cromwellian and Adolphan systems, much as Robert E. Lee's outnumbered, outgunned southern army for long confounded MacLellan's huge, but tentative, army of the Potomac.

The remnant of old Celtic, sword-wielding *La Tène* society still had a chance at victory while there was no rifling of barrels and while separate bayonets had to be fixed, after firing, to a hot barrel, under rapidly intensifying threat of death. Of great significance also was the staggered use of Highland Jacobite soldiery in a marginal

agricultural world at a time when bad harvest might mean ghastly
spring hardship — using too large a proportion of young, unpaid or
lowly-paid men in war was risky to local societies' continuance.
Campaigns had to be on and off.[26] For this reason also there was a
great value attaching to the insurance of additional meat and dairy
supply, and the denial of that to potential enemies. In times of
national military uncertainty, when there was weak occupation by
outside forces, for many Scottish Gaelic leaders, even of Norman-
Flemish origins like the Camerons, an obvious precaution was to
concentrate cattle.

If the cattle-raid story assumption is right, that this all happened in
Eoghann Dubh's time, then the story of the farms at Cregag and
Callop are taken back to 1697, to just about the dawn of modern
English records for the place. Without Somerled MacMillan's
work, hardly any non-researching reader would have easy access
to the very complicated local MacMillan lore. Any further traces,
from the place names for example, cannot be safely discerned. The
old line of intensest knowing went with the last Gaels who lived in
the old system into the second half of the eighteenth century.

     But other archival sources, and common sense, have to be
considered as bearing on this theft perpetrated on the Cregag farm
of Lochiel. These involve less complicated and speculative thinking
and point to the most plausible explanation in all of this. Had this
documentation been readily available to Somerled MacMillan he
would have arrived at a quite different conclusion. MacMillan,
however, inadvertently and usefully, did mention the name Eoghann Òg mac Iain MacMillan, seventh of Murlaggan, as cattle
reiver of the 1690s. The time and the feel of the period fifty years on
were now quite different. A major cattle *creach* may have been the
result of ungoverned mad-cap greed, but this failed heist has all the
hallmarks of a manipulative economic technique by the Camerons
in a Highland society that was largely ignored by South Britain. It
was a time of dramatic uncertainty when the winning or influencing
of MacDonald of Sleat's power was clearly vital to Jacobitism.

     But first, of course, there are fundamental weaknesses of Mac-
Millan's almost-argument, even for the 1690s as years in the time of
the *creach*. There is no knowledge from *Bygone Lochaber* of how

many beasts were the target on the Cregag farm and whose they were. This particular cattle theft however, like only a few others, survived persistently in local Lochiel lore, but is apparently absent from MacLean of Ardgour lore. Somerled MacMillan did not specify any oral source for the story other than the Drochaid Sgainneal name. Of great importance also is any assumption that the stolen cattle were anything other than the beasts at Callop. There could not have been enough Callop cows to merit the term 'large *creach*'. And, given a 'large *creach*', a new place-name surely depended on an accompanying act of bodily injury. The murder alluded to by Cameron of Lochiel at the railway hearing in London in March 1889 is probably the popular point of entry to this story if not the hinge to this creaky old door.

From a folder headed 'Lovat Letters' in a collection of Cameron of Lochiel papers, including sixty-three items registered by NRAS, there is the following:

> [2 July 1743] As to visit of Laird of Macleod and Sir Alexander Macdonald and discussion about murder of McEvanoig. Macdonald 'swore a great oath that if your [Lochiel] people would touch any of his men or take their cattle from them in their way South, that he would conveen every man and boy in arms that he was able to raise, and go with them himself to the heart of Locharkegg'.[27]

Let us assume now only that a serious crime was committed in the summer of 1743. McEvanoig, or Mac Eòghann Òig, is unidentified but the name strongly suggests that he was a MacMillan, and one of the would-be cattle thieves. MacDonald of Sleat's alarm and outrage was at the possibility of losing a herd of cattle of great value, not in the least at the death of one of the robbers. There is a touch of spirit to the letter, whatever its accuracy or underlying purpose. Maybe this was not the first attempted cattle raid on this cattle route. Cregag was unavoidably on the drove road from Àrasaig, the Morars and islands to the west. The chances of the guilty party from 'Locharkegg' not being MacMillans are not great, and obviously any escape simply had to head for Kinloch Arkaig. In those edgy times, even if the attempt was abortive, MacDonald of

Sleat must have been enraged at least partly because of the bold-faced and big-scale nature of the try.

Note also that there is the absence of any record of MacDonald's complaint at cattle theft or the murder of one of his employees in 1743. I have not found that MacDonald sought any official judgement from Donald Cameron, younger of Lochiel, the gentle Lochiel. With a strength of pro-Hanoverian Gaels in Argyll, Lowland Scotland as well as in other parts of Highland Scotland, it is unlikely that MacDonald (aware of his ancestor's estate forfeiture after the 1715 Rising) feared that the Jamesians might win and believed that it would be futile to register a complaint at a wrong done him by Lochiel. Although he died suddenly at Glenelg on 30 November 1746 (at thirty-five, cause unpublicised, with three collateral deaths/murders at the wake/funeral), there is no suggestion that MacDonald let any case wait till the occupation in 1746. In 1743 Alexander MacDonald was in the last year of a three-year contract with some Yorkshire drovers from Skipton, headed by Thomas Chamberland, to deliver and sell cattle at the Falkirk market. What appears to be a receipt for £5,000 sterling for that year measures the huge size of the herd going through Cregag farm bound for the South.[28] Then the only crime was attempted robbery, probably armed.

Lochiel's potential Jacobitism was known (unfortunately there is no knowing the part played by any anti-established Presbyterianism in his attitude, although the family had a prominent Catholic element – the Skye MacDonalds were Presbyterians but with an as-yet-unfathomed, culturally conservative Episcopal population). Lochiel's inclination to harbour, and manipulate, a cattle-stealing element was also well known. If the robbers were 'caught red-handed' as MacMillan wrote, who did the catching? The Black Watch had begun its march from its Highland base(s) to Perth in March 1743 and proceeded to London (arriving in late April 1743). There was no nearby official force capable of intervention. If McEvanoig was a drover or helper in Chamberland's service then there is the strongest case for Lochiel's openly or covertly disclaiming ownership of the Cregag farm, but surely MacDonald would never have hesitated to press for justice immediately.

The only alternative in this case is that it was a drover, or a drover's man, who killed one of the would-be cattle thieves from Locharkegg in 1743. Then one unanswered question is when ownership of Cregag was unofficially and officially ceded by Lochiel. Since no farmer at Cregag claimed for cattle losses to Cumberland's soldiery after Culloden, and since all bar one of the principals (Lochiel, Clanranald and his subordinate Glenalladale) were adults, the 1743–9 period appears the likeliest for the unofficial admission. From spring of 1746 no Lochiel gentleman had convincing legal power. If any official concession were inferable from any other person after Culloden, Alexander MacDonald's older heir, James, was born in 1742 and died in 1766 (when his younger brother, Alexander assumed the mantle). Both Ardgour and Sleat were minorities from November 1746 until 1757 and 1763 respectively. In the case of forfeited Lochiel, boundaries might be officially or unofficially decided (only to the estate's loss) and promulgated or not at the controllers' whim. The shire boundary by 1748 had been extended to include much of the estate in Argyll (as will be shown).

Lack of any evidence to the contrary suggests that this taking of life in the *creach* was by a man from near the Yorkshire Dales who was legally defending a very valuable property entrusted him by Alexander MacDonald of Sleat. Any expressible retort in Lochiel at pro-Jacobite cattle theft's being but some playful Christian (Catholic-Episcopal) Highland custom carried on without killing would have received no sympathy before or after Culloden; indeed understandable local bitterness among the MacMillans continued deep for years, and it is of great importance to note that Fassifern (whose bowmen were MacMillans) sought to assuage this when he could. Many of Lochiel's tenants, from tacksman and wadsetter to humbler folk, were impoverished in 1746 by Sackvill's, Cornwallis's and others' soldiers and it appears in suspicious retrospect that Sir Alexander MacDonald savoured the beginnings of sweet revenge before the reaper got him.

Sir Alexander MacDonald's great cattle herd would have been mustered in southern Skye and would have been shipped to Àrasaig Point — it is moot to what extent the MacMillans had earlier turned him from the old Kyle Rhea–Glenelg–Glengarry cattle route (Barrisdale and Glengarry were probably greater threats). It would have then taken the drove track to Glenfinnan and passed

through the Callop Gap on to Cregag, a large prize lowing and
farting and fertilising its way through almost at the MacMillans'
back door, at the furthest west of the Lochiel farms. Under quiet
politics, Lochiel and MacDonald might have had an understanding
about cattle droving but which, in the new circumstances Lochiel
was ready to play with, if perhaps not to the point of robbery with
ignobly fatal violence.

Where intra-Highland cattle affairs like this were concerned, one
might well value the remarks of Simon Fraser made about cattle
thievery – with the proviso that with political affairs pre-eminent,
Lovat's written words, and topics perhaps, like those of others, were
deceptive.[29] What is surprising about the NRAS26/14 collection is
how much cattle thieving was going on in the 1730s and '40s in
which the Camerons were involved – three Cameron cattle thieves
were killed. In October 1736 Lovat, a Black Watch company
commander, sent two Fraser tacksmen, his baillies and chamberlains
to demand redress for Lochiel cattle robbing. That failing, he wrote
that he would next contact the Earl of Ilay, minister of state, and
General Wade, commander-in-chief of forces in Scotland. Should
those people not gain him satisfaction he wrote that he meant to
apply to the king and the Privy Council who, he wrote, 'would be
glad of any handle to suppress a Highland Clan'. On 22 May 1740
the same source noted Lord Seaforth's watch set up against cattle
thieves and Lovat wrote that,

> Truly the rogues of your Countrey and Glengarry are ungratfull, for
> I often protected and savd their Lives [using his Black Watch
> power?], and yet they are heavy upon me as upon any man.

On 19 November 1742 Lochiel's tenants again are accused of cattle
stealing, and so are Lovat's ('by young Lentran'), and in this letter
Lovat remarked on the death of two Cameron cattle thieves. The
last letter of importance is one written by Lovat to Lochiel on 8 July
1743 to back up the one cited above. In this Lovat mentioned the
establishment of a cattle watch under MacDonald of Barrisdale, but
he also begged Lochiel not to allow his men to attack Sir Alexander
MacDonald's droves as this would lead to civil war.[30]

Leaving aside the case for Cameron expansion into MacLean country, this pre-Rising cattle-drove thievery should be seen in politico-military terms: the resented house of Hanover, the on-going war of the Austrian Succession, the Scottish Jacobite war to come and the Hanoverian persecution later in 1746. Cattle-drove thieving also had an intra-Gaelic function, to generate general pressure from below on the chief and chieftains. Cattle thieving may have been a tool to help win a vacillator like Lovat to the Jamesian fold. Both periods, in the 1680s and 1690s and the 1730s and 1740s, clearly are the thieving times whose return Somerled MacMillan's old Cameron clansman facetiously welcomed a generation after Culloden.[31] Englishman Edward Burt, in his repeatedly cited letters written from Highland Scotland from 1727 to 1736, fingered the Keppoch MacDonalds, the Camerons and the MacGregors as the prime cattle-thieving clans — Burt, like Hill, however, showed no need or wish to express subtle understanding of Highland politics. After Glencoe, the English anti-Darien reaction, the hated Union (1707) and the fairly tame Hanoverian reaction to the first serious Jacobite Rising (1715) and the Spanish interlude (1719) there was a neglect of Gaelic Scotland and no strong and effective policing – Wade's Highland force, then the Black Watch from 1729–30 were not enough and were comprised of Gaels of questionable Hanoverian allegiance. The 'gentle' Lochiel certainly was anticipating restoration, and his brothers with him and many, but not all, of his powerful subordinates. At the local level after 1746 the main query concerns Fassifern.

The Cregag *creach* was a major attempted theft, an aggressive intra-Gaelic play and inevitably a political statement that was in preparation for armed conflict. Its aim was to bring pro-Jacobite pressure from his common people on Sir Alexander. The younger Lochiel (Donald) and his brother Fassifern (John) were its engineers. Implicit in the *creach* was the hope that Sir Alexander MacDonald's political stance was not irrevocable. There was no fear of even a John Hill at Fort William this time around. The herd was guarded by MacDonald's armed Englishmen. The Cregag cattle business was, in one way, an intra-Gaelic event and preserved without the help of reports or newspapers, *inter alia* in a local place name. The murder of a MacMillan cattle thief from the Jacobite estate was nationally insignificant – Scottish law allowed that,

> the slaughter of night thieves, house-breakers, assistants in masterful depredations . . . may be committed with impunity.[32]

Property was what counted and retribution in Lochiel in 1746, for cattle thieving over the years, was systematically and thoroughly exacted on cattle herds, in national reprisal. There could be no patience with the subtleties of the old Highland society and its internal balances and reactions to wars begun outside it, but the huge importance of cattle in that society's economy was well known, and there is no doubt, from their actions, that the Hanoverian leaders in the field quickly became well aware of intra-Cameron cattle and political affairs. In 1746 there was prominent in the government plan: impoverish them all by taking their cattle, no matter at all that the preferred religious creed practised by many of the powerful in places like Glencoe and Lochiel was the English hierarchical one.[33] Six years later (1752) the first execution of a Gael in Scottish Gaeldom for cattle theft was carried out. Such a heinous business as the gentle Lochiel's entry into the Jacobite war, and at such a high military level, meant only short shrift for even those only suspected. The exiling of Cameron of Fassifern to Alnwick is simply explained, but underlying this sentence was a government awareness of the premeditated cunning and intelligence employed by him and his brother in the planning and conduct of Prince Charles's attempt at restoration. There was little dithering about the un-sheathing of the sword for King James.

Two centuries is not much time for the human memory for a major local event so the attempted cattle heist at Cregag, but more particularly the killing of a local Gael (not inconceivably the third) by an English drover, would certainly have been an unforgettable part in the prologue to the Forty-five. No wonder the old Ardgour lady remembered in 1894 the reaction of another woman to the Jamesian troops coming through that late August day long ago. The sub-legal, sub-anarchy of military law in Lochiel, on all – on wadsetters, tenants and subtenants – that followed Cumberland's victory at Culloden was surprising, as well as the thorough intelligence behind it. Lochiel's tenantry appealed for compensation presumably at least to register the thoroughness of the theft, and therein also lies an untold tale.

Whatever prominence Cumberland and later Hanoverian officers paid to the complaints of MacDonald of Sleat in 1745–6, Hanoverian reaction was rigorous and significantly concentrated in the Loch Arkaig–Glen Loy area. A 'barracks' was built at Keanlocharkeg and it was from that area, although in pre-barrack times, on 7 June 1746, that George Sackvill [*sic*] stole Fassifern's protected cows and other beasts (location unknown), and property. Cattle and other beasts and property were taken, by his majesty's soldiery, from Bunarkaig to Glendessary and Glen Pean, and while Somerled MacMillan gives the lists of items per holding and there are few dates. (Stronlea, Fassifern, Achdalieu were robbed in June 1746; Drumnasallie and one farm in Glendessary were robbed in 1746.) Notable are the facts that Captain Swettenham of Guise's regiment sent many of his reports from a base in Glen Loy and there was also a base of some sort at Bunarkaig (all Macgillonie country). These northerly focal points show an important understanding of Cameron use of MacMillans as cattle thieves, and the anti-Hanoverian vigour of the MacIllonies. Compensation claims show that Drumsallie and Corribeg were robbed of cattle, but there is no mention of Craigag, or Drumfern, or Glendylie – perhaps John Cameron had concentrated some of his beasts in one place; perhaps he had moved some out of reach. Treason (7 Anne, c. 21 [post-Union and thus English], 1707) meant attainder (19 Geo. II, cap 26, 1746) and attainder meant, among other things, loss of property. From May 1746, Lochiel and his minions were powerless over land they had held from Argyll and Gordon. The Cregag *creach* was enough to subtract the farm from the holding and for long enough without widely accessible legally precise documentation. (The later, equally-determined, force of the vengeance involved the systematic Presbyterian proselytising, both at Kilmallie and Kinlocharkaig).

I have seen no evidence that Donald (son of Charles, son of Donald) Cameron, the grandson of the 'gentle' Lochiel of the Forty-five, quibbled about or demanded the return of the Cregag farm when in 1784 the old Lochiel estate was bought back for

Donald Cameron of Lochiel (aged twenty-one in 1790) by his trustees from the Commissioners of the Annexed Estates (Ewen Fassifern was the factor). There had been radical change. The Camerons of Lochiel (and most of their people) were powerless after Culloden and stayed silent. I have found no proof of Fassifern's bankruptcy. Lochiel had a clear idea of the consequences he might bring on himself with his decision for King James in 1745.

A veil is almost lifted on this great Cregag *creach* of 1743 with the knowlege that John Cameron of Fassifern held the following farms on wadset in 23 January 1749: the 'seven Merk Land of Farsfern, Wauchin, Glendyle, Dreimfarmaloch, Clerichaig, Kainnicyle [unidentified], & Miln of Farsfern'.[34] The old mid-fifteenth-century name for Cregag, Clerichaig, persisted until 1749. The discovery by David Bruce, the surveyor of the Lochiel forfeited estate (work presumably done in 1748, the year that the gentle Lochiel died), that the 1743 *creach* was in any way connected with Fassifern's holdings must have sharply increased government suspicion that he was profoundly involved. Were the beginning date of Fassifern's wadset known, the veil would be raised clear.

If it is not known how Fassifern and Lochiel disposed of their herds at the Rising, or even if they did manage it (Fassifern lost a lot of property) – Fassifern's other holdings, of 'Inner-Skahadill, Conglen & Achafuboill' in Ardgour in 1746 were also protected, and with a protection more reliable than that given for his Lochiel holdings MacLean of Ardgour got Cregag. The limited number of MacMillans involved in the 'Forty-five suggest to me that Lochiel felt he could not force service on a family that was still defiantly outraged at the murder of McEvanoig by a Yorkshire man. It might hint also at the MacMillans' potential alternate service as providing some sort of pre-planned neutral zone. An even safer haven would have been in neutral Ardgour. Clerichaig then was a *quid pro quo*.

Argyll profited otherwise. Argyll controlled much of the Lochiel estate, through factors Patrick, Colin and Mungo Campbell, up to and after the overall control of the barons of the exchequer in 1755. At that point Lochiel's estate fell under Argyll's control and not the commissioners of the annexed estates (who elsewhere worked *gratis*). In 1770 the estate had been bought by the Crown from the superiors, the dukes of Argyll and Gordon, and then profits were taken; ironically, it was then that Argyll's (and Gordon's) 'superior' relationship with Cameron of Lochiel ceased and part of a long-established and understood hierarchical Highland land bond, even if mistrusted and resented, was broken. At least from 1755 then, religious control was in Hanoverian control. Verily, the way was open for one level of ownership and the gradual exposure of a large part of Cameron 'country' people to national standards of industry, commerce and religious thought, from which they were to have no protectors when kindness and Gaelic custom really wore thin in the early nineteenth century. (Malcolm McCaskill's and other imposed ministers' part in this conditioning is unexamined and not copiously remembered in the victorious descriptions of all that happened.)

But let's put the significance of the cattle heist into an even tighter perspective.

On 5 August 1742 a warrant was issued by the Argyll justiciary court for twenty-one men from Ardnamurchan and Sunart who were accused of the theft of nineteen tons of lead, a very large number of musket and cannon balls. The first name given was Alexander Cameron in Resipole, Ardnamurchan, the next three were McOlonichs from Acharacle, Ardnamurchan, the rest are unnamed in the abstract of the case – there is no mention of weapons involved.[35] On 21 September the same year a 'Donald MacDonald merchant in Uist' was accused of breaking down the gates of the castle of Mingary and stealing nineteen tons of lead belonging to Sir Duncan Campbell of Lochnell and transporting it to Canna.[36] On both dates the Black Watch were on service in the Highlands. The McOloniches were Mac Ghille Onfhaidhs, prominent and Jacobite Cameron tenantry. There are no letters in the Lovat letters collection dated around this time.

Somerled MacMillan wrote of the independent-mindedness of the Macgillonies and their late-seventeenth-century murder of a MacMillan near enough Achnacarry. *No Quarter Given* mentions seven known names of Cameron regiment Jacobites from Ardnamurchan and Sunart, among them Donald 'Cameron, or MacIl-lonie' from Tarbet Ardnamurchan (taken prisoner and liberated), and another 'Cameron, or MacIllonie, Tarbet, Ardnamurchan' (taken prisoner and discharged).[37] In *Bygone Lochaber,* the author named two Macgillonies, Camerons, from Tarbat, Donald and Dugall Cameron, probably brothers, who were caught during the Forty-five. He stated that they were of the Glenpeanbeag Macgillonies from west of Kinloch Arkaig.

Were one to look for another irony it would be in the muster of the Lochiel regiment. There is only one MacMillan,[38] and, while the claim is often made that MacMillans became Camerons for convenience's sake, there is no strong and broad lore of action in the Rising by many MacMillans and some were in Fassifern's debt. The undefendable killing of one of their number in 1743 by a Saxon must have made them even more contemptuous and detesting of Lochiel who was planning clearings before they emigrated to Upper Canada. In a political sense Lochiel 'country' was no simple place in the last Jacobite years.

There remain several threads to be picked up. The first concerns something that ex-British diplomat Lochiel told the House of Lords committee in 1889. He said that admission of the ownership of Cregag farm after the cattle heist had been rejected by the ancestors of Glenaladale and Lochiel. If he meant by legal adult ancestors then this happened one way or another between the summers of 1743 and 1746 or else in and after 1763 (see above). If a change in ownership happened after Culloden, when political power was becoming a daydream in Gaelic Scotland, the chances are good that Argyll had some control over the brief. Hill had had no such power in the 1690s and couldn't even get the gunboats he knew he needed. The second thread concerns the Clanranald estate. Lochiel (1835–1905) was careful, seemingly humorously, to implicate a lesser light in the Cregag case, Glenaladale, when the bigger fish, Ranald Clanranald and his son Ranald, had been the object of intense Hanoverian interest in 1746. Had this Lochiel historically correctly implicated a Glenaladale as potential owner of Cregag at the time of this theft, this might be explained as his having known of some devious effort by the government to strengthen its case for the forfeiture of Clanranald country – as I noted above, Ranald (MacDonald of) Clanranald, the Old Clanranald of the Forty-five, won clear title and control of the estate in 1751 after three years of legal argument.[39] This may have been a red herring. Cregag appears never to have been more than a pawn in Cameron–MacLean affairs.

Who was 'McEvanoig?' All that can be said with certainty is that Lovat would have been as circumspect as necessary in 1743 and that it was code for MacMillan, a cattle thieving patronymic based on Eoghann Og, seventh MacMillan of Murlaggan, who was the leader of the last MacMillan cattle raid into Skye in the last years of the seventeenth century.

No less speculative, and on a very minor level in all of this, was the changing of *sgainneal* to *sgainnir*, from scandal to scattering. The executive officer of the Ordnance Survey when the Cregag, Callop, Kinlocheil, Glenfinnan area was surveyed in 1872 was John Cameron, RE, FRS. His birth in French Flanders is un-explained but he was of the Culchenna family, Alasdair Dubh, mac Ailein, 'ic Iain, a splinter of the Callart Camerons. He was a son of Lieutenant General Sir John Cameron (1773–1844) and Amelia Brock (b. *c.* 1776) and had a brother, General Sir Duncan Alex-ander Cameron (1808–1888, veteran of the Crimea and the Waikato Maori War) who, according to an obituary in the *South-ampton Times* of 6 July 1878, was at his funeral (the surviving brother's name was wrongly given as Campbell).[40] John Cameron's influence on the acceptance of local Gaelic place names is un-known. At the time, the chief of Clan Cameron was Donald, resident at Achnacarry (the first such since the 'gentle' Lochiel of the Forty-five), MP for Inverness-shire (1868–*c.* 1885), the man who greeted Victoria in 1873, who was in 1884 to be elected chief of the Gaelic Society of Inverness, who founded the Clan Cameron society, and who obviously had interests in local history.

Why the change?

And lastly to maps and sketches: did the name MacVean Rocks, originate in the days of the great cattle droves from Mallaig – lookout points perhaps? If so, how came MacVeans to Ardgour country? Lore states that the first MacVean was brought by Lochiel *c.* 1650 as a family tutor. He married a daughter of Lochiel, presumably an unknown sister of Sir Ewen (b. 1629 and tutored separately, as heir apparent, in Campbell country). From this MacVean–Cameron marriage a descendant married into the

MacLeans of Ardgour. In Ardgour some MacVeans became tacksmen-farmers and one may reasonably postulate an important presence in Callop just before the 1745 Jacobite war.[41] The earliest recorded account of MacVeans that I have found occurs in GD112/3/9 where 'Malcolm MakVaane, [and] Gillemartin MacVaane' are among a long list of men remitted under the great seal for the 'murder of Robert MacApBrinker' (date: 19 October 1488). The Bethune name comes from the place in medieval Artois. The sketch of Cregag as an Ardgour farm, made in 1815 (RHP89887) names the new road 'Road from the isle of Sky', not the road from Loch nan Ceall, or from Mallaig, a significance obvious to Gaels if not Telford and Dick and Readdie.

The later period, including Ardgour and the emigrations

With the speculation about the Drochaid Sgainneal cattle raid and Cregag's mention in the lore of the 1745 Jacobite rising considered, speculatively, the question surfaces: what family or families were living at Calap and Cregag in 1743?

Knowledge of occupancy of the area that includes Callop and Craigag (and probably Dalrioch and Altlaig) is patchy for half a century until 1790 – for Craigag non-existent – but there is an important Fassifern link with Calap from about 1777 and a Cameron presence there in 1790 (when Alexander MacLean of Ardgour's extant estate records begin) that suggests early Fassifern control, and on until 1843 Camerons are the commonest occupants. Almost certainly in 1743 Cregag fell within the part of Cameron of Lochiel's estate that was held from the Duke of Argyll and was part of local business that the duke probably steered toward the MacLeans.[42]

The MacLeans' first, and other, family records will be used to re-create the occupation of both farms and two, perhaps three, contiguous ones, as far as possible – Dalriach, Mealdamh and Altlaig, from 1790 into the twentieth century. From these will emerge both the main changes that happened to Callop and Craigag under commercial management, but also the trickiness in accepting only written records in considering a Highland estate in the hands of non-Gaels, howsoever much sympathy they showed to the Gael. Always beneath a written record lies the consciousness of an unpowerful Gaelic-dominant, but bilingual, society accommodated by a consciousness of its own ancient classical poetry, story and science (medicine, and ship- and boat-building), perhaps also custom that had originated as law, enough to have encouraged, not long from living memory, thoughts of freedom and separateness.[43]

Having divested himself of, or otherwise detached himself from, the Lochiel West Indian plantation before the Forty-five, John Cameron, first of Fassifern (*c.* 1699–1785), appears to have concentrated his land acquisition south of Lochiel in Ardgour, and conditions were favourable. To begin with, Allan MacLean, tenth of Ardgour (1668–1756) was married to Anne Cameron, daughter of Ewen Cameron of Lochiel. Allan had relinquished the chiefship in 1732 to his son John who predeceased him in 1739 leaving a son Hugh, twelfth of Ardgour (1736–1768), who was a minor until 1757. Stable tacksmen would have been attractive to the rulers in Ardgour in difficult post-Union times. Fassifern was given protection for his farms and people at Fassifern, Wauchin, Glendylie, Conaglen, Inverscadale and Achaphubuil in May 1746, protection that the occupying military commander deliberately chose to ignore within the Lochiel estate proper. Glendylie and Conaglen, however, present definitional problems. The 1774 drawing of the forfeited estate shows that the main farm of 'Drumnasaly' included land up to the Allt Dubh Lighe, so one must assume that Fassifern held the mill, and perhaps the woodlands there from Ewan Cameron, the wadsetter, in July 1746, or his successor; or that there may have been a separate holding called Glendylie before the reorganising of the managers of the forfeited estate; or that there was an error over the name. As far as Conaglen goes, what did the holding amount to when Fassifern had it in 1746? Whether or not it had a pendicle called Calap doesn't matter, and for this reason. By 1777 a Ewen MacMillan (*c.* 1736–1781) from Kinlocharkaig, and of the old Kinlocharkaig MacMillan family, was at Callop at the express wish, one way or another, of Ewen Cameron, younger of Fassifern (the first still being quick) – MacMillan almost certainly was still fostering Ewen Cameron's son, the future Colonel John

Cameron, 'young' Fassifern (1771–1815) at Callop, until date unknown. Over three generations this MacMillan family had been in the service of three generations of Fassiferns (John, Ewen and Ewen's famous son Colonel John Cameron) – this alone was reason to suspect the first Fassifern of great foresight and cunning.[44] There is to my knowledge no link as yet between this MacMillan family and the Donald MacMillan who emigrated from Callop in 1802. The MacMillan occupation however may have been continuous from in or just before 1777 till some time before 1790. On 27 July 1790 John Cameron, unidentified, tacksman of half of the farm of Callop, gave a steelbow tack (one that included livestock) to Donald Cameron who was the tacksman of Kinlocheil for nine years starting on Whitsunday.[45]

In 1815, Cregag (including waters that drained into Lochs Shiel and Eil) was part of the estate of Colonel Alexander MacLean, thirteenth of Ardgour (1764–1855) (Alasdair mac Eoghainn), perhaps only so defined by the commissioners of the forfeited estates. Cregag is not included in a plan of part of the annexed estate of Lochiel south of Loch Arkaig dated 1772 (RHP6591),[46] which dates its acquisition/relinquishment to pre-August 1745. Was there, until the return of the Lochiel estate to the old Lochiel family in 1784, some special unwritten leasing agreement between the Ardgour MacLean owner(s) or controller(s) and Locheil that allowed the latter to continue drawing rent from Cregag? There was a long period when Alexander MacLean of Ardgour was working on his army career and he appears in retrospect to have shown little strong desire then to command Ardgour, and limit Cameron or other presence there to renters and tacksmen. Even for long after his reaching his majority in 1785 he may always have felt a diffidence about the disposition of Cregag.

The written record is insufficient and never directly reflects Gaelic thought. Most of the people of Ardgour to my knowledge became Presbyterian, as did those of Mull and Morvern and Kingairloch, in a process or processes undescribed, from Catholicism through Episcopalianism. I sense that the subject may bear study and that the emigrations conveniently mask subtleties some prefer unstudied. There may have been retentions of Catholicism and Episcopalianism here and there, particularly where Ardgour was near Catholic Moidart. Cameron country by and large is accepted as having been Protestant by 1745 but with Roman Catholic connections at many levels of society (referred to above) which induce questions about tolerance and honesty.[47] The Revd Archibald Clerk in his memoirs of Colonel John Cameron (d. Quatre Bras, 1815) wrote in 1858 that such an assemblage that gathered to inter the Fassifern colonel would never be seen again, so many had emigrated to Canada and Australia. Defining the power of the greater population to ameliorate zealotry lay outside Clerk's interest.

Looking at Cregag and Callop from the modern written record, from 1790, what was left of the older Gaelic world emerges at times, and not always directly, but the story concentrates one's thought on the rapidly deepening divide between the two Scottish, the two European, cultures, the commercial and the non-commercial. For the non- or pre-commercial, or partially commercial Gaelic world there was the benign and well-intentioned crofting system that Alexander of Ardgour set up in his Ardgour, at Clovullin, Blaich and Garvan, in the first dozen years of the nineteenth century (when there was lots of road and canal work available locally). In his early-nineteenth-century estate management there is a glimpse of the general shift away from the dominant cattle farming even while the demands and prices were high, in the person of the man who may be the first of his factors we know about, Duncan Campbell, a man who seems either to have died or, ironically, to have bankrupted himself through unwise speculation in cattle, a business that was often very tricky – Duncan appears to have been Ardgour's factor between 1800 and 15 March 1810,[48] and that was the time when MacLean introduced change on his Gaelic estate. (Duncan Campbell is described as 'former factor' in Ardgour on 15 March 1810 (NRAS3583, bundle 19) and as 'late Drover at Stronechrigan' in 1813 (NRAS3583, bundle 2). Also, in the Robert Brown correspondence there is a letter, 9 March 1804, from Campbell at 'Ardgour, Glenscadle', (factor to factor) dealing with the claim against him for debt by 'Trumsgarry'. Campbell claimed to owe Trumsgarry nothing (NRAS2177, bundle 1522). Trumsgarry appears to have been in Clanranald's Benbecula.) MacLean of Ardgour's name, however, is not associated with the greedy brutality of using Gaels almost as forced labour to make kelp, and that is what began in around 1790 for Ranald George MacDonald of Clanranald's people.[49]

Inferring from a general description of the population make-up of Ardgour that is taken from a speech made by Alexander MacLean himself on 31 August 1850 which contains his reminiscences back to 1780,[50] it appears that a Gaelic cattle economy was allowed to continue relatively unmanaged in Ardgour, people repeatedly subdividing farmland, until the French Revolutionary War. Improving measures on the neighbouring Cameron forfeited estate (till 1784), basically evicting people, must have been well known. When his circumstances goaded him, during the Napoleonic Wars, Alexander MacLean of Ardgour was like Fassifern and other powerful men in the area, bound irrevocably to the commercial system and to upper-class English and North British society – the Regency period that was costly for many an extravagant Highland chief and chieftain ran from 1811 until 1820. On 17 March 1806 Alexander MacLean received a written valuation from his factor Duncan Campbell at Stronechrigan of rent of sheep-farms in Ardgour, a report which suggested another for 1808, with increases proposed.[51] In 1810 MacLean was either in or just about to begin service as lieutenant-colonel in the Argyll Militia.[52] In 1810 he gave up Stevenson House near Haddington and moved to Keith House in Tranent near Edinburgh which he leased from his wife's half-brother James Hope, third Earl of Hopetoun (1741–1816).[53] In 1812 he had two sons at Harrow. He had made an offer to Peter Oliver from West Shiels in the Borders of a nineteen-year lease of Inversanda and Gerridh as a sheep-farm (NRAS3583/B, bundle 19 – Oliver took Inversanda without Gerridh); MacLean had bought Inverscaddle farm from Ewen of Fassifern by 31 July 1811 (NRAS3583/B, bundle 2) for £15,000 and clearly was running his estate commercially, with a good steady rent coming in from crofters working on the road and canal schemes nearby, and with sheep-farming beginning to feature profitably.[54] There is a sense of his need to retake his estate in all of this. His capitalising for friends and relatives, on his position and contacts, may be seen in the GD51 records, which deal with patronage in the East India Company. The estate and later records were retained for legal reasons and are still privately held – I am unaware of any material that has not been catalogued for the National Archives. In human terms there is much besides.

More important to me is that the estate records do not often expose Ardgour's sympathy for the Gaelic tradition on his estate, which existed and is not to be sniffed at. He is widely believed to have understood and accommodated the old non-commercial demographic element in a way not unlike Captain John of Glenaladale in Prince Edward Island. What proportion of the population on his estate the old Gaelic Highland population made up at any one time is missing from the record, although one might carefully assess something of its pecuniary value (and MacLean's generosity) at different times.[55] To what extent Ardgour was a refuge for those cleared by people like Patrick Sellar in Morvern is unclear to me. I guess that the Ardgour MacLeans were sympathetic to poor Gaels and proud of holding true that old bond. (If I recall Calum MacLean's book *The Highlands* aright, the MacLeans of Ardgour were among the last, if not the only chiefly family *c.* 1950 who still spoke Gaelic.) MacLean clearly used Cameron renters of his estate evenly, on his reclaimed estate.

As in North Morar into the 1830s, the concept of tacksman covered what in the 1841 census were 'farmers' and not necessarily controllers of hundreds or thousands of acres as is assumed in articles such as 'Clanranald's Tacksmen', which includes people like Captain John MacDonald of Glenaladale, and the MacDonalds of Borrodale, Rhu and South Morar. A Donald MacMillan from 'Callop, Glenfinnan' was in the MacMillan emigration to what is now Ontario from Fort William in 1802,[56] but one cannot deduce anything about him. At Whitsunday 1810 Callop was occupied by a Martin Cameron and in that year he obtained an eleven-year tack for himself and his son Ewen. Both men, date unknown, had been tenants at 'Glasforin' (perhaps Glas Mhorain) on the south side of Loch Shiel. Alexander MacLean signed the tack document in Edinburgh in 1811. If this tack agreement covered the last eleven years of a nineteen-year unwritten deal then it is possible that Martin Cameron left Glasforin for Callop in 1802. Perhaps he and his family even lived at Callop.[57]

On 20 March 1821 Alexander MacVean at Drumfearn farm in

Ardgour (south of the Dubh Lighe) got the lease of Callop through the factor, Patrick Henderson. The rate went up from £70 to £78 per annum and those vacating the place, or the right to control it, were Martin and Paul Cameron. Who lived where is not implicit in these nineteenth-century deals, although it seems that Alexander MacVean was actually living at Drumfearn on 20 March 1821.[58] The arrangement he lived there under appears to have carried until 1831 because he is described as possessing Drumfearn in 1831, and because of family records cited below. On Whitsunday 1831 John Cameron and another John Cameron (at Drumsallie) took Drumfearn on a twelve-year lease (until Whitsun 1843).

On Whitsunday 1836 (the year of the first of the two famines in the Highlands) Alexander MacLean of Ardgour let the farm at Callop to the surgeon Ewen Cameron, Achdalieu, and to John Cameron junior, Drumnasallie, for nine years at the same rent, £78 per annum. They may not have continued until 1845 because the records show that a Donald Cameron was at Callop on 19 May 1843 and that that year a Duncan MacGregor made an offer for the place to Ardgour on a complicated rent of wool and wedders. On 22 May 1843 James MacGregor, Ardgour's factor, granted Duncan, a tenant at Blarnaclerach (Priest's or Cleric's Field, south-west of Fort William[59]), a five-year lease at £57 10s per annum. There appears to have been no MacGregor collusion – the 1841 census, for example, shows an eighty-five-year-old, locally born Angus MacGregor in the second home at Druimarbin, near Blarnaclerach (and another MacGregor family listed in the fifth), and at High Bridge to the north, in home five, a forty-five-year-old, non-locally-born James MacGregor, 'independent' (who shared the home with John (25), a gamekeeper, and Charles and William, cattle dealers[60]). In any case, economic conditions on that corner, and over all the Ardgour estate were not promising from the late 1830s – James MacGregor's salary was reduced from £105 to £50 per annum in 1837[61] – and there is no explanatory comment in the family record. On the other hand, government bounties were made available in 1832 to the poor wishing to emigrate and by 1837 this influenced Ardgour.

So, from 1790 until 1843, with one exception (Alexander

MacVean), Callop was leased by tack or otherwise, by Camerons. This is all that suggests that Cregag too might have been accepted by the MacLeans as a Cameron farm, under old Gaelic thinking, and under MacLean ownership, until a record for 1829. Then, for five years Duncan MacGregor held Callop and, one assumes, used it primarily as a sheep-farm. Then on 21 May 1848 a letter of offer for Callop was delivered to either or both the factor, James MacGregor, and Alexander the owner. It came from Malcolm Boyd and offered £70 a year. He held the property on 14 April 1850 when, from Fort William, he wrote offering £65 for it. He was there in 1851 and renewed a deal for the farm in 1854 at the same cost. In 1858 most of northern Ardgour, including Callop and Cregag, was sold to the Earl of Morton and in that year John Mitchell, an outsider, held Callop. The 'Calape' farm in 1858 amounted to 2,909 acres imperial, no postage stamp.

Among the persisting niggling questions for me are: was there a mill on the Callop farm on the tributary near the shingle ford I crossed in dry weather, just west of the little bridge over the Callop River and what was it used for? *Tearlach* MacFarlane and Hugh Cheape, who know the area intimately, describe the tributary just before it reaches the shingly ford as a lade, and the rocky assemblage as evidence that there had been a mill there (Drumsallie mill was less than a mile off). I remember no relic of a building there, but I don't remember having explored. There is no evidence of a building on the 1872 six-inch map, suggesting either that there was no structure there, or else that what might have been was some simple, outdoor structure not meriting inclusion. One other approach to the questions lies in MacLean of Ardgour documents NRAS3583, bundle 20.

The top item is given as 'Papers mainly as to farm of Callap and mill at Camusasig [near Corran Ferry]'. There is plenty of record of the tacksmen at the mill at Camusasig, from its beginning in 1836 to the last nine-year tack given, which began on 6 March 1849. All the 'Callap' data is about a farm, not a mill. So if there were a mill of any kind it was the project of one or more of the earls of Morton. Inasmuch as Archibald McCallum, Glasgow, was dickering with Ardgour in 1839 to take on the Camusasig mill with a view to starting a woollen manufactory, an early use for a Morton of a mill

at Callop could well have had to do with a woollen industry. After
the sheep industry went down a bit, the only kind of mill for which
one might guess a profitable use was a sawmill. One might have
provided lumber for the new lodge in the 1870s, and perhaps also
for the main Callop farm building. The obvious temporary usage of
a sawmill, or other power source, later would have been for the
building of the West Highland Railway branch from Fort William
to Mallaig *c.* 1900.

In all of these Ardgour records there is less data dealing with
Cregag. However, tellingly perhaps, according to a 'state of
intromissions of P. Henderson as Factor upon the Estate of Ardgour
the Property of Alex Maclean Esqr of Ardgour' from Whitsunday
1829 to Whit 1830, the renter of 'Cregaig' was 'Sir Dun Cameron',
third of Fassifern (1775–1863), who surely never lived there. Sir
Duncan's rent was £50 and it remained at that figure until at least
1838 if an added note on the page attaching to the 1815 sketch is
correct. Fassifern's tenancy may have involved the controlling of
the isthmus and the easiest portage between the Dubh Lighe and
the Callop rivers. If a good profit was to be made in those days from
the export of canned salmon from Loch Eil and from the River
Shiel, Alexander MacLean either felt the press of creditors, not to
gain directly, or some sense of bond with the traditional owners of
Cregag farm. Revd Archibald Clerk in or *circa* 1838, writing in the
'lake' section of his NSA report of the parish of Ardnamurchan,
noted specifically about the 'inland lake', Loch Shiel, in the parish
of Ardnamurchan,

> Fishermen from the east [North Sea] have pulled their boats
> overland from Loch Shiel [*recte* Loch Eil] into the lake, and, finding
> their way on its waters into the western sea, have taken a full cargo
> of fish before companions, who took the more circuitous route,
> arrived at the fishing station.[62]

This practice had probably gone on since the opening of the
Caledonian Canal and certainly, assuming nothing about the
ethnicity of the fishermen, Highlanders knew exactly about *portaging* from the uncounted Scottish Gaels in the North West

Company and then the Hudson Bay Company in colonial Canada. If it were a response to North Sea weather conditions then the procedure was intermittent. How or if this trade were facilitated with the deepening perhaps of the Dubh Lighe and sub-tributary of the Callop nearest the Dubh Lighe is not known. How long *portaging* went on is not known either. The boats must have been small, many locally built. The market they served (presumably indirectly, through Mallaig or Tobermory or some other gathering point) was either points north in Scotland and/or the Greater Glasgow area (pre-Edinburgh-to-Glasgow railway, 1846[63]), Liverpool and overseas. In any case, at least some part of the Cregag border with the neighbouring farms of Altlaig and Dalreoch and Callop was used by stranger-fishermen, and potentially commanded some mulct or income.

In Victorian times there are at least three easily accessible sources showing what the Earl of Morton had in mind for Callop and the Cregag appendix in 1874, the year after the Scotophile queen's visit to Glenfinnan. Those immediate post-visit years in Glenfinnan were an optimistic building period (church, school and 'the castle'), and the development of Callop must have seemed to the rich as an intelligent Highland adaptation – others might have seen it as an entrenchment of outsider-owned improvement (with tacit royal favour) down to chimneyed stone houses for shepherds high up the glens. Information from the 1881 census suggests that there was, in Callop and Craigag's case, an apparently gentle shift from a mixture of subsistence and the dominating sheep-farming, to a tripartite rural life with the appearance of hunting and shooting with local people, those who were left, providing the ancillary services.

Craigag and Callop became Sholto John Douglas (1813 or 1818–1884), the eighteenth Earl of Morton's Victorian shooting estate, and one that lay partially beyond traditional old Ardgour, allowing tradition to reach back to June 1633. For many local Gaels born around 1820, the changes visible in 1881 might have looked more hopeful than in the intensest of sheep and emigration times, although the attraction for Highlanders to urban Britain and overseas remained powerful.

Accounts referred to above show that the shooting lodge on the

eighteenth Earl of Morton's Conaglen estate was initially known as
'Calass' (Calap) – there is a photograph held by the National
Museum of Scotland of a gamekeeper and his gillies at the 'Callop
estate' *c.* 1913.[64] The third piece of evidence is the building lying to
the south-east of the lodge by the little stream, called above a
storage building. The only reference I have found to this building
lies in a 3 December 1991 record of the transfer of less than an acre
of land on 25 November of that year – the record gives '0.84 acre,
to south-east of THE OLD FORGE, CRAIGAG, bounded on the
north-west by old road from Fort William to Mallaig and on south-
east, east and north-east by new road from Fort William to Mallaig,
part of lands and estate of CONAGLEN.'[65] The forge is marked by
symbol only on the OS 1895 survey for the one-inch map of 1902.
It was not there in 1872 when the six-inch map survey was done.
The well-heeled tenants occupied the lodge in shooting season(s)
and the deer-stalker guide lived on one of what in 1881 were four
homes in the census's 'Callop'. When the forge was built, who the
smiths were and if they doubled as stable keepers, remains to be
discovered – no smith is given in the 1881 census. The focus of
their attentions would have been on bating and shoeing horses.
Perhaps it was the last of them that made the little makeshift iron
bridge that I remember over the burn. The marked but all-but-
unused road or lane on the flat, which I remember cycling and
walking on, leading to the forge from the old road just after the
high point of land to the east, as shown on the one-inch map of
1902, suggests that in late Victorian times the shooting lodge
experiment either was working well or showed promise. What
Morton considered the bounds of Callop estate remain unclear to
me but are probably implied by the census-taker's term 'Callop' –
presumably most of the stalking and shooting was done in Ardgour.

From this, it is tempting to think that the name 'Craigag' was
only applied to the lodge part of the 'estate' when the original
Cregag farm by the Callop River ceased to be farmed, or when the
Earl of Morton sold the Cona Glen estate, lodge and Callop
included in 1953. It is equally tempting to think that the Earl
of Morton built the slate-roofed Callop farmhouse which I knew,
in the mid-1870s when he decided to start the shooting estate
business in the area – it is a relatively modern building with squared

ends and with a cow byre and hay mow where a garage might be today, as I recall (and I remember a cow's being milked there and a tortoise-shell kitten getting a *bus*-full of warm, bubbly milk squirted at it). Perhaps however it was contemporary with the shepherds' Coire Thollaidh stone house up the Finnan and the building up the Gleann Dubh Lighe.

From the cartographic record

From the Clerk of Kilmallie *Sròn na creagaig* reference in *Bygone Lochaber,* which pertains to the early days of the Bonnie Prince Charlie Jacobite Revolution of 1745–6, there are census mentions of Craigag; otherwise there are only stray mentions in the written record of either Craigag or Callop. My missing photographs taken from the shoulder by Craigag Lodge in 1970 are important to me because they show a place as I (think I) remember it just after the war. Today, a Forestry-Commission-planted army of boreal forest thirty-odd years old, like plush, in neat infantry rows, shoulder to shoulder, cool, dark air between, beginning at the roadside half a mile south-west of the road tunnel under the railway, near Joe MacLeod and Joe MacVinish's bothy in the cutting, runs almost clinging to the east bank of the Callop and Allt na Cruaiche, running up almost as far as Doire Mór on Meall nan Damh. There seems to be little just as regimented as these resolute rows to be found in the new forest that modern economics are forcing upon many blocks of Nova Scotia (including Cape Breton – Christmas trees excepted, sometimes). I had the sad feeling in 2002 that I had brought my son Seumas all the way east to an ancient geology to sense the old heathery, myrtle-ly resonance of Druim Fada, Fassifern, Corribeg and Ceann Loch Iall, to experience the little hills and turns of the little one-lane road, with passing places, near Drumsallie, to travel, slowly, over the old wooden bridge over the Dubh Lighe (Drochaid Sgainneal) under the remnant of an old deciduous forest, only to be confronted with a forest that he knew only too well already, made up of what resembled the spruces, firs, balsams and larches of Nova Scotia (we saw no sign of the spruce budworm). The neo- and seemingly mono-species forest began in the west just south of where the road dipped under the railway east of our old bramble-picking embankment and Joe MacLeod and Joe MacVinish's bothy, and ran eastward in a line along the south bank of the Dubh Lighe beyond the Drumfern [Druim fearn] farm (Ardgour) to Garvan [Garbhan] (also Ardgour). It thickly cloaked the eastern part of little neck of land where Lochan Dubh Tòrr an Tairbeirt is, and the *'toireasgair'* peat hag, and it reached south up the Callop and Allt na Cruaiche tributary almost to Doire Mór just to the east of the track over to Conaglen of the Mares. Strange too, I must have been home again just before the trees were planted because I have a memory of the same area, with broad, scoring parallel furrows a yard or two apart running south into the hills almost to the Doire Mór.

Druim Fada hadn't changed, and I dare say were one to walk the modern road, from Annat say, past Fassifern, to the turn-off for Drumsallie farm at the head of Locheil, there would be the same sense of Highland aromas, now mixed with boreal mole-cules and hydrocarbon exhausts at peak travel times; many of the same houses perhaps, a glimpse of the walking days of yore, certainly including the immutable railway line. It was just that for years I had imagined dropping him and his younger brother off at Annat, driving ahead to the boulder, and letting them walk or cycle to catch up with me, no words spoken, no paternal dictation at all. I left it too late. Homes had trickled west from Annat changing the appearance and feel of the place into a suburb of discreet occupation.[66] And, in 2002, when Seumas and I reached the new and sweeping turn-off to Drumsallie, we found ourselves in what to us was an impressive European pulp forest. To the southward it started on the far bank of the Dubh Lighe. To the north, beginning on the west bank of the Fionn Lighe, it reached from the new roadside far north up the valleys of the Fionn Lighe and the Dubh Lighe and, skirting Craigag Lodge, as far west as the railway tunnel.

Where the road and railway ran close together, at the bramble embankment, the trees had drawn in on the south and formed a chasm higher than the sides of Joe MacLeod-Joe MacVinish railway bothy cutting. The forest ran proudly along to the southern bounds of Craigag and it was overwhelmingly unexpected in the evening light. If there is no symbiotic relationship with bracken (and if the spores soon or eventually die for want of light) then the forest will have controlled that plant, and rushes, and grasses, but the future farmer will face conifer-induced podzols, not oak and alder and birch-derived soils. The new forest near Craigag does not belong to the Scottish Forestry Commission and there was still enough untreed bottomland near where the boulder had been to make comparisons to memories.

Somewhere I had read that the last of Cameron of Locheil's oak forest had been consumed in the making of ammunition boxes for the Great War but otherwise I had not associated the north shore of Locheil with boreal forest, pine perhaps excepted. Clerk mentioned the holly hedge at Fassifern until *c.* 1850, the 'truly magnificent beeches' bordering Kilmallie churchyard (*Memoir,* 1 and 2), and the huge and ancient ash thirty feet from Lochiel, and near a burn at Kilmallie, which had fallen to perceptive malice in 1746.[67] Timothy Pont's map of 'Lochabir' (*c.* 1610) is not very informative about the west end of Loch Eil (unless those few tree symbols given with no legend had contemporary meaning) but there is a topographical notice attributed to him that describes plenty of great 'firrwood' about Loch Eil, possibly on the south shore. On the north 'syd thereof great store of fair oaken wood, and sp[e]ceally one fair wood, there are in Loch-yioll manie small glennis fitt for pasture.' As with Doire Mór behind Callop farm, one is left to wonder if Pont assumed that the reader would know that such woods were sod banked and/or walled and protected from thieves and nibblers. Perhaps archaeology will answer that question, although what is known about the old woods that are at present being protected by local people, about sixty-six hectares behind Trislaig and Achaphubil in Ardgour, is that indeed woods were assiduously protected by wall and topping fencing.[68] Ardgour, presumably like Locheil and other estate users and owners, was keen on growing hard and softwood forest, for economic and ornamental reasons and he recorded having enclosed some.[69]

For convenience one main step out of chronological order, the next reference, from Thomson's 1832 *Atlas,* and therein Johnston's 1820 survey of Inverness-shire, shows four local farm places, Cregag, Altlaig, Callop and Dalreoch. The first two lie in Inver-

ness-shire, the other two in Argyllshire. There is no indication that
clearer cartographical treatment was given to either shire. Ironically, the only place of the four in which no building is discernible
is Cregag in Inverness-shire; the area is marked as wooded.
Although the tributaries of the main rivers, the Callop and the
Dubh Lighe, are not named, there are four buildings identified for
Callop, two on either side of what can only be described as a
symbolic tributary on the west of the Callop. On the other side of
the Callop there is a building belonging to Dalreoch, and to the
north of the lochan in Inverness-shire a building is marked for
Altlaig. The people were amnicolous.[70] No farm boundaries are
shown. The two mountains separating Callop from Loch Shiel are
called Dubh Ghlas. Johnston did not trace the Callop tributaries
exactly as they are shown on any readily available post-1950
Ordnance Survey map, to which one must note simply, but with
diffidence, that streams and rivers, in certain circumstances, change
their courses, and that mapping tools and techniques have improved since 1820.

   Aside from the inclusion of the place names Dalrioch and
Altlaig in the Johnston survey, there is an unusual hydrographic
feature there, which may have a useful explanation. A long
stream is drawn, tumbling down the hillside, which feeds Lochan
Dubh from Glas Bhein in the south (in Ardgour) – it is the only
stream the mappers included (although the modern 1:50,000
Landranger sheet shows three other, much smaller feeder streams,
all from the south). Johnston however represented this unnamed
main feeder stream as forked, the main course rising near the peak
of Glas Bheinn, its subordinate stream joining from the east about
a third of the way to Lochan Dubh. This is how the Landranger
map represents that principal feeder stream. This feature would
have been visible from the road in 1820, since Glas Bheinn
reaches over 1,900 feet. What is unusual is that the lochan was
represented by Johnston as draining to start with much as it does
today, from one outlet on its west side, but this in 1820 quickly
formed an S, or an E, going to the north then turning in a north-
easterly curve to join the Dubh Lighe just north of the home at
Altlaig (to the south of West Drimsallie). This is the only map
that shows *Lochan Dubh* draining into Loch Eil – MacCulloch's

map of 1840 has the lochan draining into the Callop. The Landranger map with its modern accuracy shows a much more complicated meander after the stream leaves the lochan, a meander which joins the Callop just to the east of where the wooden bridge I remember crossed the river. This meander course, however, is joined by a sub-tributary from the north-east, which swings from the north just about where the railway rises over the dipping road, only a hundred yards or so from the Dubh Lighe.

One might suggest that in boggy country, what the Revd Alexander Fraser described in 1792 as 'soft moss', Johnston made a mistake – but there is another explanation. He could not have travelled the road to gather the information for the *Atlas* because he would have been very near where the lochan's outlet met the Dubh Lighe and would never have made such an error. Just south of that juncture of road and river the mapper marked the home at Altlaig (there are two ten-metre/thirty-three foot prominences nearby, Tòrr Linne Dhùghail and Tòrr an Tairbeirt (OS six-inch) and if it were on either and not at the roadside it would have been on the first, the nearer one). The simplest and most obvious explanation for the error is that he availed himself of recently made plans of the Ardgour farms and misinterpreted the information he found there – in his introduction to the *Atlas,* John Thomson wrote that William Johnson had worked 'from estate surveys, &c. &c.' The 1815 coloured sketch of the Cregag farm is important in explaining the Johnston placing of the outlet from the lochan emptying into the Dubh Lighe and not the Callop.

From the final plan of the estate made in 1815, Johnston clearly got his knowledge of the four farms Cregag, Altlaig, Callop and Dalriach (although just from the earlier representation of Cregag these too would have been obvious to him). The mapper's source could also have been Alexander MacLean of Ardgour himself, or his factor John Cumming of Achdalieu (factor from *c.* 1810–*c.* 1817), or possibly from Sir Duncan Cameron of Fassifern whose seat was nearby. The 1815 Cregag sketch shows the farm holding bounded for most of its length on the north by 'Alt Chroich' (marked but unnamed on the six-inch OS map surveyed in 1872) and the Locheil estate. On the west it is delineated from the 'Lands of Glen-finnan' by an unnamed river (Allt na Crìche) and a lochan

lying between the road and the Callop (Lochan na Crìche –
someone pencilled or inked in 'Calap Loch'). The southern line
is the Callop River (with no allowance for a large wooded 'island'
roughly where the tributary Allt na h-Àiridh meets the Callop near
my wooden bridge). To the south-east, the line is with Dalriach
and is the tributary Dubhaidh for a hundred yards or so until it is
joined by its sub-tributary from the north (unnamed on the six-
inch map). From there Cregag is divided from Altlaig by a line that
runs north a short distance before curving to the north-east (surely
along the sub-tributary of the Dubhaidh); while this sub-tributary
turns north a hundred yards or more from the Dubh Lighe, the
Cregag boundary continues to the north-eastward to meet the
Dubh Lighe at Torr Linne Dugail [The Hill of Dougal's Run]. The
remainder of the Cregag border runs up the Dubh Lighe to 'Alt
Chroich' and pencilled or inked in beyond the Cregag line is 'by
Drimfern' (conceivably a rental by 'Drimfern' based in Ardgour of
this part of the Cameron of Lochiel estate).

The line between Cregag farm and Altlaig was assumed by
Johnston to have followed the sub-tributary of the Dubhaidh and
thus they wrongly show Lochan Dubh Tòrr an Tairbeirt draining
in a broad horseshoe into the Dubh Lighe and Lochiel.

Also, although one cannot be certain, the placing of the name
'Cregag' on the coloured 1815 sketch suggests that the farm
building then stood south of the new road, north of the Callop
and not far west of the Dubhaidh, in the south-east corner of the
holding. I knew of no other big rock near the wooden bridge in
the 1940s, so the one I knew lay about mid-south. The Cregag
holding in 1815 amounted to 505 English acres, 3 of which were of
arable (presumably my wren's-nest lowland and plough-and-spade
arable), about 50 of green pasture, about 236 of 'benty' pasture,[71]
about 47 of mossy pasture, about 47 of natural wood, about 4 of
plantation, about 104 of moss, and about 3 of (Dick and Readdie)
roads. The sketch shows the new road but offers no name for the
bridge over the Dubh Lighe given in the six-inch map of 1872 as
Drochaid Sgainnir (there is also on the 1872 map a Dail na Sgainnir
marked on the east side of the Dubh Lighe a little to the north).
The 1815 map gives only the descriptive 'Innish Slige' for the
crook of wooded Cregag land where the Alt Chroich meets the

Dubh Lighe – at a stretch *innis* might be read as a cattle rest, and *slige*, apart from shelly, as bent timber (of a boat). Neither Ardgour nor Fassifern need have bothered to give Lowland mappers the name of the crossing. However the name of the Cregag boundary tributary Alt Chroich may denote stream of the cattle herd.

The Johnston error in tributary mapping however leaves an interesting red herring. Although the hill, Tòrr an Tairbeirt, of the mossy isthmus lies to the east of the lochan, and the modern OS contours point to an inevitable discharge of the Dubhaidh into the Callop, there is one implausible argument in favour of its having at one time drained initially west, then north, then north-east to join the Dubh Lighe. It has to do with the West Highland Railway Mallaig extension.

By 1897, the railway had reached the head of Loch Eil without major problems – requirements had been brought by water and the geography along the shore was all but level – but from the bridge over the Dubh Lighe the only economical way to reach Glenfinnan Summit at over one hundred feet altitude and only about two miles away, was by embankment, cuttings and a tunnel and a viaduct over the mighty sweep over the Finnan River. The rock at the MacLeod–MacVinish bothy cutting, and the tunnel (Kinlocheil and Moinian Group metamorphosed sediments of great age) is not easy to drill, cut and blast, and Concrete Bob McAlpine's son Malcolm conceived the idea of a water-driven turbine to produce the needed compressed air instead of the older use of the steam itself to power equipment. The story of his getting the idea from his Helensburgh dentist is given in John Thomas's *The West Highland Railway* (p. 94). According to Thomas, he built a seven-foot dam across Loch Dubh and by the end of 1897 the water-powered air compressor was going full-tilt, twenty-four hours a day and was much more efficient than the system it replaced. (A sawmill nearby is not inconceivable?)

The 1951 OS map, with its fifty-foot contours, deters one from thinking that the lochan might ever have drained into Loch Eil. The Landranger map contouring (using just over 33-foot intervals) however appears to suggest that the Johnston 'surveying' could almost have been accurate and that the McAlpine's

working to build the embankment to get the line on to the
Cregag shoulder altered the drainage of what is a Rannochy-type
piece of country, a dead-looking lochan in a treeless morass, Blàr
Creagach. I never tried to fish the lochan's outlet to the Callop. I
never wanted to try to get to the lochan itself; both lay in
uninviting, hostile, boggy and dangerous country. In the days of a
farm at Altlaig and another at Dalrioch there may have been some
control over the drainage. I remember nothing artificial about the
lochan, no dam for example.

The four farms, Cregag, Altlaig, Callop and Dalriach, are all
mentioned and sketched in the 1813 and 1815 plan of the Ardgour
estate; only two, Cregag and Callop are included in the list of
Ardgour farms paying rent to Alexander MacLean from Whitsun
1829 to 1830. Altlaig and Dalriach may have been consolidated
with the other two named farms and been the beginning-to-be-
forgotten 'pendicles' referred to above. If there were simple
consolidation then no person need have been completely displaced
– however the 1841 census shows only one house at Callop and no
MacVeans there. It appears almost safe to say that an old MacVean
presence had at last gone from the north-west of Ardgour, and that
it had once been significant. There is not enough literately con-
firmable information on the placing of the MacVeans within
Ardgour over the century, 1650–1750, or their exact relationships
to the two chiefly families, Cameron of Lochiel and MacLean of
Ardgour, to make categorical statements about their importance to
either chief in clan land affairs and politics, but, given some
background understanding taken from 1760 to 1870, plausible
speculations may be fairly made. If local pendicle place names were
being forgotten as farms were consolidated in the 1820s, one is
entitled to wonder why the two 'MacBheathain' place names in
and near Callop survived till the 1870s OS survey. They appear to
be old names; some memorable service, or function, an event or
events now forgotten, must have fixed these names into the local
collective memory as late as the 1870s. The MacVeans somehow
are associated with the Ardgour–Clanranald borderland. To me
their disappearance is a sadness.

The MacBheathain people at Callop and in Ardgour

In the century from 1760 to 1860, particularly starting with a death record on a gravestone in 1803, there is a genealogical record from which the inferences of earlier times may also be conjectured.[72] On 30 October 1803 a Mary MacBean (Màiri nighean Iain) aged nineteen, second or third child of John McVean (d. 1826) and Anne Dallas (predeceased John in 1826), died and was buried at the McLean burial ground in Ardgour. The chiselling on the gravestone states that it was laid by the order of her father 'John MacBean Tacksman Drumfern'. The year before the new road, MacVeans were at Drumfern. Mary MacBean's birth record (4 Jan. 1784) for the parish of Kilmallie prefers to write the name as McVean, allowing for the aspiration. The Kilmallie record of the baptism (20 January 1784) at Craigveachan, in Glen Scaddle, suggests that Anne Dallas, or John MacVean may have had a parent or parents farming there (NB the birth of the first child to Anne Dallas, Betty (1782), is associated with Keil, Ardgour; of the other four, three were baptised at Craigveachan and the fourth was either born or baptised there; there is no record discovered yet of Dallases in Ardgour; the name however occurred in Badenoch whence two Dallas Jacobites in the 1745, and elsewhere in Scotland) and there was a parish of Dallas in county Elgin.[73]

Where Callop to the west of Drumfern is concerned, one of the same family of MacVeans, Allan (1824–1896), (Ailean mac Alasdair 'ic Iain) was born there. He went to Glasgow University then took courses at the Free Church College in Edinburgh before emigrating to Portland Bay, Victoria, Australia in 1852 as a minister (in which state he had two brothers, John Hugh and John, and sisters Margaret and Mary). In a letter to Allan at Glasgow from John Z. Huie 8 February 1848 at Port Phillip, Victoria, concerning Allan's possibly becoming a minister in the Australian Free Church in Victoria, Huie referred to Allan's having mentioned his command of Gaelic and his wish to minister to Gaels in the state.[74] While Allan's father Alexander MacVean was born at Drumfern (1785, son of John MacVean, tacksman there) he (Alexander) is associated in adult life with Aryhoulan in Ardgour, having certainly obtained the farm from Alexander MacLean of Ardgour when he (MacLean)

left Drumfern. It is noteworthy, however, that the baptisms of six
of Alexander MacVean's children were conducted at Drumfern,
with Ewen having been born and baptised there in 1820, and
Donald born there in 1822. The habit was to have the grand-
children baptised in their paternal grandparents' home. The last of
Alexander MacVean's children baptised at Drumfern was Annie
MacVean in 1830 (two others were born afterwards, in 1832 and
1835 but there is no record of any event for them at Drumfern).[75]
In 1841 the 'farmer' at Drumfern was Dugald MacLachlan (65). By
1841 the MacVeans were gone for ever from Drumfern and
Callop, although some of them continued to hold profitable farms
elsewhere in Ardgour, most of them based on sheep. I had never
heard of MacVeans in that part of the Highlands.

Alexander MacLean thirteenth of Ardgour, particularly from
about 1800, brought most of his estate into the commercial world.
He also effected changes for his poor Gaelic population from about
the same time, essentially shifting them from the old runrig system
with more and more folk per acre farming in the old ways, to the
personal shore croft holdings with kelp for fertiliser and the chance to
catch herring. In that, and for other undoubted kindnesses, like some
of the Fraser chiefs who owned North Morar, MacLean is remembered as a considerate, forgiving and generous landlord. In this,
however, he was profoundly helped,[76] or trapped, by the government wages earned by rank and file on the Caledonian Canal and the
road to Loch-na-Gaul − an 1825 memorandum in bundle 8 of
NRAS3583 shows that (1) the crofting system had been adopted *c.*
1803 to stem the tide of emigration of ordinary Highlanders; (2) it
really only worked because there were government jobs locally, or a
herring fishery; and (3) without that work, crofting was not viable.[77]

Now after a Trial of 20 years, it is found that the Lands of Blaich,
which were only suited to the crofting system while the Caledonian
Canal and Parly roads were going on, or while there is a good
Herring fishing. The two former have ceased altogether as regards
employment to the Blaich men . . . Crofters cannot thrive but in
the neighbourhood of constant employ either in public works,
manufactures or fishing. No crofter with a few acres of arable Land,
and 2 or 4 cows can, without foreign aid, pay any rent at all.

MacLean of Ardgour:

> but for the cruelty of dispossessing these people, . . . would have
> abandoned crofting and being much against his interest to continue
> it . . . has given up the introduction of crofting other Farms upon
> this conviction.

Give him his well-earned due, Ardgour forgave rents from 1818 (a
good herring year) till 1825 and invented his own public works, on
roads, fences, woods, to give his Gaelic poor a chance to stay rather
than go.[78] At the same time, however, some of his commercial and
potentially even more commercial farms, however, were put on
the market to lease (see below). He began work on a new house in
1825, which took five years to complete and cost over £4,000.

Where commercial farming on Ardgour is concerned, when he
was in his seventies (from 1834), there was the noticeable economic
downturn (that may have been, or was responsible for more than
halving the factor's salary). In 1837 the five-year-old bounty system
for the displacement of unadaptable, non-commercial people from
Britain to the economic hinterlands of the empire took hold. On 8
May 1838 Dr Boyter, a naval surgeon and government emigration
agent for Australia, arrived in Fort William and, according to the
Inverness Courier encountered,

> Thousands of enterprising Gaels . . . around the Caledonian Hotel,
> anxious to quit the land of their forefathers to go and possess the
> unbounded pastures of Australia.[79]

In 1838 the flow of government-assisted passengers to Australia
strengthened. Nine ships with 2,161 government bounty emigrants
left Scottish ports that year, as well as 1,054 'private' bounty people
and unassisted emigrants (total 3,215, Gaelic-speaking portion
unknown). Apparently, however, 1,200 people signed up under
the Colonial Act of 1835 at Fort William for assisted passage to
Australia; a huge number of people, surely mostly Gaels – note, this
was six years before the first naming census). How many evictions,
or how much misery, were averted by this scheme are nowhere
speculated on, nor government alterative spending ideas. No

government ships sailed for Australia after 1841 and the bounty system was suspended in 1843,[80] but a far-off destination had become fixed in people's minds (as North America had been from 1770 to 1840). Craigag and Callop, as Highland Gaelic traditional places, were withering into commercial accounts in the age of coal, however much MacLean may have rued it.

Many were the MacVeans who went to Australia, mostly after the bounty system had been suspended, but some remained in Ardgour and did very well as main tenant sheep-farmers. The obvious affection MacLean (d. 1855) had for old Ardgour strongly suggests that the outsiders that he brought in to the estate in the 1840s were brought to replace the outflow of enterprising people, like many of the MacVeans, but, getting on in years, at last he may indeed have felt more driven to the inevitable eroding of what was a centuries-old Highland population going back to the Lordship perhaps. He left a son an estate in debt and among the part the next Alexander MacLean had to sell was the strange Cregag appendix.

The family of Alexander, son of John, MacVean included two Scottish-educated Free Church ministers, a Scottish medical doctor and several successful farmers in Ardgour and Australia. They were socially prominent in Ardgour rural society before and after sheep-farming. For what it is worth, there are 'to let' advertisements in the Edinburgh-published newspaper *The Scotsman*, for Inverscadle, Stronchregan and Dalendrian (as one holding) in 1823, for Aryhoulan and Glenscaddle in 1828, for Craigveachan in 1829, for Davidoch in 1829, and for Narachan farm, also in 1829 – all farms are in the same general area. Aryhoulan is associated with Alexander MacVean (1785–1870) in the 1841 and 1851 censuses and his gravestone describes him as tacksman of the place. His sons John Hugh (b. 1817), Hugh (b. 1820) and Peter (b. 1828) were all born at Aryhoulan, and his daughter Elizabeth MacVean was living there with him in 1841. To my knowledge the old home is gone.

The official older document, the 1815 plan of Ardgour, NAS RHP89887, was in the possession of Mrs R.M. (Fiona) MacLean of Ardgour when the NAS holding was indexed. It is a survey made by James Wingate of Alloa in 1815 of the barony of Ardgour, then owned by Alexander MacLean, thirteenth of Ardgour (d. 1855).

Thirty-one places are named, starting in the north-west of the estate, travelling east then south and south-south-west ending at Inversanda below Corran Ferry and Cladh a' Mhuilinn [Clovulin].[81] The first nine are '(1) reduced plan of Ardgour; (2) Cregag; (3) Callop (Calap); (4) Dalriach; (5) Mealdabh; (6) Altlaig; (7) Drumfern; (8) North Garvan (Garbhan); (9) South Garvan.' Cregag belonged to MacLean of Ardgour in 1815. Included also, however, are '(13) Achaphubuill (Achphubil) . . . (17) Inverscaddle (Inverscadale), (18) Corlarach and Craundalich or Conaglen,' all of which were among John Cameron of Fassifern's farms and listed as exempt from Hanoverian plunder in May 1746. (Inverscadale, or a farm there, or a house there, was occupied by the last of the old Murlaggan line in 1761, courtesy of, or rent paid to, John Cameron of Fassifern. In 1767 John Cameron drew up a post-nuptial contract for his newly wed eldest son Duncan wherein he infefted Duncan and his male heirs in the lands of Inverscaddle, Conaglen and Achafouble – such an agreement need not bespeak ownership, although the Langlands map of Argyllshire in 1801 shows a 'gentleman's seat' at Inverscaddle, labelled 'Ewen Cameron Esq.'[82] The MacLeans of Ardgour only regained Inverscaddle from Ewen in 1810/11. The term 'Conaglen of the mares' comes from a collection of Fassifern household accounts, GD202/44, which includes a list of names, ages and prices of mares bought at Conaglen in 1755.) Fassifern's legal landowning superior appears to have been Alexander MacLean of Ardgour.

From the point of view of the poor Gael, Alexander MacLean of Ardgour comes down the years as a kindly man. He was an ex-English-army dragoon officer, whose nineteenth-century view of estate management blended the required stark commercialism with unusual sympathy for the ordinary Gael. His earlier chiefship, he implied himself, allowed the traditional system of land-division and subdivision to go unchecked to the point where old tenants were becoming land impoverished. He became a resident chief (with a second home in Tranent); he spoke Gaelic. While the Gaelic-speaking people in Morvern to the south suffered radically in the transition to modern land use, from about 1819 on,[83] Alexander MacLean's Ardgour held more to a variant of the older tradition. Sadly there was no such steady Christian compromise possible in the early Victorian years and his regained old Ardgour only lasted until 1858.

There was emigration of the folk of middling status and of lesser standing from Ardgour. There is a record of an emigration from Fort William on 28 August 1849, 'chiefly tenants of Maclean of Ardgour; with a few families from the lands of Lochiel . . . a large proportion of them . . . young unmarried people' bound for Australia – a large number of the tenantry of both Lochiel and Ardgour turned out to see them off and a very touching and pathetic scene it was, even in the dark of night.[84] The brothers John Hugh and John MacVean were at the time in Victoria – they did not lead a multi-family emigration. Not quite a decade later, in 1858, the northern part of Ardgour had to be sold by Alexander MacLean, fourteenth of Ardgour (1799–1872).

Alexander the thirteenth, nonetheless, is remembered in the chiefly family as a most remarkable man who sought to avoid the disintegration of the society he knew intimately. He publicly stated his dislike for emigration and acted to keep his people on his estate. To do so, like Thomas Fraser of Lovat in North Morar and other contemporary chiefs, he encouraged new farming techniques to derive the most produce for a growing population – in this he was in line with the general conversion from community runrig farming in the Highlands. While rigs were obvious at the head of Loch Shiel, I remember none on the Callop arable or on the pasture below Cregag.[85] As a man of about ninety, perhaps under pressure, perhaps simply anticipating Ardgour's future under his non-scrimping heir, as well as fast-changing circumstances that he knew were bound to force him to sell the northern part of Ardgour, Alexander thirteenth of Ardgour assisted the passages of twenty-eight people to Australia in 1854. It appears like an act of compassion. MacLean's assisted passages to nine of those people from Duisky on Loch Eil seem to have been linked with the accession of Duisky by the farmer, John Mitchell (or his subordinate) in 1853. Duisky, including a building that had been built by Donald MacLean who by 1853 was in Australia, when Mitchell got it had been held by Angus and Donald McLachlan. The McLachlans, in a letter to Ardgour dated 15 March 1853, sought repayment for the cost of a wire fence they'd had to put up to keep Mitchell of Inverscadle's sheep out –

they hadn't been able to find anyone to patrol the border.[86] For them the writing was on the wall, as indeed it now was for the north-west corner of the old Ardgour estate, including Callop and Cregag. Although Alexander MacLean's mother, Elizabeth Houston of Jordanhill, by Glasgow had been the first non-Gael in many generations to marry an Ardgour MacLean, he was a Gael, although where he learned to speak Gaelic is not on record.[87]

The flavour of Lochaber and Ardgour, from John Cameron of Fassifern's (d. *c.* 1785) time was increasingly commercial, and part of that outgoing commercial Fassifern line was embedded in Inverscaddle in Ardgour till 1810, with Ewen Cameron (d. 1828) selling the property to MacLean in 1810.[88] Alexander MacLean could never have avoided being part of that commercial world. The records of James McAlpine, a merchant and trader at Corpach, for 1822–3, show that Colonel Alexander MacLean of Ardgour was a co-partner in the lease of the forest of Locheil, with sawmill and timber floating rights – an advertisement for a person to take charge of the Ardgour sawmills appears in *The Scotsman* of 7 April 1826.[89] During his life MacLean was a keen planter of trees and cannot but have been involved in the maintenance of the old forest at Treslaig. It was he, as a man in his seventies, who introduced in essence non-traditional-Ardgour 'farmers' some time around 1841. His financial situation must have dictated that he introduce commercially viable farming or sell out then.

The changes that happened in Callop and Drimfern between 1830 and 1841 reflect the rigours of bringing a Highland farm into the commercial world. Alone, the records may not appear to reflect any radical disruption in the Ardgour estate – and at least some unchanging occupation was not inconceivable despite changing leasers – but had the records for the eighteenth century been available I think there would have been greater stability in the main farmers. Between 1830 and 1841 the name MacVean disappears from two farms, from Callop and from Drimfern (both held by Alexander MacVean), and this was typical. During these years also, the thirteenth MacLean of Ardgour introduced eight 'farmers' who lived at Inverscaddle, apparently as speculating bachelors – six were not locally born. With them lived two female servants, one locally born, and three other men (two given as agricultural labourers), all from the area.

In P. Henderson's intromission as factor on Alexander Mac-Lean's Ardgour estate, 1829–30, Alexander MacVean paid £248 per annum for Callop (£78), Drimfern (£145) and 'fishing' (£25). There were only six holdings of the eighteen on the estate in that year whose rents were higher than MacVean paid for Drumfern, and, the fishing aside, there were only four rentals that were more than £223. He either died or moved away between 1830 and 1841. His sons Alexander MacVean (1813–1873) and grandson Donald MacVean (1822–1874) stayed in Ardgour and were prominent farmers/tacksmen. The 1841 census gives Alexander Mac-Vein (53) as a 'farmer'. He is at Aryhoulan [Àiridh Shualain/ Shuarlain] in Ardgour. He and his wife and their nine children (aged from 6 to 25 years) were all born locally. Their home was listed first and there were a further eight people living under the same roof, for a total of nineteen people; this was probably the 'gentleman's seat' marked on Langlands' map of 1801. Aryhoulan farm and house are in the depositional lowland plain of the combined Cona (to the north) and Scaddle rivers, which empty as one into Inverscaddle Bay in what is now known as Loch Linnhe.

There was in that 1841 census also another locally born Alexander MacVein (25); he lived at 'Lentnafrais' (Leathad nam Fias,[90] OS, 1:50,000) in Glen Scaddle. The other MacVein was Donald (45) who is listed in Conaglen. Then the 1861 census shows a Donald MacVein (51), a 'crofter' born in Kilmallie parish, living with his wife and family, and a servant (Catherine MacVein, 26) at Tomacharich in Kilmonivaig parish. How these MacVeans/Mac-Veins are related to John MacVean, tacksman of Drumfern in 1803 and 1830 is not known. They were though, the spine of Alexander's rural Ardgour.

After the old cattle economy had had its day and commercialism was entrenched, the next radical change in Ardgour came between 1841 and 1858 and the first simple hint is in the 1841 census. There the first house in Inverscaddle, neighbouring MacVein at Aryhoulin, was headed by a John Mitchell (25), a farmer (possible age, 25 to 29); next named is Duncan Mitchell (30), also a farmer; the other farmers were Walter (35) and Andrew MacFarlane (30), Duncan Smith (30), John MacKenzie (45), William Todd (17), and John MacPherson (15).[91] Of those eight farmers, MacKenzie and Mac-Pherson were born in Inverness-shire. The three other men, Dougald MacLachlan, Donald MacIntyre and Robert Robertson, all also appear to have been Inverness-shire-born Highlanders. Inverscaddle House had thirteen residents in 1841. John Mitchell's lease of Inverscaddle ran for seventeen years at £450 per annum from 1841 (to 1858). He took the farm from a Morvern man, Hugh MacDougall, whose nineteen-year lease, at £600 per annum, had begun in 1826 and was cut short by about four years. Turning the pages back, according to Ardgour estate records, Inverscaddle, Aryhoulan and Achaphubuil were granted to Charles MacLean, uncle and heir of Allan MacLean, seventh of Ardgour, in 1604. John Cameron, first of Fassifern, held and rented Inverscaddle in 1764 when he was in Alnwick. In 1771 Inverscaddle was the home of his son Ewen Cameron and his wife, as well as the birthplace of Colonel John Cameron. In 1811, Alexander, thirteenth of Ardgour, bought Inverscaddle and its large acreage (*c.* 15,000) from Ewen Cameron for £15,000. This purchase appears to have been the redemption of a wadset on the property that seems to have gone back to the early 1760s, at least (although the farm was among Fassifern's protected ones in 1746). In 1764 Fassifern was drawing rents from tenants of Inverscaddle but he was also paying feu, something paid by a vassal to his superior. Presumably Alexander of Ardgour was flourishing financially in 1811 and could regain the old farm. In the prospectus for the sale of the northern part of Ardgour, now called Conaglen, in 1858, a 'John Mitchell Esq.' held by a long lease the eight farms of 'Inverscadle, Conaglen, Dalindrein, Stronchrigan, South Duisky, Dalriach, Mealdambh and Calape', about 30,468 acres *in toto*. The lease ran until 'Whitsunday, and separation of crop from the ground 1872.' (This suggests a farm each for the 'farmers' mentioned in the 1841 census at Inverscadle.) NRAS3583/B, bundle 21 states that Mitchell got a new nineteen-year lease of Inverscadle, Dalindrein, Stronchregan, croft no. 1 at Trislaig and Duisky on Whitsunday 1853.[92] NAS RHP747/1–3, three copies of 'the lands of Inverscadale, Strongrigan and others,' in 1858, in the papers of the Earl of Morton, drawn by T. Strachan in Edinburgh and lithographed by Schenck and Macfarlane of Edinburgh, show the estate Morton bought to comprise Callop, Cregag, Altlaig, Drumfern, Dalriach, Mealdabh, North and South Garvan, North and South Duisky, Blaich, Achaphubuil, Trislaig, Stronchreggan, Dalindrein,[93] Inverscaddle, Corlarach and Craundalich (both in Conaglen). This represented the northern part of the old MacLean of Ardgour estate (with the exception of parts sold to the Forestry Commission, this holding, called Conaglen, remains much the same today, although it is now owned by John Guthrie who lives in Yorkshire). Inverscaddle was the main farm and that fact dictated the initial naming of the purchase from Ardgour. By 1864 Sholto John Douglas the Earl of Morton's holding in northern Ardgour was called the estate of Conaglen.[94] An unusual feature of domestic architecture, surely reflecting Morton taste, marks the east and the west of the new Conaglen estate, the M or double-roof. The present ruin of a two-storey stone house at Aryhoulin in Conaglen estate was built in 1858. The other, still lived in, is my old home, Craigag Lodge, built about twenty years later.

Without the six-inch maps of 1872 showing the two Clach mhic Bheathain [MacVean rocks] on (one almost on) the Callop farm one might only posit a Cameron presence south of the Callop. So much of the story of Gaelic Scotland is well-nigh impossible to tell.

1872 also appears to have been a turning point for the new owner, the Earl of Morton.

Until and after the Morton shooting lodge experiment

When Callop was still part of the colonel's estate, in 1841, there was only one home there (headed by a Donald Cameron (45) who had a wife, seven children, a servant, and a Marjory Cameron (70), all of whom had been born in the parish of Kilmallie).[95] His description in the 1841 census as 'farmer' suggests that he had taken over the lease from the surgeon Ewen Cameron, Achdalieu (who, with another, had a nine-year lease from 1836). However, the next place the census taker visited was 'Dalnoch' where there was also only one home; here were recorded locally born Duncan Cameron (40) and his wife (21) living with their infant son Martin, a servant and an older Cameron man who was born outside the parish. There was no Altlaig distinguished in the 1841 census. Also, a possible relationship between Callop, Dalrioch and Cregag is seen in the description of Donald Cameron at Callop as 'farmer' and Duncan Cameron at Dalrioch and Angus MacInnis at Craigag as 'agricultural labourers'. Callop was the main holding in the area and had been at least since whenever Cregag fell to MacLean of Ardgour, probably long antedating that obscure transfer.[96] All three farms, Cregag, Dalriach and Callop, were situated in the high, above flood land of the Callop river.

Altlaig however is listed, in combination with Drimfern, in the 1858 rental which was created as a sales prospectus (both were held on lease until 1872 by a Mrs Cameron and the (combined) extent was 2,046 acres). In that list of rentals 'Cregaig' was tenanted by 'Angus MacDonald Esq.' (Glenaladale?)[97] with no lease and for just under £46 per annum, down £4 2s 6d from what Sir Duncan Cameron of Fassifern was paying in 1829–30. I have not chosen to discover what happened to John Mitchell and the other seven 'farmers' of the 1841 census when the Earl of Morton, presumably Sholto John Douglas (1813 or 1818–1884), eighteenth earl, bought Conaglen in 1858.[98]

In 1861, when Callop was the Earl of Morton's, there was no Dalrioch (or Altlaig) mentioned by the census taker but there were two homes at Callop and one at Craigag. The first Callop house was occupied by Allan Cameron (40) and his unmarried sister Christina who was his housekeeper, both born in the huge neighbouring parish of Ardnamurchan, as well as a Kilmallie-born boarder. Callop had entered its penultimate phase. Allan Cameron was a gamekeeper and his occupancy continued in what clearly was an expanding and modern Callop under Morton. The other home was occupied by a shepherd, Duncan Morrison (born locally in Kilmallie parish which included the northern part of Ardgour), his wife, two daughters and a servant, Ann Corbett, an old Clanranald name; the wife (27) and older daughter (6) and the servant were all born in Ardnamurchan but the younger daughter, aged four, Chirsty, was born in Kilmallie parish. The character of Callop had changed into a sheep-farming and deer-stalking entity. Craigag was occupied in 1861 by a Morvern-born weaver of wool

(Alexander MacMaster aged 42), his wife (40) who was born in Arasaig, and their five children, aged from twelve to two, all born in the parish of Ardnamurchan.

In 1881, when the 'Calass' lodge (and perhaps the new main gamekeeper's farm at Callop had been built) there were four homes at what the census-taker was satisfied to call Callop.[99] No other place or farm name is given. Allan Cameron (59) the gamekeeper was still there with his spinster housekeeper sister, but now there was another single sister, Ann (57), who was the dairymaid (the stone house that stood at Callop in 1946 had a dairy, as well as a hay mow), and a servant boy Neil Cameron. Allan Cameron's was the fourth home listed. In the second was James Grieve, a sixty-six-year-old shepherd born in Kilmonivaig parish, his wife, a Glenelg parish woman, and their son aged twenty-six, who had been born at Loch Broom. By this time, as the occupants at Gleann Dubh Lighe to the north show over the years from 1841, there was free-trading of shepherds going on perhaps as woolly get-rich notions faced harder realities. The other two homes were occupied by Samuel MacDonald (72), a 'crofter', and his wife (70), both born in Glenelg parish, their son (36), a seaman, who had been born in Morvern, and a grandson (19) who had been born in Kilmallie parish. The fourth home was headed by a widow Isabella Mac-Varish (58), also a crofter, but born in Kilmonivaig parish to the east; her daughter Mary MacVarish, next named (20 and single) was also born in Kilmonivaig, but her son Duncan MacVarish (26) had been born in Appin; the last of the family was four-year-old grandson Alexander who had been born in Ardnamurchan parish.[100]

The presence of two crofting families may point to some success of the sheep and deer-stalking business or to a readiness on the earl's part to find sustenance for traditional farming families. It is apparent to me that this 'Callop' included at least two homes at my Callop (Allan Cameron's and the shepherd's), one at Dalrioch on the east side of the Callop River opposite Callop proper, and one at Cregag to the north of the river just after it is joined by the Dubhaidh.

The total population at Callop in 1881 was fifteen, up from eight in 1861, but down one from the sixteen of 1841 (when Dalrioch was included separately). If the two crofting farms of 1881 were as productive as Donald Cameron's farm in 1841 then the produce was not being used to feed large families. A simple guess might be that lodge shooting guests at Cregag relied on the two crofts on the Callop side for produce, perhaps for peat. None of those twenty-eight ordinary folk from the Ardgour estate who were assisted by Colonel Alexander MacLean in 1854 to sail on the *Derry Castle* to Australia gave Callop as his or her home.[101] (Ninety-four others were assisted by Donald Cameron of Locheil, a man who, according to Somerled MacMillan, was one in a long line of Locheils to shrug off ordinary, unneeded local people.)

My 1970 photographs showed a Callop, and land from the pasture on the north side of the old road, that not only was on the verge of a new land use, but that was also quite different from the scene that had existed at the end of the Napoleonic Wars in 1815 and in 1820 when Johnston was gathering cartographic data for the 1832 atlas. In 1970 there were no obvious signs of the homes that had existed at Callop, Dalrioch and Altlaig. A new, modern economy of simply deer hunting and minor subsistence had replaced the old family one of subsistence, and it in its turn had withered away to a feeble skeleton of what even that had been in 1881. I have not studied the influence of the Crofters' Act in 1886 on the peopling of Callop.

9

The Callop river and the road and the Glenfinnan station

Just a little west of the wooden bridge to Sarah MacVarish's there was a longish stretch of water over smooth pebbles and stones along the north bank where the current still cut and it was deep enough for swimmers. It ended gently, and there the river was easily fordable over a depth of well-worn shingles, if there hadn't been much rain, that is. Just about here was where the little tributary that flowed by the MacVarish home joined the Callop and in good weather even the accumulated two waters made no serious difficulty for a boy crossing, barefoot or in Wellington boots. Although there was one shingly shore westward (on the Ardgour side), this patch of well-worn pebbles and stones was the loch's high-water mark in deluge times (when loch waters perhaps lapped Creagag itself). It was a *barrachois*. At the loch end a long, thin muddy spit marked the partner depositional feature.

Then, somewhere not far west again, the river turned a little to the northward and cut deeply into the south bank this time, leaving a perfect run for brown trout and salmon parr, deep water, a wooded overhanging bank to hide under, with tree roots, lots of food-rich water fresh off the hills. The riverbank was smooth. At the end of this run, near the last shingly patch, I lost a chrome-plated penknife in the deep water close to a big sunken tree root. I couldn't swim, and the water had a different, more threatening look, so the knife stayed there. I can still see it lying on the bottom, shining at me, five feet down, nearly sixty years ago; the river had begun to be more than a river although it wasn't sure and I had no words for that. And knives were important to a boy, for freeing hooks, for cutting hazel arrows.

But my favourite pool was on the north, the Craigag side, a little further west again where the hills were still tight from the south. There was no fording to get to this run. You crossed the road at the big rock at the end of the Craigag driveway and made across a short tussocky reach for the trees of the clefted valley bottom across to the south-west a bit – there are alder trees there now and the other vegetation is rank and tall. I remember hazels. The pool and its run began just after the deep little rivulet joined it, the rivulet that emerged from the hills and on to the pasture below the lodge at the storage building, the burn that the six-day trail motorbikes crossed near the strange building – indeed that rivulet may have been joined in the trees by another, swelling its breadth and deepening it. I can't remember how the little stream crossed the pasture, or where it was bridged by the road (but it had to have been) – it was only a foot or so wide and had the quality of a deep but narrow chasm. The best place to cross the stream was where two young hazels grew, one on either side of the stream maybe a yard apart. I see the frayed edges of hazel calyces clasping green nuts. It was a deep, inlet-like tributary that had not changed its course for a very long time. Like the Callop itself, here, it had a different character, one that bespoke retreated loch and fast down erosion. The little hazel trees provided good footing (and excellent straight arrows) and once over, if you crept stealthily to the riverbank, you could intrude a worm on a hook to what I assumed to have been unsuspecting prey. The riverbank was not rank but grassy, although I never saw a sheep or goat grazing there. I used to risk a look to make sure my hook was not on the bottom and often I saw a trout make its fatal dart. Many little trout I caught there, not a few parr, and at least one eel – eels resist arrest formidably and it was good to have a knife handy. Across the pool were the last shingles, and to the left you could see the tail end of the penknife run. The river was slower flowing but still sometimes active and carving its way through the ancient sediments it had brought down from the mountains, but it had begun to change, and after the hazel pool almost suddenly it gathered into a deep unchanging pool whose end was far away near Acharacle.

The river turned in a sharp turn to the south, and on the northern side there were, as there still are, the older deciduous trees that dressed the valley bottom. Here the Callop was perhaps ten or twelve feet deep, and in its lower waters cold at all times. I never fished there. It swirled silently and forbiddingly and gathered itself, letting go its sediments; it was the loch in what was soon a complicated river mouth of pools among the cat's-tails, a horseshoe inlet, all on the Ardgour side, and a thin line of deposition pointing to the woody island at the top of the loch (whose shape probably pointed to a different entry for the Callop years earlier). Now there were just two unchanging riverbanks. On its south bank at pen-knife pool Meall na h-Àiridh was still quite tight from the south. The south bank was narrow. The hill rose quite sharply, rocky and heathery and with Scotch pines here and there. To the north, across the little road, the valley bottom was also grown narrower. The trees were spaced well enough and grew at the hill-foot in mosses or grasses where the deer often slept at night. The woods ran up the hillside to cover the railway tunnel. Any boat could easily have sailed as far as the sharp curve pool and maybe a little further. If men portaged to Loch Eil it would have been somewhere about here, where the pattern of shingles and deeps began, whatever the river's course in days gone by, that the men would have had to get out and guide their vessels over shingly patches to get to Lochan Dubh Tòrr an Tairbeirt or else transfer to smaller, more easily dragged craft.

There can have been no easy way along the northern bank of the Callop to reach the sharp turn pool from my favourite fishing run – it was loch–river transition territory – because I only remember reaching the deep swirling pool from the road. The little road, however, passed quite close to the pool and there was a little cleared track through the woods to reach it (still obvious in 2002); it must have been the starting point for fishing expeditions on Loch Shiel from the lodge. My memory tells me also that from about the deep pool one could see the beginning of the confusion of cat's-tails on the southern bank where it widened again and drew back a little from the river, but that view may have opened a little nearer the last turn to the loch. That southern bank turned into a frightening place, unknown, clad in deep clogging vegetation taller than a boy – I don't remember it any other way although I must have seen it winter and summer. I was never on that side of the Callop there.

I walked the road and saw the deep pool through the trees twice every school day while I lived at Craigag. Perhaps naturally I have many more memories of walking home than of going to school, not that school was unpleasant or troublesome, more than that once. Coming home, when you had crossed the bridge over the Finnan and the old field flat at the head of Loch Shiel, you rounded the twist, the switchback leaving the loch, with just room for the narrow little one-lane road. Then you were in the Callop gap; I remember trees that are not shown on the one-inch OS map. I do not remember, for example, seeing the train on the track high up the hill to the north. In those trees the little road twisted, rising and falling a little, and there was a little clearing to the left, on the north side, with a grassy track of a sort into it a few yards. I remember this because in this little clearing there stood what was to me a large angular rock, of some striated schist or gneiss, and one of the exposed faces had a sheet of mica which yielded great big flakes almost big enough for the see-through part of one of those old wood stoves I remember in Inverness county. This one had been blasted, although at the time it just looked new and out of place and unexplained. If the OS maps are correct, there were at least three cuttings blasted for the railway between the tunnel and the viaduct, all of them not far to the north of the old road in the valley. Judging by its ups and downs and twists, the old road had avoided blasting here (except probably at the last turn before Loch Shiel). A blasted boulder, more likely many, however, could well have tumbled, or been tumbled, down the hillside from the railway workings at any time over the some forty-five years that the line had been there. Perhaps the track into the boulder had been made as an access to rock and gravel for the upkeep of the road or the building or renovating or strengthening of the quay at the switchback where the Dalilea and Acharacle boat docked.[1] I wish I had been taken down the loch but my mother almost surely did not know about Glenaladale or Dalilea House, although I know she knew about the Eilean Fhionnain burying ground (as 'the Green Isle').

Somewhere between the mica rock and the deep pool, according to the six-inch map, in the trees to the north of the Callop, was where Lochan na Crìche gathered the waters of Allt na Crìche from the north before disgorging into the Callop. The 1813 plan of Cregag farm shows the pool, although unnamed in 1813, so it was not a freak of the winter and spring of 1872; someone had pencilled or inked in 'Callop Loch' as a name for it on the 1813 drawing, proving again that what I call the Cregag appendix was once simply part of Callop farm. (As an accepted boundary, one might assume the lochan's permanence, although it may have resulted from Dick and Readdie's need to elevate the new road above average flood levels.) I passed this way often but I have no memory of 'Callop Loch', Lochan na Crìche, under any name, just to the west of the big deep pool. I suppose it may have been drained by the 1940s, but I don't remember the border stream Allt na Crìche either. It must have been a tiny stream.

There is one unusual Gaelic naming feature that appears in the 1813 and the 1872 maps. The big wooded 'island' in the Callop, referred to above, is shown in the 1872 map as Eilean Mòr [Big Island] but is not in fact an island. It is a tongue of land. Another 'island' is indicated on the same map as marking the northern limits of Dalriach where there is a tongue of land, called Eilean Fearna [Alder Tree Island], created by the Callop to the west and the Dubhaidh to the east. The term 'Innse Fearna' is given to the tongue of higher land between the Callop tributaries Allt na Cruaiche and Allt na Teanga Duibhe.

As you passed from Glenfinnan into Cregag, past the track to the big pool on a summer day that smelled of a hundred greens, trudging eastward, going home, that little few hundred yards of deep valley before the wooded Craigag shoulder and the big boulder round the corner could get quite hot; it was always humid, so a stranger might have felt drowsy there. The road that John Ford tended was potholed and sometimes hard on bare feet and big toe nails. I remember once the drowsy summer sun melting the tar and tar bubbles had to be burst – butter took the tar off later. There was a ditch on the left near the old grey granite mile-stone marker and its mossy sides, not very deep, were emerald green and home to newts. Sometimes a roe deer would dart into the denser trees and scamper up the hill. It was about there, in the mornings, that we used to see the roundish depressions left by the deer overnight; little wonder the poachers were attracted here. I don't know what John Ford did – I don't remember a filled pothole, but why would I have cared – but he cannot have earned much, kindly soul (if he was evasive it may have been for fear of passing on tuberculosis). Cars very seldom met or passed us on the road to or from school so perhaps just finding a little bit of the old road in 2002 was enough. I suspect that those old mile-stone markers went the way of Creagag itself when the new two-lane highway was blasted through.

I cannot remember ever having walked much further than the Stagehouse Inn at the west end of Glenfinnan, just after the blending of the low road and the higher one past the church and the school. I was local. At about that meeting, near the Stage-house, on the low road coming in from the loch-side, was the house where John 'the post' and the Chirsties lived. And Angie 'the bar' MacDonald lived near there too.[2] (Dobbin Blythe lived up there too, maybe in the last house on the high side of the main road – to me, Dobbin's house looked oddly urban, like something in Murrayfield.) Down further on the old road in Glenfinnan was Archie MacKellaig's where the great big stuffed salmon hung on the wall above the door going in, and from there, taking a path to the right brought you to the big Glenaladale House, on its own in my days. There was another large stone building there too, a little stable-ish, my memory of which has never been strong. At any rate, at the junction of the low and high roads was also where the lane to the station turned off to the north-east; it was almost a crossroads. On the right at the turn to the station from the high road I remember trees, pines I suspect, and I think they were just about opposite the hall where Archie MacKellaig taught some of us 'Highland' dancing, where we played whist sometimes, moving from table to table, and where the amateur dramatics society rehearsed *The Admirable Crichton*. I can't see the outside of the building, just a few whist tables and Archie MacKellaig in an orangey-coloured kilt giving an oddly controlled, very high kick. Maybe there was a stage.

Up from the hall, on the left and upper side of the lane, I think I remember two homes, modern, perhaps two-storey, built to an older formula than Dobbin's, and the uppermost, near the line, was John Monaghan, the station master's – I can still see his wife standing in the doorway. I don't remember any houses on the right side going up; perhaps it was wooded to the top. I remember also that the approach the lane took was from the low road where it met the high and that the lane to the station ran from south-west to north-east over its short distance. This approach lane, built probably in or just before 1898, gave access to the low road, not the high, which is one suggestion that the section of high road from the crossroads at the Finnan, up to the church and the school and then on to upper almost-crossroads near the Stagehouse, was the less significant in Glenfinnan around 1900, and relatively new. John Ford's tar-paper shack – really I can only summon up an edge or two of the black tar-paper sticking out somehow – stood on the upper side of the high road, alone, apart from the low road houses and buildings, set into a cutting of some sort in the hill that, I learned many years later in Judique, is still there – few people today remember John the roadman. His home was on our right going west from Miss Fraser's school to Janet's little shop behind John Monaghan's station. From near John Ford's, the view down the loch may have offered much more of the Ardgour side than the Moidart one but it was from even higher up than the church's and was nothing less than spectacular when the weather was good. The steam train behind his bothy ran through a deep cutting so the traveller missed this panorama of Meall na h-Àiridh and Meall a' Bhainne, with Feadan Mhic Bheathainn in between, then Sgor nan Cearc, although I later learned that some trains (presumably going east to Fort William with the grade) stopped on Concrete Bob's viaduct to breathe in the deep and fragrant heresy of Jacobitism and thoughts of a people about whom they knew nothing.

When Seumas and I drove the high road three years ago I was struck by the absence of thick woods around the church, and the presence of trees across the road from John Ford's, blocking the great view he and we had enjoyed in bygone days. I liked Glenfinnan much more when the church was hidden away like a jewel, calling a silent MacDonald cry for succour down the long, lonely loch, and linked simply with physical creation, and the view from John Ford's humbler home, raising its voice in blatant and unimpeded praise.

I remember the station at Glenfinnan, up that little lane, but not in any detail. What was fascinating to me was John Monaghan standing at the end of his platform and exchanging tablets with the man in the through train. Each held out a large hoop with a leather sporran-like appendage at the bottom and no matter how fast the train was travelling I never saw one dropped. Lickety split! Lickety split! It never occurred to me that that night the engine might be in Glasgow, across a world, in unhallowed air. John Monaghan had a very important job in those days, station master on the West Highland, much better than the pass at Corrour by lonely, dammed Loch Treig [Loch Forsake], or the desolate, peaty, lochan-dotted Rannoch Moor pass. My brothers found old John's 'Glay Fee' for Glenfinnan as interesting as I did the message hoop exchange, and when we found ourselves reminiscing in South Paris Maine in 1995 (in another oak forest whose first European people had left too but not so long ago – Finns) the topic came up like new, and brought distant looks, and smiles of sadness for something valuable lost to the scurryings of time. Someone remembered the trail of cigarette ash down John Monaghan's black uniform. It wasn't until sitting with Pat, his younger daughter, at Kinlocheil, in Joe MacLeod's daughter's home, that I suddenly remembered the three-legged greyhound hurpling home up the line! Not quite gone yet is the strange dank, stale, coally smell of railway stations in those days but not at Glenfinnan. Like the peat, it is almost gone.

The last time John Monaghan came up in my conversation was in late September or early October 2005, in Judique, warm and green with golden rod and asters still blooming. A white, comfortable car had pulled into our little drive one day. It was Buddy.[3] I hadn't met Buddy for a year or two although we only live about a mile apart, if that. He is still kept very busy playing the fiddle. He had known that I wanted a couple of copies of his latest CD, the one made with his niece Natalie (Creignish), and thought to bring them himself to save me the trouble. We sat for an hour in our little living room and reminisced. Not surprisingly we got on to railways – Buddy worked all his life for the railway in Nova Scotia and had been a station master himself – and when I told him about old John Monaghan at Glenfinnan station in the days of steam and rationing, he immediately asked me if John worked the telegraph. I didn't know. I don't remember him tapping out messages but Buddy figured that he had to have. Buddy you see turned eighty-one on 18 October 2005 and, though John Monaghan was born in 1895 (he died in 1983), their railway experiences must have been much the same. They would have enjoyed one another, especially in Buddy's younger days.

And howsoever strange that recent reminiscence may seem, there are many links between Àrasaig and the Morars and Cape Breton and north-east Nova Scotia. The great gap, from 1820 to 1900, is only a gap, when it is one, for Scotland. The more important continuity lies in places like Judique and Mabou and Sou'-West Margaree, and Judique. Maybe five or six years ago Buddy and I met and greeted each other near the extravagant (mostly public expense) new hall in Judique. Buddy told me with a hint of excitement in his voice of having not long before learned that Freddie had told him of meeting a Garanaich MacDonell in one of the Morars who knew keenly of brothers of his grandfather who had settled in Judique during the great emigrations! Everyone in Judique, and around, knows the Garanaich MacDonells – perhaps not everyone in the Morars does though. Freddie MacDonald, Boston, is the son of an apothecary who'd been born and raised in what is now Centennial, south of Judique and inland a mile or two.

It happened that I had been talking to Freddie too – he comes home from the Boston states almost every summer to a little cottage on Route 19[4] at Long Point south of Judique and if we can Patsy and I drop in for a chat. (Freddie met Ted Williams and other New England luminaries. Although Freddie was a young victim of polio, he had fought in the US navy at the Normandy landings, and had done countless other things, councilman in Boston, he ran a dance orchestra. He tells endless stories, sometimes over a bottle of beer.) After many adventures in Greater Glasgow, Freddie got to Àrasaig and Morar, maybe not looking for relatives but with a keen eye out, and ear. His old father had told him not to try to speak Gaelic because his powerful Boston twang would grate on people's ears. He found his way late one night to a house, which I reckon might have been near Bracara in North Morar. There, having been invited in, he saw an old man with a fiddle in one hand and a bow in the other at the top of a flight of stairs. This old man, to Freddie's utmost surprise, knew people in Judique north, and was related to them quite closely. Buddy and I had independently shared Freddie's delight. Ah, dear Buddy MacMaster, what a contribution he has made! Such a remarkable talent! Such an amazing repertoire, tune on tune all night long! Complete and highly talented immersion in an old consciousness. There was no one like him in my old Glenfinnan, although my mother once told me, almost by mistake, that Calum the gamekeeper had played the fiddle. And Freddie: who would think hearing his New England accent that he is a bearer of Inverness county lore, but he is.

10

On the old roads in October 2002

Seumas and I visited Glenfinnan late in October 2002. The road to the isles, west from the Lochy, for the first time, was almost alien below the hills. It had a number I've forgotten. If I struggle it is more to forget than remember. The old road, when I sensed its forlorn call, has here and there been left as little loops off to the north, disappearing sometimes into nowhere. In vain I looked for the little stone house on the west side of the stream up from the old bridge at Corribeg. The little woody hills and twists before Drumsallie were gone. There was a new bridge to the south of the wooden one at or near Drochaid Sgainneal, the approach to which reminded me of nothing at all, the old character was gone. This was transit through rural suburb not travel through little communities of man, each with its own tales and its known potential. It wasn't until we reached where the road went under the railway, just east of where Joe MacLeod and Joe MacVinish's railway bothy had been, maybe still was, with the chalybeate seep, that I suddenly realised where I was, how far we'd got. The craving for European modernity with pothole-less, smooth black top and painted borders was here at least successfully challenged by the costs involved in building a new railway bridge from scratch – the *Jacobite*, an old steam engine, draws the summer tourists west on the old line from Fort William to Mallaig, fleeced they doubtless are at every stop, and no John maybe lingering in warm society at the Stagehouse till the last minute, no message exchange, and no three-legged greyhound limping home up the line. Otherwise, at that old McAlpine railway bridge, for a few yards we might as well have been in boreal Canada or Sweden. How many Lowlanders, how many foreigners, have driven through sensing nothing! Here the dense green forest on the north and south reached darkly to the roadside like an arboreal coniferous venturi, but then, a little further on, the south again was suddenly forestless as I remembered it. But we could see the forest edge. It ran into the hills on the west bank of the Callop and its continuation, Allt na Cruaiche, up the hillside almost to where Doire Mòr had been. Had I known it at the time I could have told Seumas that the Dalriach and Altlaig farms had been wooded at last, and the old peat hag too.

We drove up the new driveway to Craigag and were kindly shown around the old lodge. In Nova Scotia it would be a heritage building. With a few little changes inside, it was much the same, but light switches not wicks, no hint of dankness. The old outhouse with the corrugated or metal roof was still there too, where once we had accidentally cornered a terrified wild cat. The big birch tree at the back had only recently blown down – no one had counted the rings but it was probably over a century old, a sprout pushing up into the drizzle when the first trains went through. At the gate and to the east on the peaty flat there were tall twenty- to thirty-year-old coniferous trees of some sort (Corrie's bones, had they lasted by some miracle in all the acids, were being troubled by new roots, I told the owner and she told us that a dog of Gavin Maxwell's lay out there in the earth somewhere as well). On the other side of the lane, at the gate, the rhododendrons were still there, tall as trees and proscriptive of all undergrowth – they must have been at least eighty years old (unless they have some unusual regenerative process). The whole experience moved me sometimes to joyous reflection but more often to sorrow, not at the trees which enclosed peculiarly, so much as at the remarkable power of the automobile. The old dozen or so miles from the Lochy to Craigag was now a matter of minutes, a town of modern buildings thinning into something sub-suburban that I didn't recognise, where it had once been a soothing and unhasty journey on a passing-place one-lane road, Annat farm distinctively bucolic, as well as a big hotel near the road somewhere in that area and other reference places. Travelling west, from the Lochy, past an outward-bound woody enclave at Corpach, past Kinlocheil, past Torebane, just over the Fionn Lighe at Drochaid an Earanaich [The Irishman's

Bridge], the new turn for (Lochiel) Drumsallie and (Ardgour) Drumfern was now a fast sweep, an exit the like of which you still don't see on right-handers on the 'Ceilidh Trail' from Plaster Cove/MacMillan's Point to Bay Saint Lawrence and Meat Cove at the northern tip of Cape Breton. It was all modern, part of a great European web of speedy convenience, wasteful marketing fever of shallow conception, a form of arrogant condemnation of alternatives.

Near Craigag, late on a grey afternoon, we got out of the car in what had been a tussocky pasture nearly sixty years earlier, where I had found the wren's nest, gentle country, used but not exploited, where orchids grew, adding their subtle scents. The old cow pasture had not been used by beasts owned by man for years. It was not exploited, mind you. Worse, it was neglected and bore, to me, a taint of waste. There was no litter, but it was clotted and dense with rank grassy and reedy growth about two feet high, not the seemingly impenetrable and hostile golden rod, seeded asters, meadow sweet, and wild rose and bramble tangle, and rising white spruces I know on deserted farms in Cape Breton, but it looked to me like some rural analogue of the sort of unwanted European weeds, probably nettles, found on deserted city sites and old roofless homes. It was as though the road's price, once out of the new, brazen, dark, needly forest, was almost a hundred yards on either side where the only vegetation that could withstand toxic spraying mocked the past – I hasten to add that I have no idea if anyone sprayed there for budworm, tree-attacking beetles, midges, clegs and ticks or anything else (a technique used, I suspect, in unpopulated and populated parts of the forested country in rural north-eastern Nova Scotia to keep the power lines clear). The tall rank growth on the flat below Craigag Lodge struck me as hopelessly forlorn and insulting to man's greater ingenuity, not altogether unlike those vast acreages of wounded, neglected clear-cut in rural Nova Scotia, just over the hill from the tourist roads through the almost last north-east deciduous forests.[1] It faded however into wet, sad alder trees to the west and I could not imagine the hazelly riverbank I had fished from not far away. Yellowhammers, I learned, were a bird of the past, and gold-crested wrens unremembered.

Then I saw a little piece of the old road and we stumbled to reach it. It lay *in situ*, in its old wider sweep to the south of the new highway, nearer the Callop. It was built on what was about three feet of elevation, to keep it above the flooding – surely as much a part of Thomas Telford's road-building system of the early nineteenth century as MacAdam's a little later (cambered crushed gravel on a rock base). Its ragged exposure in profile may have meant that here was where a little unnoticed bridge had once carried over the stream from the old empty Craigag forge. The old road was so narrow – about as wide as the twelve-foot wide Strontian roads built in the 1730s to serve the lead mines. Only in out-of-the-way places could the old one-laner have survived, even have been neglected for want of a John Ford. From the old road for a moment to the east I could just make out the little hill crest where the path to Callop had turned south, where the old Cregag buildings had been (though I did not know it at the time). I could remember another time. There, standing on the old road I realised that the great big boulder that had given a centuries-old Locheil farm its name, that had been first of all the individual Ardgour farms listed in the plan of 1813 (listed as number 2 after the general estate map), as well as the tongue of hill below the lodge, perhaps Sròn na Creagaige, had stood silently in the way of progress. They had been blasted away, no picks and shovels this time my lads, not in any insult to the withered but regenerating Gaelic world, but in some plaintive cry to be allowed into the world of unrestrained growth and final improvement and another stasis of minor understanding like the ultra-confident, know-it-all Victorian, colonial one that had preceded Albert Einstein's new observations of the physical world. We seem to progress in those manic fits, always more destructive overall and pointing to novel concepts of money and consumption. I wish I had the old milestone marker from a little west of the lane-end but I guess that the road had run over it in its haste as well.

Seumas loved Glenfinnan, but he found the little old-world road up Gleann Ruadh [Glen Roy], past Bohuntine in Keppoch, Lochaber even more redolent of something quite unexpected and suggestive of the mannerly old that we have shed, and I had told him about even in my silences. What! Kindness you say! Only fools . . . We saw that long glen in the dying light of another

day when non-tourist cows with shit on their rears were crossing
the little road in the lower slopes of 'Beinn a' Mhonicag' (Beinn a'
Mhoineagaig/Hill of the Pea-pod?) to reach their old stone byre.
The ancient MacDonald voices from Mabou, I made them echo
for him between the parallel roads and he understood what had
happened so long ago, to the people of Bohuntine, of Cranachan in
Glen Roy, and to the folk in places along the Spean like Keppoch,
Achluachrach, Achnacoichine, Tulloch, Murlaggan, Clianaig, In-
verroy, Killiechonate. So profound had been the removals and
emigrations from Catholic, Jacobite Keppoch.

At a high place up the glen, past the last farm, we stopped to look
to the south and the snow-streaked, cloudy mountain tops, then to
the north where the valley sides pressed in. North, there were signs
of the old times, of older life, at Achavady (Achadh a' Mhadaidh/
The Fox's Field) where men had farmed a little. Then a dark-
coloured car headed past travelling north. Its driver was a young,
gaunt and white-faced, unsmiling young woman who didn't wave.
We watched her car gradually make its way down the contours of
the treeless mountains of the Glen Roy National Nature Reserve,
below the three parallel roads, below Coire nan Eun [Corrie of the
Birds], to the valley bottom. Then we drove after it. At what looks
like the end of this long primary mountain valley, where the river
Turret joins from a degree or two west of north, and the Roy cants
to the north-east then east (and Leckroy/Leac Ruadh and Annat,
another Annat), was a tuft of woods encircling a large house. This
was Brae Roy Lodge. It had the appearance of an almost guarded,
daunting refuge, the less patient and more cynical might have called
it a socio-linguistic diaphragm greeting a well-worthy *feadan*. We
saw one like it called Glenfinnan Lodge up the river Finnan just
north of Corryhully. We knocked on neither door. There they
sometimes sit, these strange people – *Who Owns Scotland* names
many of them and gives their far-away home addresses – listening
to the wind, waiting, waiting, subconsciously distancing, subordi-
nating, fearing for all I know; if any don't wave, and if any look
down, it is only because they don't know how to look up from a
modern fantasy. In the case of Glen Roy, even the secondary folk,
often Gaelic-speaking Highland shepherds, who came in from the
outside after the first great leavings of from about 1790 to 1830, are

no longer the power they were. That glen is a tale of two declines, two flights. To understand the older Gaelic Glen Roy people, there are still folk of the old stock there, but it is only in greater Mabou, Cape Breton, that the knowledge is richest (and intensely musical, complete with the last subtleties of the last Gaelic-Scottish rhythms). Modern rich estate owners, wherever they come from, cannot be expected to learn to hear the echoes. Not all of the modern Scottish Gaels are ready to graft in the anachronisms of *seann Alba bheadarrach,* not even if cleverly laid before them. The New World seems but a crass, retarded aberration in this shrivelled and stilted world.

Although I know what happened to many of the old Roman Catholic Keppoch folk, the old Catholic and Jacobite tenantry, try as I might, and have, I have found no certain Glenfinnan consciousness anywhere in the New World except in Prince Edward Island where Captain John Glenalladale (Mac Iain Òig, no Fear a' Ghlinne) people settled. On the northern shore of Port Phillip in Victoria is Melbourne and so far it seems that the Glenfinnan people diffused there and elsewhere and leave no trace I have discovered. Where Callop is concerned, at least members of the MacVean family who lived there for some years in the early years of the nineteenth century are aware of their story and the place almost lives on in the land of sun. And many of the MacPhees in Australia know exactly who they are.

Where Craigag is concerned, the old Cregag farm of before the lodge of the 1870s, there is perhaps only one obscure reference that I will include and which crops up in J.L. MacDougall's *History of Inverness County.* In this case, as in others, one is forced to speculate, but always there is the strong realisation that MacDougall's remarkable reporting work on hundreds of families, Catholic and Protestant, was ingenuous and always is presented sufficiently without comment or bias that a great deal may be learned, and mooted, about old Gaelic society in immigrant times from it, if one will but consider carefully, often in the context of his silences, when you spot them. What MacDougall knew and supposed as a matter of course, even as a rigorously trained Nova Scotia lawyer, is difficult to imagine today – more British by far, but further yet, much more Highland.

A Donald Cameron married a Marjory Cummings 'at Craigie about 130 miles from Fort William.' They had a son Hugh, Eobhan a Chreagan who emigrated, married to a Christina Laidlaw with a family, to the Strait area of Cape Breton on the ship *Aurora* in 1827.[2] Dealing with Hugh first, he and his wife and nine children settled at General Line, which is in the hinterland of Port Hastings and Creignish (now an almost empty hinterland). According to MacDougall, one of Eobhan a Chreagan's family, George Cameron, was born in 1820 in Lochaber and became a stone mason.[3] So, considering that Cumming is a prominent Achdalieu name (on the north shore of Loch Eil) (as well as a Badenoch name, both of Norman origin), and that the old Cregag farm on the height of land just north of the confluence of the Callop and Allt Dubhaidh lies about sixteen miles from Fort William, in modern miles,[4] it is not inconceivable that MacDougall simply had no sense of distances in Scotland, or his printer added a zero to be on the safe side and this couple were actually married at the old Cregag farmhouse. The name 'Eobhan a Chreagan' is as suggestive of Cregag as is Somerled MacMillan's term 'Stronchreagaig' (but perhaps also of Inverailort/Sròn a' Chreagain). One hundred and thirty miles from Fort William, you see, describes a circumference that includes Edinburgh and the north of Caithness and Sutherland. Not only did MacDougall write that Eobhan a Chreagan had been born in Lochaber (which does not include Inverailort), but the Laidlaws, although Lowland in name, were living in Lochaber date unknown until 1826 and were in the sheep business – several members of this Laidlaw family in Lochaber, in two generations, emigrated on the *Aurora* in 1826 and a Laidlaw still lives in Troy, Cape Breton at the St Lawrence end of the Gut of Canso.[5]

Now, concerning the marriage at Craigie: the 'Craigie' memory that J.L. MacDougall tapped in Inverness county, Cape Breton, presumably in the first quarter of the twentieth century, but possibly earlier, concerned a marriage that must have taken place about 1780. According to the genealogical work of Dr Robert Cameron in New South Wales, the first issue of Donald Cameron and Marjorie Cumming was Alexander Cameron, who was baptised on 10 March 1781. The second child he gave as Ewen (to wit

Hugh, or MacDougall's 'Eobhan a Chreagan') who was born in 1783. In 1780 I know with certainty only that Cregag was not the property of Cameron of Lochiel; that John Cumming, (either the then or later) fifth of Achdalieu, had only been married for about a year (his father, John, fourth, perhaps still lived, with all his memories of Locheil in the Forty-five[6]). If Dr Cameron is correct and Marjorie Cumming of Artlewn was a daughter of a George Cumming and a Christina McLachlan, then her relationship to the third, fourth and fifth Cummings of Achdalieu is unknown but close. (Artlewn is a corruption of Achdalieu or one of its ortho-graphic variants, the 'Aychetilay' or 'Asterlow' of 2006.) Cregag may have been the home of one of the Achdalieu Cummings, presumably George, and, for what it may be worth, the only likely George Cumming to emerge from the electronic indexing of the holdings of the National Archives of Scotland, eighteen years earlier (1762) was a drover in Corpach, the farm abutting Achdalieu to the east.[7] He would have had dealings with the Lochaber Laidlaws.

The train journey north
and straggling thoughts

Looking at the 1970 photograph of Craigag (with its ugly, poorly
proportioned outbuilding, unchanged, and its utility pole), the
thing that stands out as different today is the trees on the north side
of the line. I remember our picking a cupful of blaeberries on that
slope and there were either no trees or very few – blaeberries didn't
do very well because heather and bracken choked them out. The
1951 one-inch OS map shows a brake of deciduous trees at
Drochaid Sgainnir but none behind Craigag, which, by my lights,
is correct. The change has not come about because of the ex-
termination or severe control of wild goats or rabbits. The goats we
saw always were much higher up the mountains and hills on the
skyline, a badger's sett nearby in a cleft in a rock, and one wild cat,
but no rabbits or hares. I never saw that sheep-bane, the fox, so
efficient had been the gamekeepers in the later days of the golden
fleece. I never saw sheep on the hillside north of Craigag. There
were deer in plenty and maybe greater control of their numbers
had let some forest return.

But the most obvious reason may be the change from steam to
diesel trains.

I have a strong memory of the sparks from the old steam engine
setting the northern hillside alight in the most memorable and
dramatic fashion (always the train climbing up from the east). There
must have been dry spells when the bracken got sharp as a razor – it
is the razor cuts, not the blazing sun, that I remember. The fires
seemed to be at night so must have been in the late autumn. And
the flames never started on the south side. Maybe there was a slight
camber in the line or maybe it was a wind from the south that took

the sparks into the northern tinder. There was no panic and there was no fire service; there were no aeroplanes anywhere near, and helicopters might as well have been uninvented. The bracken and heather fire took its course. In that part of the country, rain seemed to be an almost daily occurrence so there were none of the disasters to which Mediterranean climates and vegetations are prone with their long dry summers. The flames seemed to envelop the entire hillside in a crackling drama, but nothing much came of it, except more and reinvigorated bracken and heather next year, and no trees. The tart aromas of the burning stay with me, and I remember the blackness of what had been russety brown after the heather had flowered and the bracken had dried to skin-slitting sharpness. *The Scotsman* records that I've read, which run to 1950, only mention the one hillside fire of May 1897,[1] no autumn one in steam railway times from 1901 to 1950.

At least twice we visited Edinburgh on the North British's West Highland Railway during my Glenfinnan years. In my lifetime, until the final socialist amalgamation of the last independents some years after the war, the North British Railway company controlled our journey from Edinburgh to Glenfinnan – it never occurred to me that I lived in a North Britain (or that many of the streets in the capital were named for hostiles and the NB stood champion of the east end of Princes Street). The West Highland Railway, which began its haul to Àrasaig in a sooty, greasy, stale Glasgow station, was part of the North British Railway company but ran distinctly coloured and appointed trains and carriages. The selectiveness of my childhood memories of the old steam trains is dominated by the fact that I think I only remember the northward journey, and of that, because of the schedule, really only the start, a snippet or two midway perhaps, and an hour to an hour and a half at the end from the cold and lonely pre-dawn. The train I remember leaving Edinburgh left the dull charcoaled roof-light of Waverley Station at that end of the Princes Street where the North British Hotel stood, above the station, near the GPO and the archives – 'Don't be vague, ask for Haig!' the hoarding used to proclaim above the stairs from Princes Street down to the platforms. The train left in the evening and then chugged out of Glasgow at past my bedtime. I could never sleep well on those bristly benches and when I did it was only for a few hours. I remember some of the stations, Ardlui, Crianlarich, Tyndrum and Glenorchy, and Rannoch, but none of the spectacular scenery from the Gareloch and Loch Long. I remember waking up in a pale grey dawn to see Rannoch Moor for the first time. I never saw the real lost Rannoch in sunlight, its lochans a-glitter to the far-away mountain fringes. The train slowed maddeningly, then ground to a halt and a wait, apparently nowhere. Nothing could have been bleaker and more disturbing at dawn, almost shunting, false starts, metal plates creaking, no progress, no reason. The experience must have deepened my sense of the inaccessibility and distinctness of truly Highland Scotland.

Just before the old Campbell farm at Achalader, north of Glenorchy, the road I later got to know well twisted up the Black Mount heading for King's House and the eastern gateway to Glencoe, all high along the western limits of the great empty Rannoch moor, east of the gathering Glencoe massif (and the old Wade road). The rail line on the other hand broke away, curving right past the Achalader farm, an important old Campbell farm controlling the old drove road, and then crossed and climbed up what I remember as the barest, emptiest of boggy, lochan-dotted moors I have ever seen. Rather than finding a way, as Wade's old military road did, up the Black Mount on to the high western rim of Rannoch to the west of the modern road I cycled, negotiating what would have been a staggering descent to Glencoe, and blasting a path along the shore of Loch Linnhe past Corran Narrows, railway engineering economics dictated following easier gradients, crossing the moor itself making for a height at the marches of Badenoch and Lochaber, heading west along the Spean, on top of the gorge, and then coming south into Fort William from Spean Bridge. Gaelic Scotland's saddest glen only endures the road. I only have a few memories of the moor but the general impression is ingrained – when I saw the fringes of Dartmoor a few years later, on visits to the torrs from Bovey Tracey in Devon, it looked less rain-drenched, less hopeless and forbidding. And Crewe Junction, a lonely industrial train complex at four on a summer's morning, where miles of cold, shiny railway lines met among the platforms, even Crewe Junction and its lostness lacked the threat of the open moor.

There was a railway stop at Rannoch Moor in the middle of nowhere, but not yet the high point of Scotland's central barren. Rannoch station, what I saw of it, was forlorn, half-awake and depressing, although a few people lived there. It could only have been manned by lovers of solitariness and the shroud – I have never read a memoir of a life working or a childhood spent there.[2] Rannoch Moor was a place where train travel slowed down, among unmappable morainic little hummocks and bogs, often to a stop, stuck it seemed for no reason in some Highland muskeg. The high moor hinterland of Saint Anthony at the north of the Great North Peninsula of Newfoundland is a little like it south of the truly treeless north; otherwise, you would have to travel in the summer in the Canadian or Russian arctic to find similar conditions. I don't know if we were on a siding to let a south-bound through.[3] In the early minutes of dawn crossing Rannoch I saw the only vertical wooden snow fences I saw before I came to Canada, and the most desolate moorland in the world. Even the fences were derelict and gapped. I remember snow. I think I remember native red deer. At last the train jolted clear from its stops, plates grating, but still it was up a gradient, still in the depths of the moor. The high point was Corrour (Coire Odhar/Brown Corrie) near the south end of a long unforgettably naked, exposed loch, a place to live that many would not choose before Siberia or the Sahara where death would come more quickly. I can't remember the train stopping at Corrour, although some old timetables say that it used to. If it did, that could only have re-emphasised Rannoch. And yet once the wester part including Loch Treig was well forested.

Loch Treig was like a last exclamation point before the richness of Keppoch country into which it drained (and Keppoch too had been denuded of much of its Highland folk by 1850). *Treig – an treig thu, chlann mo chinnidh mi*, the brave Keppoch said, or words to that tragic effect. It was a long and narrow loch in almost treeless country, like Rannoch in general; I've only seen the place in early morning greyness, never direct sunlight. I remember no large trees by Treig's edges and those edges were the edges of an almost lost reservoir. It was harshly artificial, like a prison yard, stripped and desperate in the winds, left as a reminder to unlucky humanity.[4]

Rannoch moor is nothing if not memorable, and if hunted Jacobites fled there after Culloden, few would have chosen to follow them far had it been on a grey and cloudy day. The navvies who built the line walked miles out, risking life itself, just for a night's fun away from the pall.

I remember the swaying of the West Highland Railway cars and the shifting and creaking plates between the carriages, the third- and first-class compartments. I remember (I think) the netting overhead for luggage, the five-pound-fine notice for pulling the emergency cable that ran the length of the train, the painting in each compartment, and the mirror. The almost abnormal Kilimanjaro and Fuji symmetry of Beinn Dorain south of Glenorchy, I remember that too, the long, gentle curve in the early light of dawn. I cycled the road nearby it a number of times too but couldn't associate it with Donnchadh Bàn until twenty years later. Those old West Highland trains were not well sealed and while the country couldn't impose itself as it did if you cycled, still the wild was only a step away and seemed nearer than it does today from any rubbery-sealed vehicle.

About ten years after we left Craigag, about 1961, the steam engines were taken off the British Rail system (which had taken over the old and proud British Railways/West Highland Railway) and were replaced by diesel locomotives. Gone were the tiny little flecks of burnt coal you got in your eyes when you poked your head out of a carriage door on a curve to see ahead. Gone was the patter of little cinders on the carriage roofs as the engine strained up to passes like Glen Orchy, and gone for ever were the roman candles of sparks that set our hillside ablaze just about Joe MacLeod and Joe MacVinish's bothy. I've never asked anyone who lived further up the line if they remembered any annual firing of the westerly Àrasaig hillsides. A footnote, from which I deduce that there indeed may have been many heather and bracken fires in the area in steam-train times, comes from the mention in March 2003 of an impending action by the owners of the modern Glenfinnan estate, for £100,000 sterling, from some unnamed person or institution for timber losses sustained in a fire on the property in February.[5]

I never travelled on the old railway line further than Glenfinnan.

I don't know who John Monaghan's cronies were, only that he was a sociable character whose oldest daughter was a doctor and his younger a beautiful blond friend of mine who grew to love theatre. What I saw of it further on came from either my first motorcycle, which I had in the late 1950s, or a car a dozen years later when the lost exposures of Callop were made. My father came home to Craigag when he could, by train. I remember too my mother telling me that the fireman used to kick off coal for our fire at Craigag in the wintertime. I had never associated the kindness with anything until I took Seumas to the old house in late 2002 and the owner or occupier of what is now a small hotel, an outsider I had never heard of, told me, perhaps us, thoughtfully, that my mother had used some visible charm to induce the man on the train to boot off a few bits of black diamond. (In rural Scotch Inverness county, Cape Breton, only sharpened malice would have prompted such a reminiscence, and one of the general enduring prides lies in understanding others' sensitivities. Had I somehow insulted the lady I wonder . . . but the memory had lasted and been handed on for at least half a century, reaching the outsider many years later, which was impressive in a way.)

The arson fire in May 1897 can only have happened after an unusual and prolonged dry spell. The normal weather was characterised by west coast frontal rains from huge masses of grey clouds packing in, unbroken or defined, often relentlessly, from the Atlantic – the opposite of the neatly arranged, strung-out clouds that pass over Nova Scotia and the Maritimes all at the same altitude. Rainfall of over eighty inches a year was normal near the Atlantic. In five years there I have no memory of a dry spell of any length. River floods were therefore more statistically likely, although I remember only one time when Glenfinnan was not reachable by the paved descendant of the old Dick and Readdie road; it was probably in 1949. *The Scotsman* archive shows there to have been two floods that year. The first happened around 19 January; the second happened in the early hours of Monday, Boxing Day. There might have been no reporting had it not been for an ambulance from Àrasaig heading for Inverness with a sick patient getting stuck in the flood waters. This happened about two miles from Glenfinnan, which means that it was at a low point somewhere near the Craigag lane-end. Luckily for the patient, Angus MacDonald from the Stagehouse in Glenfinnan was driving home from Fort William in the early hours. He saw the predicament and drove the hotel's lorry into the water and pushed the ambulance on to a clear piece of road. This was our Angie 'the bar', who only died a few years ago.

Just over ten years earlier, in 1938, there were at least two floodings, one that Adam photographed on 3 April, and another in November 1938 when there was a rain of monsoonal proportions, near six inches of rain in six days, which caused Loch Shiel's level to rise dramatically, overflowing to a depth of several feet on to the road at Craigag. On Thursday night of 25 September 1890, homes at Glenfinnan and at Corpach (on Loch Eil) were flooded to a depth of up to four feet. The funnels at Eilean Fhionnain and Corran could not handle it. Callop farm is never known to me to have flooded and it is obvious that the original Cregag buildings also were sited above high-water mark; if not, then 1890's flood may mark the end of a very old building site.

My father and my brothers had visitors to Craigag (my mother none that I remember). The younger people, from Dollar Academy – I remember a Henderson and Peter Rae – climbed the mountains and explored. My father's friends included a now-mysterious Attlee, and Iain Campbell. I have no memory of Attlee's face, or of any little kindness shown to a boy, but I know he was a birdwatcher and had arrived to try to spot what we called the gold-crested wren (*Regulidae Regulus regulus anglorum*), a tiny bird, king of the English, Europe's smallest, equalling in size the wren of the *Troglodytae* tribe, which was stamped on one side of the farthing. Attlee, whoever he was, whatever his relationship to the socialist prime minister, was probably as alert to see the firecrest (*Regulidae Regulus ignicapillus ignicapillus*) (whose upper half is a bit greener than its cousin). Both tiny birds like larch and fir woods and surely Attlee had some prior knowledge of his chances of spotting one or other, or both, using Craigag as a base. I don't know if he saw either.

The Scottish misnaming of the gold-crested wren lay beyond my realising until I saw a pair of preoccupied little birds near the common pasture up in the hills east of Kingsville in Inverness

County, Cape Breton in about 1980. The snow had gone, even from the deeper woods by the warm and dusty little dirt road. The little birds were intent on mating and the brilliant red crest of the male was flaunted unmistakably. This was the second smallest of Canadian visiting birds, the ruby-crested kinglet, or *roitelet à couronne rubis* (*Regulidae Regulus satrapa*) and its identity is not always easy to establish. But, in the happy thraldom of procreation the creature gleefully displays its magnificent crowning glory. The more modern of my bird books allowed me to deduce certainly that it was much the same bird as Scotland's gold-crested wren, belonging to the *Regulidae* tribe. It does not have the kicked-up little tail of the wrens and looks more like a British willow warbler or a chiff-chaff. (The only bird that is smaller in Nova Scotia, a visitor too, is the ruby-throated hummingbird, *le colibri,* light unto something else.)

Iain Campbell worked with my father at the *Daily Mail* (which in those days was at Tanfield where the Water of Leith was crossed by one of the modern roads down to Granton on the Forth – it was a three-hayp'nny one from the top of Granton road on the tram). Iain was a younger man with black, curly hair and he was trapped in fascination with the Gaelic world early. He married a Gaelic-speaking woman from Lewis, I think, and eventually took my father's job at the paper, going on later to edit a newspaper in Holland. I remember him taking photographs at Glenfinnan, one in particular of Willie, Tim and me near Drochaid Sgainneal with the old oak tree in the background; that same tree has furnished me with my concept of a Lochiel oak tree, ancient and gnarly. Thinking back, that old oak stood somewhere near where the Altlaig farm would have been, on the edge of Blàr Creagach [Rocky field/peat bog]. My Iain Campbell is gone.

I have no idea how poor we were when we lived at Craigag, probably not very compared to others but I was unaware of any reverse snobbery, or the burden of any expectation about me. I remember the kindnesses. I was quite unaware of Highland personal sensitivity and pride, or that these had been misunderstood weaknesses at times (these I was to discover in socially conservative rural Cape Breton many years later).

I learned about painted ladies and fritillaries and swallow-tails from a summer holiday spent with a cousin in Bovey Tracey, but I learned about browns and blues on a hillside south of Glenfinnan. I picked up a practice chanter from my oldest brother. From the younger I got an interest in catching trout and on one occasion that I cannot forget he took me fishing with him on a little lochan called on the map Lochan nan Sleubhach [Lochan of the Slaves(?)], high in the hills above a patch of woods on the northern shore of Loch Shiel. I have no idea who the slaves were. To reach the lochan you had to cross the Slatach River, I forget where, and then, the map suggests, follow Allt na h-Aire [Shieling Burn] diagonally to the south to its source. I don't remember the bridge or the climb but I remember the lochan at the top. At its northern end there lay the shallows and from there on that sunny day, as we approached, a handful of good-looking brown trout whipped away into the deeper water. I don't remember if Tim caught any fish, but what I remember is at least one rocky outcrop on the other side of the lochan, part of *Meall a' Bhrodainn* [Hill of the Goad]. On the way down I learned about tiny meadow blues and browns.

Since that time every time I happen on a description of one of the local Jacobite MacDonalds, surely a Glenaladale, watching the Hanoverian redcoats driving cattle from his land in 1746, in my mind's eye I am up near the source of Allt na h-Aire and my anger and outrage is still sharp and unmodified. This was the essence of the spirit which was laughed at in Edinburgh, as though such remarkable military bravery by what was a small portion of one half of the population of Scotland amounted to nothing whatever and deserved no mention (and Edinburgh is called the capital of Scotland). Such a radical division in Scottish society, so driven by pro-English bigotry and ignorance, the last irony having been the championing of modern Scotland for its Presbyterian-inspired education system! For that and other reasons I boarded a plane in Prestwick on the edge of Burns country on 27 January 1966 and was gone.

In 1970, traffic still used the main street in Fort William and the old railway station with its impressive entry was still down near the water on the north-west corner of a little square you came to as you entered the town from the Onich and Ballachulish road. Although I never saw it knowing what it was, I think that part of the old original fort may still have existed as late as 1970 as well, the one that the Jacobites were unable to take in 1746 not long before the end (and most of which was destroyed to accommodate the West Highland Railway). In 2002 the West Highland Railway station was gone and where the lines and yard had been, Fort William had built a new broad ring road with roundabouts to let people drive through non-stop. A newer, even more destructive obeisance. I'm not sure if the Belford hospital was still there in 2002, or the playing field where I first heard a bagpipe band, from the inside. The main street was for pedestrians only and I could not find more than one of the old shops I thought I remembered; the name MacLennan comes to mind and a middle-aged son perhaps. Fort William had been a Highland place, or more accurately, a place with Highlanders in 1950, but in 2002, while I know there were still Gaelic-speakers living there, it was more obviously now a commercial place where time flew by in English and to the rhythms of different registers. I heard no Highland accents.

Notes

1 The lost negatives of Callop, Ardgour

1. Within half a mile there is John Dan MacDonald, Gael, veteran of World War Two. In general, the most culturally conservative NS Gaels who taught me were found in the Roman Catholic areas, the descendants of immigrants from South Uist, Moidart, the Morars, Knoydart, Àrasaig, Lochaber, Strathglass. NB I have only found one emigrant from Callop to anywhere in the New World and he went to Ontario and he was a young single MacMillan man.

2. One shift from the old Gaelic culture to the modern capitalist one, not at all an uncomplicated shift, is given in Gaskell's *Morvern Transformed*.

3. In 1825 Alexander MacLean of Ardgour had for several years forgiven the rents of many of his Blaich crofters and an objective statement of their economic plight, made by his lawyer, Walter Ferrier WS, in August 1825, noted that even with a few acres to cultivate and with anything from two to four cows (and probably a few sheep on the hill as well) they could pay no rent at all. NRAS3583, bundle 8 (pertaining to the setting of teinds by Ardgour, which was related to MacLean's estate income).

4. See '*Memorandum* between NIALL DIARMID CAMPBELL, DUKE of ARGYLL, and sold [*sic*] acting Trustee under Deed of Trust by SHOLTO GEORGE WATSON DOUGLAS, EARL of MORTON . . .' Dated 25 November 1924, in Search Sheet, county of Inverness, 1568, H545 in the Sasine Register. NB The recorded origins of the Douglas family appear to have been in Moray, although they are associated with Lowland Scotland. The name is a Gaelic name. (Tearlach MacFarlane and Ronnie MacKellaig, when their respective children were young and had wandered off in the area of Callop, found the remaining shell of Dalriach. See MacFarlane, letter, 5 January 2007).

5. That the name might have been Blàr Creagaig or any other variant (Blàr Clachaig for example) is speculation. NB The OS six-inch map of the area gives a knoll south-east of the lochan as Tòrr an Lochain while William Roy, identifying the more isolated feature to the east of the loch gave 'Tornatorbert'. See Roy, sheet 23/1.

6. According to Kurt C. Duwe, the 1891 census for Glenfinnan and Loch Iall shows fifty-one households with the top three occupations of the breadwinners: twenty-five shepherds and gamekeepers; eleven crofters, farmers and fishermen; and seven workers (including predominantly farm and domestic servants). See Duwe, '*Alba 1891: Gàidhlig* (Scottish Gaelic) Local Profile.' November 2006 (used with kind permission).

7. Norman MacLeod had *Iain Òg* say this in one of the hillside chats, of the rough Lowland firs in the 1830s, '*a tha iad a nis a' cur air gach cnoc mu na tighean ùra, air an cumadh mar gu-n tigeadh iad o làimh tàilleir, agus a' seasamh 'n an sreathan dòigheil, guala ri gualainn, mar air an fhaiche.*' ['That they are now putting on every hill about the new homes, keeping them as from the hand of a tailor, and standing in neat lines, shoulder to shoulder, as on the parade.'] See MacLeod, *Caraid nan Gàidheal*, p. 21.

8. A pamphlet report of a committee of the Highland Society of Scotland, after the harvest of 1825, included observations on the use of the Flemish scythe. The flaughter spade was the skimmer of the top vegetation, in the Saxon vocabulary, and, since turf was used for walls and roofs, it or a variant must have been used in Gaelic Scotland.

9. There is a collection of Donald MacCulloch photographs in St Andrews University's special collections.

10. According to Tearlach MacFarlane, Joe's grand-uncle was Donald MacLeod, the Glenaladale estate gardener for whom Gatehouse in Glenfinnan was built. See MacFarlane letter, 27 April 2007.

11. According to the occupant of Craigag in October 2002.

12. Robert M. Adam photographed in black and white in the Glenfinnan area in 1920, 1933, 1937, 1938, 1952, 1955 and 1956. While his exposures are important in showing forest and a few tree types, they also contain valuable glimpses of land use and local architecture. The R.M. Adam collection is held by the library archive of the University of St Andrews. (Adam's Callop in flood exposures unfortunately do not show the loch water's easterly limit.)

13. Previously Ardgour and Ardnamurchan and Sunart and Morvern had been in Inverness-shire. See the 70th act in *The Acts of the Parliaments of Scotland*, vol. 5, June 1633, p. 80. Archibald, seventh earl, had contrived to destroy the Clann Iain MacDonalds of Ardnamurchan in favour of himself and his line before he faded into continental (Spanish) Catholicism in 1618. Archibald his successor ran the Argyll estate and had the country boundary changed. His wife was Lady Margaret Douglas, daughter of William, second Earl of Morton. NB Robert Gordon (and R. Morden's) map of Scotland in *c.* 1690 gives *inter alia* the shires of 'Innerarra' and 'Innerness' with the former containing the following 'countries': 'Argile, Laern, Cantire, Ylla, Iura, Mul, Wyst, Teriff, Coll, and Lismore,' and the latter (Innerness) embracing 'Lochabyr, South Part of Ross, and Badenoth.' The Herman Moll map of Scotland, 1745, shows the Inverness–Argyll boundary in the Sound of Mull.

14. Sally MacPhee, Brisbane, has a photograph of a plus-foured Keith MacPhee, visiting from Australia, standing at the gable end of an old stone building in Torebane in 1920. The walls stand perhaps four feet tall and the roofing is modern. The MacPhees first appear at Torebane/Corribeg in the person of Duncan (given as sixty in the 1841 census). Their strong presence in Glengarry County, Ontario, was surely influenced by the Murlagan and Glenpean MacMillan emigration from Kinloch Arkaig and environs to Upper Canada in 1802.

15. See John Thomas, *The West Highland Railway,* p. 56.

16. See Fenton and Walker, *The Rural Architecture of Scotland.* NB The records of the Arisaig and Moidart Parish Council, under the chairmanship of Col. John Andrew MacDonald of Glenaladale show, for 4 May 1896, 'Inspector authorised to have Widow McMillan's house thatched.' See Robertson, 'Arisaig and Moidart Parish Council Minutes.' NB The 1841 census for Clovullin, Ardgour shows eighteen homes (the same number as shown in Admiralty Chart 1426), and elsewhere one can deduce that almost all of the homes were either stone or otherwise meriting recording from ship-board in Loch Linnhe. In 'Trinsleg' there were twelve homes in the census while the chart shows ten. (Bailechelish slate quarries were nearby.)

17. At least part of the main graveyard near Corran in Ardgour was paved over recently. What part dyked enclosuring played in the emigrations from this area is not established, but in Houghgarry, North Uist in 1786 there was a distinct problem. A Duncan Macqueen there complained that he was being fined for cattle straying on to others' land noting that it was inevitable 'where there is no dyke yet.' He also wrote that 'if a dyke has to be built and the cattle confined it will mean that some will be unable to pay their rent.' See NRAS3273/4249. The road-building project must have struck would-be enclosers as fortuitous and indeed Boisdale's mason built a march/boundary dyke between Àrasaig and Allar in 1800. See NRAS2177/B1508.

18. A *fang* (n.f) is generally accepted to be a sheepfold. In Perthshire, according to Dwelly's dictionary, *fang* described also a cattle pen. Allt an Fhaing presents *fang* as a masculine noun, perhaps a derogatory subtlety.

19. Samuel Lewis noted in 1846, that at high tide, seagoing vessels of six or seven tons burden could easily reach Glenfinnan. See Lewis, *Topographical dictionary of Scotland,* 'Ardnamurchan' section.

20. See Sasine Register, county of Inverness, Search Sheet 1568, H545.

21. See letters from Tearlach MacFarlane, 8 November 2006 and 5 January 2007.

22. Lundy is not an uncommon Gaelic place name in Scotland. NB Queen Victoria walked from Abinger's mansion to a neatly squared stone farm building at Lundy Bridge in the fall of 1873.

23. I am indebted to McGill-Queen's University Press for including a photograph I made of Margaret MacLean in *Old and New World Highland Bagpiping* (in John Zucchi's Studies in Ethnic History series), 2002.

24. The distinctly Flemish origins of the Camerons, Campbells, Bethunes, Comines and many other medieval incomers to the north is here acknowledged but the generic 'Norman' has been used simply for the sake of brevity.

25. I have this translation from *Seumas* Watson, Queensville, Cape Breton.

26. An ardent academic disquisition of the evils of Scottish Presbyterian theocracy in Covenanting times is found in M.E.M. Donaldson's *Scotland's Suppressed History*. (John Telfer Dunbar noted that Donaldson's statements were never refuted. See *Herself*, p. 30).

27. Under the parish heading there is no mention of Alexander Fraser in *Fasti Ecclesiae*, vol. 8, p. 344. Neither did Hew Scott include Revd Malcolm McCaskill at Kilmallie in the 1750s, suggesting to the curious a convenient oversight, to the cynical a period of rigorous conversion without sufficient outside observation.

28. NAS RH4/93/1.

29. The subject of the persistence of Celtic law into the diaspora years of the nineteenth century, at the popular un-literate level of custom, is not well studied. One possible example is quite insufficient but the following one from Ardnamurchan is an interesting reminder of older times and attitudes. On 19 July 1837 Duncan MacLachlan (Glendrian) and Christy Henderson (Achnaha) 'were jointly fined three pounds for illicit sex. She was his late wife's sister.' See MacLean, *Night Falls on Ardnamurchan*, p. 40. (The amount of the fine itself suggests radically discountenanced/threatening behaviour to the Presbyterian church.)

30. R. Andrew McDonald's *Outlaws of Medieval Scotland: Challenges to the Canmore Kings, 1058–1266* (2003) studies the reaction of people in $^{11}/_{12}$ of what is thought of as Scotland (plus or minus parts of what is modern England) to the incursion of alien polity and religious practices in the second half of the eleventh century (beginning with the Hungarian-born, Saxon princess wife of the Gaelic King Malcolm III (Ceann Mór), Margaret, but most notably with the Norman and Normanesque incursions sponsored by their youngest son King David I in the twelfth century (*reg.* 1124–1153). The identities of 'a variety of native warlords and discontented dynasts' are identified but inevitably a profounder overview is denied for want of corroborating written evidence from the losing side. See *Outlaws*, p. ix. The reporting available was non-'Scottish' Gaelic. There persists for me in its pages and wisdom a slightly distorted ethno- and politico-centricness, which, while praising the scholarship of W.F. Skene and E.W. Robertson, follows a post-Celtic thread.

     In his study of King Robert *de Brus* Barrow wrote that at the battle of 'Bannok Burn' on 24 June 1314 'The Highlanders, islesmen and others serving under the king's own standard, chafing with impatience [as one may imagine] at not yet having taken any part, now rushed upon the enemy in a rage.' See Barrow, *Robert Bruce*, p. 325. This idea has been repeated *ad nauseam* in Scottish histories with no satisfactory evidence as to which Highland leaders were present or the numbers of Gaels they led, or if Highlanders actually formed the majority of the king's brigade; presumably the others were people from *de Brus*'s properties. The element of post-facto, deliberate, manipulative inclusion of Gaels, in 'national' events such as this, and in the often-offered Gaelic origins of what were, almost certainly, early Norman and Flemish families in Scotland (like Forbes, Fraser, Chisholm, Cumming, Bethune/ Beaton, Campbell and Cameron), is very seldom emphasised.

Even in a scholarly collection of studies, like Jennifer M. Brown's *Scottish Society in the Fifteenth Century* (1977), there seems to have to have been down-grading distortion found in an introductory phrase of hers like (Dr John W.M. Bannerman) 'Here . . . provides the opportunity to look at a local society in detail and in depth. It is a fascinating study.' Bannerman's own words about the territory of the Lordship of the Isles are, 'a province of Scotland is being considered here.' Gaelic Scotland cannot be so jealously segregated.

31. Campbell interest in Cameron leadership, including inter-marriages and other bondings, is noticeable in the seventeenth century. Eoghan Dubh Cameron (b. 1629) was a son of a daughter of Campbell of Glenfalloch. Eoghan Dubh's son John Cameron of Locheil married a daughter of Campbell of Lochnell (by whom he fathered Donald, Dr Archie, Fassifern, and Fr Alexander Cameron, most active Jacobites in 1745–46).

32. See Allardyce, *Historical Papers,* p. 534.

33. The earliest 'Oban [and] a cave' comes from the William Roy map of the area, drawn up between 1749 and 1755. See Roy, Sheet 12/4.

34. Thomas Kitchin's 'A new and complete map of Scotland and islands thereto belonging' (1773) mentions 'Raitland', 'Ardglash', 'Meobole', 'Oban', and below Oban, 'a cave'. William Roy's map (1749–1755) shows 'Oban a cave' and 'Retallan', *inter alia*.

John MacDonald Esquire of Borrodale (*c.* 1754–1830), around 1815, had a plan of his lands of Achranich drawn up by Alexander Langlands, lithographer. NRAS656/1/15. Achranich was a farm in south Morvern at the head of Loch Aline on the Ardtornish side. It had belonged until bankruptcy in 1775 to the Camerons of Glendessary and reflected the once-close marriage and Gaelic political ties between Morvern and the Camerons. Langlands was responsible for the 1801 map of Argyll referred to below. See Maudlin, 'Tradition and change . . . houses in Morvern.' NB Morvern, in Argyllshire since 1633, hitherto part of Inverness-shire, was peopled by many Jacobite MacLeans for the most part until 1745–6 but belonged to the Duke of Argyll. Archibald Campbell, the third Duke of Argyll, in retaliation for Drimnin MacLean loyalty to King James, re-set his huge property almost completely under Campbell tacksmen in and from 1754.

35. NRAS2177, bundle 1522. Letters to Robert Brown (Jan–Mar 1804). Borrodale's new house at Achranich by Loch Aline in southern Morvern was built *c.* 1815.

36. Highland farming co-operatives. There was at least one club farm in Morvern, Keppoch, and Glenelg in the first half of the nineteenth century.

A letter from Colonel David Robertson Macdonald to Clanranald's factor in 1806 or 1807 shows the last throes of 'let's keep 'em out'. 'The offers are as yet entirely from the old set who will wish to keep strangers at a distance in hopes of getting Clanranald's lands and mine at a very low rent.' NRAS2177, bundle 1532.

37. From 'Miann a Bhaird Aosda' ['The Wish of the Ancient Bard'], in *Sar-Obair*, p. 14 (my translation).

38. RMA H-922. St Andrews University photographic archives.

2 *Craigag*/*Cregag*/*Creagag*/Craigegg

1. Interestingly, 'Craigag' is positioned south of the road in the Bartholomew half-inch map series, Number 50, 'Arisaig and Lochaber', 1972. The source used appears to have been the OS six-inch series surveyed in the 1870s. (There is no Craigag, or Calap, Lodge shown although it had been there for almost a century.) There was a tendency among cartographers to copy without checking.

2. Sholto George Watson Douglas, nineteenth Earl of Douglas 'disponed away by disp. to The West Highland Railway Coy' 10 564/1000 acres (of his 35,825-acre Conaglen estate). The record is dated 28 May 1900 in the Search Sheet, County of Inverness, 1568, folio H542. The deal was that the railway must not build any building to the east of Craigag Lodge nearer than the 'Burn'.

3. Meoble in South Morar, for example, was advertised as a sheep-farm to let, beginning Whitsunday next after September 1879, 24,000 acres 'suitable for a deer forest', 'already well stock with Deer', with shootings and fishings. *The Scotsman*, 17 Sept. 1879. The six-inch OS map of Meoble shows the sheepfolds. In one part of Argyllshire, lore of the nineteenth century written in 1966 by Donald Cameron/Alasdair MacLean states that some families were 'forced to build the stone dykes'. See *Field of Sighing*, p. 51. The folk to be cleared did a last, forced service for the clearers. (The game-shooting phenomenon began early in the nineteenth century in many places.)

4. NAS GD253/129/19, a bundle of fifty-two documents to which I have chosen not to buy access.

5. The prospectus for the sale of 'The estates of Inverscadle, Stronchrigan, and others 1858' estimated the value of the shooting rent at £250, and later mentioned the shooting lodge at Blaich. Craigag Lodge, and fishing with the use of a boat on Loch Shiel, were advertised for rent until July, in *The Scotsman* of 28 April 1934. Applications were invited by 'Hon. R. Douglas, Dalendrien [Ardgour], Fort William.'

6. 'Càrn' a stone, and its derivative *càrnach*, conceivably hinting at a quarry, seem plausible suggestions for a meaning of Lochan na Càrnaich. The genitive sense conveyed by the phrase, *lochan na càrnach* may suggest an alternate meaning. Carnach is a common Highland place name. The Clanranald–Cameron line would have been an important place for a sheep dyke. My brother Tim wrote that he wet fly-fished the lochan many times in the late 1940s and mentioned dykes. Lots of trout meant small trout. The fishing would have been part of the advertised attraction of

Craigag Lodge from the 1870s. NAS GD150/3820 (Papers of the earls of Morton 1250–1940) show a march fence was set up between Cregag and Glenfinnan in 1881.

7. Another Allt na Crìche drains from the north into Loch Eilt (known *c.* 1800 as Loch Ranach) at Arienskill in Àrasaig, and another lies just north of Fort Augustus, and an Allt Lochan nan Trì Chriochan drains into the west end of Loch Beoraid in South Morar. There is also an Alta na Crìche that joins the Feshie river above that river's junction with the Spey; it is known cartographically also as Allt a' Mharcaidh. (See, Munro and Munro, *Acts,* p. 148). NB The modern Glenfinnan estate includes land to the east of the old Gaelic border, reaching to the Dubh Lighe but not including Craigag.

8. I could not use Mahmoud Abdurrhaman Raif's 1804 map of Scotland with Arabic script. I have discovered no motive for this inclusion of Highland Scotland in a Muslim's map. Two notes that I can think to add are the high number of Scotch Gaels who fought the French near enough Alexandria in 1801, the number who were taken alive (deliberately) by Mehmet Ali at El Hamet in the Nile Delta in 1806, and the fitfully fluctuating interest on the part of the sultan in modernising the army of the Porte at about that time.

9. 'Proposals for cantoning', in Allardyce, *Historical Papers*, ch. 36, vol. 2.

10. GD201/1/281. Papers of the MacDonald Family of Clanranald, title deeds, contracts, bonds etc., 1520–1859.

11. Broad-leaved trees were the accompanying symbol to a slated-roof house to indicate a 'gentleman's seat' in George Langlands & Son's map of Argyllshire in 1801.

In the Old Statistical Account, Revd Archibald Clerk, writing the Ardnamurchan parish entry in 1838 (possibly including 1839) described three schemes for the protection of woodland. Young trees were sometimes enclosed for seven to ten years; sometimes cattle were kept out for fifteen to twenty years with or without careful pasturing at times; some woods were permanently enclosed. See OSA, vol. 7, 150. A Donald MacArthur, Portbane (east end of Loch Tay) is on record as complaining for not being completely paid 'for quarrying stones to build a dyke round a clump of firs planted in Ardradnaig this previous year [1792].' See NAS GD112/11/3/3/85, 4 Nov. 1793.

In improver/commercial times, Alexander MacLean of Ardgour had his gardener, Hugh Kennedy, keep a record of tree planting from 1805 to 1834 and on the 'Farm of Cuill in Ardgour,' between February 1810 and 10 April 1812, 373,300 trees were planted. They were ornamentals but the motive was primarily commercial.

According to Fiona MacLean, in 1809, 94,000 seedlings were obtained from the 'Nursery at Oban' and 61,00 from the nursery at Cuil in Ardgour. In 1810, 81,000 three-year old treelets were used from the Cuil nursery and 165,000 'thorus' were obtained from Oban, 120,000 of which were transplanted to the Cuil nursery. Thenceforward all seedlings planted out were from the Ardgour nursery at Cuil. E-mail from Fiona MacLean, 1 November 2006.

In or just before 1835 MacLean had enclosed and planted 'several spots' with firs.

OSA, vol. 14, p. 120. In 1838 there was a market for railway ties/sleepers, planks and deals (from which MacLean could have profited). The market for ties existed in 1868 and 1869 and probably was attractive until the end of the nineteenth century. In 1856 a comparative study was made of the cost of fencing with larch or wire. See NRAS3583/B, bundle 39. No Hugh Kennedy appears in the 1841 census, from 'Inversander' to Cregag. (At home number eight at Achaphubuil/Achadh a' Phubuil there lived a widow Mary Kennedy (60) whose oldest son living at home was a weaver, Ewan [Eoghan/Hugh] Kennedy; at the only home in Dalandrain there was Donald Kennedy, 'ag lab' 55, Ann, 50 and (son?) Ewan, 20, in a group of six below the parents). NB Lloyd Laing wrote that birch, alder and willow were used as winter fodder in the Norwegian pastoral economy *c.* 700. See Laing, *The Archaeology of Late Celtic Britain and Ireland,* p. 179.

12. The holly may have been an escape, or descendant of an escape from the holly hedge that till not long before 1858 surrounded Fassifern House. See Clerk, *Memoir,* p. 13.

13. In 1746 the glen was called 'Glendylie' by the governor of Fort William, Alexander Campbell.

14. See Revd Angus MacLean entry in the NSA, for Ardnamurchan parish, 1838, NSA vol. 7, p. 162. Forestation was the first of two main physical differences that would have been noticed by a visit by the author of the OSA entry of about forty years earlier, in the 1790s. The other would have been the barrenness of what had been the old 'outfield arable'. NSA vol. 7, p. 162.

15. GD201/5/1231/42. The broken line used in the six-inch OS maps marked the ditches.

16. Sir John Murray (1841–1914), the moving force in the bathymetrical survey of the freshwater lochs of Scotland, was born in Coburg, Ontario, son of a Scottish immigrant.

17. On the north Morar estate owned by General Simon Fraser there is a record of the local people using, *gratis,* the wood on the estate in the 1770s – perhaps to Fraser it was superfluous to the woods around Beaufort Castle in richer country near Inverness. Nearer to Loch Shiel, on Loch Sunart but in Ardnamurchan to the south, a wood-keeper's house is marked on Alexander Bruce's *Plan of Loch Sunart* in 1733. The 1841 census of Dalilea on the north shore of Loch Shiel, in Moidart, shows a locally born Alex Smith, boat carpenter. Loch Shiel was the old highway.

     As Gaelic populations moved and were forced away from the farm, fewer people were available to keep hill sheep from cattle grazings/shielings and garden lands thus speeding the transition from bovine to ovine.

18. In the old Gaelic world a traveller's rights crossing another's land included taking wood enough for a fire.

19. M.E.M. Donaldson looking out from the railway station, presumably *c.* 1922, noted a preponderance of larches in Glenfinnan. See *Wandering,* p. 23.

20. *Sgainneal,* scandal, is a masculine noun (a quo, *dail (an) sgainneil*); *sgainneart,*

scattering, is feminine (a quo *dail (na) sgainneirt*).

21. Since the Union of 1707, Scots had no intra-Scottish recourse, as the common man had no intrudable claim to make on land ownership since the annullment of the heritable jurisdictions after the Forty-five.

22. John Cameron of Fassifern's sworn statement, made in 1750, for losses suffered at the hands of the men of the Duke of Cumberland in 1746 and 1747, is to be read in NAS E768 papers and in Somerled MacMillan's *Bygone Lochaber*. The latter also touches on the suspicion against him of conniving to have the Locheil estate pass into the hands of an old, autochthonous Gaelic family, the Macgillonies. Fassifern did many years' court-decreed exile in England. The post-Culloden animus shown by Hanoverian forces against farms on the Locheil estate was honed by the fact that Locheil's superior was the Hanoverian Duke of Argyll who resented free political and military expression, and by the fact that the two families, for whatever reason and at whoever's instigation, were intertwined by several important marriages.

23. John Cameron held Fassifern from his brother Locheil and the latter held the bulk of Cameron estate from the Duke of Argyll, and had done since the Earl of Argyll arranged the acquisition in the early seventeenth century (see MacMillan, *Bygone Lochaber*. See also Campbell, *History,* vol. 2, p. 154). From 1675 at least until 1718, Fassifern had been a wadset holding of a MacLachlan family, and its loss to them has remained beyond my enquiry. (The *c.* 1710 Robert Johnson map of Fort William gives the place 'Fashi-Fairn' (along with 'Asterlow' and 'Annet'). The notion of ownership has to be carefully considered in eighteenth-century Highland Scotland for there were many levels of something akin to ownership below the superior or Crown. Papers of the forfeited estates show that, between 1751 and 1769, John of Fassifern was taking rents from the farms at Corpach and Achnacarry and paying feu duty for his wadset of Fassifern.

    The terminology used by John Cowley in his 1734 map of the Duke of Argyll's heritable dukedom and justiciary territories, islands, superiorities and jurisdictions carefully delineate that on land that 'belonged' to the duke, other people 'possess'd' holdings. 'Swenart' for example, was 'Possess'd by Camerons.' Most of the lordship of Morvern belonged to the duke but was 'Possess'd all by Camerons' and Sir Alexander Murray's Ardnamurchan was 'almost wholly Possess'd by Campbells and their Followers'. Cowley's map was published in Sir Alexander Murray of Stanhope's *The true interest of Great Britain,* in 1740.

24. 'Water of Finallie' from GD201/5/1231/42, p. 15. Both Gleann an t-Sùileig and Allt an t-Sùileig use a masculine definite genitive form of the feminine *sùileag*.

25. See MacMillan, *Bygone Lochaber,* p. 139.

26. Dungallon was either first cousin to John of Fassifern or first cousin once removed. Dungallon had a slated gentleman's house at Glen Hurich in Sunart, Ardnamurchan parish.

    The Scottish Record Society's 'Commissariot of Edinburgh Consistorial Processes and Decreets 1658–1800' shows that Alexander Cameron of Dungallon (d. 1759) had a daughter Christian who married, at Fort William, 27 January 1767,

David Carnegie (Lord Rosehill, dvpsp/*decessit vita patris sine prole*/died childless in his father's lifetime) eldest son of the Earl of Northesk whose estate was near Arbroath in Angus. Upward social mobility via the Lowland gentry was widespread and may have affected estate management and attitudes to the traditional tenantry in Sunart. NB www.thepeerage.com claims that David, Lord Rosehill (1749–1788), married in August 1768 one Catherine Cameron who was also known as 'Mary Cheer'.

27. Alexander Cameron of Drumnasallie, a Jacobite captain, sixth in the list of Cameron officers in 1745, was killed in early 1746 at Fort William. His brother, Evan/Ewan, died of wounds taken at Culloden, in 1750. See *No Quarter Given*, p. 35.

28. Between the road at the southern edge of the woodland and the river Dubh Lighe was given in the six-inch map as Lòn Druim na Saille; to the south of the river the flat land was called Lòn Druim na Fearna.

29. The presence of stalwart old willows in Inverness county still makes me wonder if the bark or other parts were used by Highlanders for medicinal purposes. I have no evidence that it or any part was, and none but one tenuous suggestion for Cameron country just north of Loch Eil. The first MacVean to settle in Cameron country came from Skye in the mid seventeenth century, as tutor to the Lochiel family, according to MacVean lore. MacVean is perhaps a version of Beaton and the best-known Beaton family in Skye was a line of hereditary medical doctors.

30. NAS GD170/1588 (1789) and GD170/1057 (1763-1767). In the same GD170 collection there is a letter from '?P' Cameron, 20 November 1787, at Calloch, to Alexander Campbell of Barcaldine, writer, explaining that he, Cameron, had a licence for brewing, and that he wanted (to buy) barley. NB John of Fassifern had a son Peter. The same Barcaldine, in 1785, received, and saved, a letter from a Hector Gillies, Peneygoun, in which Gillies made an offer to buy barley. There were marriage ties between the prominent Camerons and middling Campbells. For example, Alexander Campbell of Barcaldine (1745–1800) had a sister (Louisa) who was married to John's son, Ewen Cameron of Fassifern (1740–1828), and a brother Hugh Campbell married to a daughter of a Fassifern. At the Annat in Appin, near Barcaldine, a family of brewers called Carmichael flourished in some secure leasing tenure in the late sixteenth century in the (long-established?) person of a 'Gillemechaell McEwne VcGillechallum VcEwne VcUnche VcGilleme-chaell', between 21 December 1595 and 27 January 1596. See, GD170/44. A member of this Carmichael family is recorded in Glasgow in the eighteenth century.

31. Another chalybeate spring is shown on the six-inch map at *Drochaid Druim na Saille*. This bridge was reported as 'Auchadalea' by the reporter of Queen Victoria's visit to Kinlocheil in early September 1873. This appears to be an anglicised version of Achadh an Dail Lighe [Field of the Valley of the Lighe]. Here, where the queen turned back for Inverlochy, was described to her as where Locheil bit the thrapple out of a Sassenach enemy.

32. John Guthrie, owner of the Conaglen estate and son of the man who bought it in

1959 from a Michael Mason, noted that in 1959 Craigag was 'the one property that was not included.' Michael Mason had bought the Conaglen estate from the Earl of Morton in 1953 and owned it till 1959. He was the Michael Henry Mason who wrote seven travel books between 1924 and 1934 including *Deserts Idle* (1928) in which there is a hint that the author knew Highland Perthshire. John Guthrie wrote that Mason, whose home was in Eynsham Park, Oxfordshire, was thought to have worked in British intelligence during the war and was a friend of Ian Fleming. Guthrie added that there had been, a few years ago, speculation that Mason had been Fleming's inspiration for James Bond. (Mason's son David, born 1951, began his novel *Shadow over Babylon* with a Highland deer-stalking incident on an estate whose access was a one-lane road with passing places.) The other connection with James Bond comes through Captain Bill Sykes, a trainer of special agents who was based at Àrasaig during the war (1942–4), and a friend of Major Gavin Maxwell. Sykes was an expert on throttling and is reported to have been the model for one of Fleming's nefarious characters.

33. NRAS3583/B, bundle 6. 1844 appears to have been the first year of an income having been recorded for shooting on Ardgour. NB A single-storey, three-bay cottage built of harled rubble on boulder footings, in Blaich, in 1817 was converted into a Church of Scotland church (then a mission church). It was in decaying condition, with a slate roof, and an attempt to sell it had failed in 2005. It was owned or managed by the Scottish Civil Trust.

34. Old (Ranald) Clanranald (d. 1766), who had gone to court over the technical illegality of the forfeiture of his estate in 1748 won it back in 1751, and from later land dispositions within the estate it appears that Bruce's holding(s) were conditional upon the victory of the barons of exchequer. On the surface Clanranald's land dealings look like clever bribes.

35. That Cregag farm may once have been in Argyllshire seems to be implicit in the following: 'Extract Interim (In Duplicate) Decr. By Lords of Council and Session in Petition of said Sholto George Watson Douglas, Earl of Morton, – inter alia, approving of instrument of Disentail (dated 13 Feb. 1907) by said Earl, – of lands and Farms of Inverscadle, Conaglen, and others, in Parish of Kilmallie and Counties of Argyll and Inverness (formerly in County of Argyll alone) in which said Earl is infeft conform to Exract Decr. Of Sp.Serv. Recorded in this Register (County of Argyll) 4 Dec. 1885.' Search Sheet, county of Inverness, 1568, folio H543.

36. The steel engraving by Joseph Swan (1796–1872) of the original painting of the Glenfinnan monument by John Fleming (1794–1845), entitled *Loch Shiel (Argyll-shire) from Tor-a-Chant, looking South West* that was published in 1834 in *The Lakes of Scotland,* shows, from three-quarters, a two-storey, three-bayed, slate-roofed, two chimneyed (at each gable end), harled and white-washed house. Three upstairs windows face the loch to the building's east, and there appear to be three on the ground floor level. The building resembles the Langlands symbol for a gentleman's

seat, but giving more windows. It was typical of late eighteenth-century modern/ improver houses. If it was a different building to the one Glenaladale occupied in 1873, remains should be discoverable. 'Tor-a-Chant' is nowhere else identified. The degree of liberty taken by Glaswegian engraver, copperplate printer, lithographer and lithographic printer Swan with Fleming's accurate representations is not known but compromises were probably needed.

37. Colonel Alexander MacLean of Ardgour's factor in 1826, Patrick Henderson (factor from *c.* 1817 to Martinmas 1833), wrote to Ardgour 'as to assumed old and new place names of lands in Ardgour estate, and with copy letter from Donald Currie, schoolmaster at Strontian, of 1 December 1826.' A letter from Ardgour of 19 December that year, recipient unknown, dealt with 'place-names which were parts and pendicles of other farms'. NRAS3583/B, bundle 8.

38. NSA, vol. 14, p. 123. Parish of Kilmallie entry by Revd Donald M'Gillivray, 1835.

39. Thomson and Johnston marked the old road as ending just over the river 'Camme' south of Bunacaimb in 1820, now given as Allt cam carach, the boundary between Àrasaig and South Morar, on the Landranger OS map.

40. The 1872 survey shows useful heights but with 'approximate Mean Water at Liverpool' as the standard, but does not give contours.

41. In 1881 a Margaret MacGregor (41), wife, seven children, a tutor, a barmaid, a waiter, two housemaids and a cook were enumerated in the census in Banavie.

42. In 1842 the Campell Marquess of Breadalbane denied to drovers the use of the old traditional drovers' stance at Inverouran and Inverveach near Bridge of Orchy. This threatened the Ardgour and Clanranald and Cameron droves of cattle and sheep heading south via the Black Mount on the fringe of Rannoch Moor. See NRAS 3583, bundle 28. The case dragged on for several years and is a marker for the death of an old tradition. An unpaved relic of the old style of road still exists in the Ariundle area. It lies, slightly cambered perhaps, between two foot-wide containings, with the ditch on the upper side.

43. MacVeans were associated with both properties. The other Mac Bheathain place name is Stob mhic Bheathain between Glen Scaddle and Cona Glen in interior Ardgour.

44. Kilmallie is now part of Corpach and lying just east of the Lochiel Annat.

45. The 1861 census gives the only Hugh MacLachlan as head of household nine and aged 64. (This is the same Revd Archibald Clerk who wrote the Ardnamurchan OSA report.)

46. Assuming that Glenfinnan was on an old cattle droving route, as A.R.B. Haldane implies in *The Drove Roads of Scotland* (p. 71), then it is possible that in good weather cattle forded nearer the mouth of the Finnan than the footbridge. The location of the rest, or stance, may have been the flat headlands. Apparent boundaries shown on the six-inch map of the 1870s, especially the short straight one at the sharp corner, may have been, first and foremost herd containments. I remember rig outlines at the

east of the headland but the rigs on the hills of *Tom na h-Aire* in 1920 suggest the main dry-land higher arable.

47. R.M. Adam's 1955 photograph shows the switchback nature of the corner and betrays enough evidence of the steepness of the slope at the apex to leave one sure that the road would have taken the corner rather than cutting up through the trees. See RMA, H11106A.

   Coming in the other direction that turn was the magical inner door to Clanranald. It has only recently been blasted away for ever to accommodate a two-lane blacktop and long transport trucks/fish lorries, tourist buses and caravans.

48. The narrows separating Moidart and Sunart, all but blocked by *Eilean Fhianain*, could not let the rains and melting snows escape fast enough from the main loch. This had two effects. The first was to cause the level of the main body of Loch Shiel to rise, flooding the headland and the Callop valley to the north-east. The second was to inundate Claish Moss in the smaller, west–east part of the loch from *Eilean Fhianain* to Acharacle. I have no record of Claish's ever having been farmed or lived on.

3 Getting away from Saxon Scotland, and early impressions

1. Adam's 1920 photograph, *View from a knoll*, seems to show no building where the shop was. A.J. Valentine photograph, JV-D2503 (Lib. U. St Andrews), shows a 1957 version of the shop, painted white and with a gate, which was then called 'Prince Charlie's tearooms'. There was a car park lot in front, with a few black cars.

2. For some outside observers of course, late-eighteenth-century Highlanders were gaunt and haggard, uninventive, beggarly poor and imprisoned, only vaguely employed, and in an economic and social trough of despondency.

3. These Munros were from the parish of Fearn in Easter Ross and there there is a Castlehaven.

4 Iseabal Friseal, Glenfinnan

1. Giusachan still lay in the parish of Ardnamurchan in 1902. The parish then ran from the Callop in the north and included the wooded Eilean Fhionnain. It was abutted to the east by Ardgour parish. An indication of Cameron distribution in 1746 is seen in the suggestions made by Donald Campbell of Airds to 'Lord Justice Clerk of Scotland' Andrew Fletcher, and the Earl of Albemarle, that 100 government soldiers be stationed at Strontian, another 100 at Kinlocharkaig, 70 at the head of Lochyell, 50 at Achnacarry, 50 at Highbridge and 60 in Glencoe. See 'Scheme for Civilising the Clan Cameron', 3 October 1746. The military significance of the lead ore at

Strontian is overlooked and will be addressed later.

2. The six-inch map including Giusachan, surveyed in 1874, shows that the bridge over the river at Giusachan is Drochaid na Craoibhe Daraich [Bridge of the Oak Tree], and that the bay created to the south-west of the little delta is Camas na Craoibhe Daraich [Bay of the Oak Tree].

3. Fergus Kelly wrote that one of the few rights that men of appropriate social status in early Irish society had over private property was the right to cut wood enough to cook with (presumably while travelling). See Kelly, *Guide to Early Irish Law,* p. 106. James Riddell and the Earl of Morton (presumably George Sholto Douglas (1789–1858)) had prominent places in the group of select Scotsmen who greeted HM Queen Victoria at Edinburgh in 1850. See *Anderson's History of Edinburgh,* pp. 567–8. NB W.A. Speck described the collecting of firewood in the Great Park (presumably Windsor Forest) as 'an immemorial [English] custom.' It was a custom that met with the disapproval of the new (Windsor) forest ranger in 1746, William, Duke of Cumberland. See Speck, *The Butcher,* p. 202.

4. The persecution of Revd John MacCalman, minister of Kilchrenan & Dalavich, in Barcaldine, in 1685 and 1708 illustrates the heatedness (I presume he was a Presbyterian). See SC54/17/3/2 and SC54/17/4/8/1.

   The citation dating to 1736, 'There are here and sometimes Three Popish Priests for ordinary travelling through this parish [Kilmallie] and in the Neighbourhood, and it is not possible for the Minister thereof to be so often among them as necessary', shows the widespread popularity of Roman Catholicism in Kilmallie and explains the thoroughness of the post-1746 Presbyterian reaction, both at the minister and the catechist level. See 'A State of Popery in Scotland' NAS CH1/5/119, p.11 (cited in Prunier, *Anti-Catholic Strategies,* p. 93).

   While Hew Scott's self-imposed mandate does not explore the imposure of ministers in the forfeited estates by outside controllers after Culloden, Kilmallie's list of ministers shows this local religious powerlessness. See *Fasti,* vol. 4, pp. 134 and 135.

5. In 1755, from Webster's census returns, there is the report by Reverend William Grant, Kilmonivaig parish (presumably to William Ross, agent of the Church of Scotland and clerk to the SSPCK) which notes 'so many papists, people Outlaw'd & of bad fame in the parish.' Kilmonivaig abuts Kilmallie to the east. See Prunier, *Anti-Catholic Strategies,* p. 51. (Source: NAS RH15/105/9.)

6. CS96/3377 (1811–12) and 3378 (1812–17). Sederunt books pertaining to James MacDonald. In 1813, perhaps until 1817, his superior was Alexander MacDonald of Glenalladale (who was succeeded by his first cousin once removed, Angus Mac-Donald Esq. of Glenaladale, son of John of Borrodale), GD201/1/341.

7. John Cameron, RE, (b. St Amand, French Flanders, 31 March 1817, d. 30 June 1878) was in charge of the Dublin office of the OS from 1846 to 1852; he was executive officer of the survey from 1852 to 1873. He was made director general on 11 August 1875, a post he held till his death. The OS six-inch map of Glenfinnan

was published, under his watch, on 31 March 1877 and he is credited as Major General John Cameron, RE, CB, FRS. See Seymour, *History of the Ordnance Survey*, p. 167. Cameron left the OS in 1874 when promoted to major general but returned as director in 1875. Sackler Archive of the Royal Society, GB117 EC/1868/08. (Military List, 2nd Lt. 10 Dec. 1834). He died a brevet lieutenant general.

8. William Roy's pre-1755 map gives two places in the area, 'Taynaslatich' (Tigh na Slataich) and 'Garbole' (Garbh Allt?). The latter lay east of the Finnan and to the south of where the railway viaduct is today, presumably above the high flood-water mark. See, Search Sheet, 12/5.

9. The pronunciation of the Gaelic place names such as Omhanaich and Sròn an t-Sìthein for example, have more syllables than their English equivalents, Onich and Strontian – one reason for the observation of many Lowland Scots that Gaelic is a slowly-spoken language.

10. On 26 June 2006 there was no record of the exact date of construction of 'the castle' among the papers of the Scottish Catholic Archives in Edinburgh. See letter to the author from Caroline Cradock, SCA.

11. The priest's youngest spinster sister, Jane MacDonald, surely the *chatelaine* at the Glenaladale House, died aged 70, on 16 December 1874. After Revd Donald died, Glenaladale House and estate were let by John of Glenaladale (*c.*1838–1916) for fourteen years beginning in August 1896 to Major Sir Theodore Francis Brinckman, 3rd Bt (1862–1937), who, in 1895, had remarried and who planned a pheasant-raising business for his Highland estate. Brinckman's name appears in *The Scotsman*, 3 March 1898, as the instigator of a court case against the West Highland Railway extension. He claimed damages of £4,550 for his loss to the railway of seventy-four acres of his rented property (for which he was paying £1,000 per annum). The case lapsed, apparently because the major was called to service in the South African/Boer War.

12. Roy's map shows no home or field markings here so either he wasn't there because of the Clanranald challenge (1748–51) over forfeiture or those rigs were latter-day workings.

13. The Revd Alexander Campbell, who wrote the Old Statistical Account of the parish of Ardnamurchan in the 1790s, admitted that the parish actually con-tained five old 'countries', Ardnamurchan peninsula, Sunart, Moidart, Àrasaig and South Morar. Ardnamurchan parish lay in two Highland counties, Argyll and Inverness.

14. With the building of the new big house Angus moved the family from Borrodale in Àrasaig to Glenfinnan; he was 'proprietor' of the first house at Borrodale in 1861 (among seventeen people). In the 1881 census, the sixth household in Glenfinnan, the one that included Fr Donald MacDonald, also included the priest's nephew John (43), John's mother (a 65-year-old lady born in Edinburgh) and a dairymaid and a cook among the five servants.

15. Joseph Swan's etching, painted by John Fleming, some time in the mid-1830s (see

Leighton's *Views of the Lakes of Scotland*, 1837) seems to show to small sailing vessels close to shore about where the present big house wharf is. NB There is a claim made at the Glenfinnan Jacobite monument exhibit that, having landed on 19 August 1745, the royal party crossed a river and climbed to the top of a prominent hill to unfurl their invasion statement. The six-inch map of the 1870s shows a boathouse in the little bay to the south-west of the Slatach river. Had the party landed there, or even on the deep-water side of the Slatach, the west side, then the only river they had to cross to reach the knoll behind the modern school was the Slatach.

16. From Canon Bernard Canning's *Irish-born secular priests in Scotland, 1829–1979*. Fr Patrick Joseph O'Regan D.D. (1904–1971), born at Ratharoon, Bandon in county Cork, was educated at the Scots College in Rome and ordained at Rome, for Argyll and the Isles, in 1930. He served as a curate at St Columba's, Edinburgh in 1930–1, then as parish priest at St Mary's, Benbecula (1931–40), at Saint Mary and Saint Finnan's, Glenfinnan (1940–62), and at The Visitation, Taynuilt, Argyll (1962–71). He was largely responsible for the South Ford Bridge, named after him, joining Benbecula and South Uist. His entry in the obituaries in *Catholic Directory for Scotland,* 1972, expands on Fr O'Regan's (then unaccepted) theory of the birthplace of St Patrick at Banavie, and adds that O'Regan suffered nervous breakdowns and bad health at Glenfinnan, the site of 'the huge church at Glenfinnan' where he had found it hard trying 'to maintain the fabric of this colossal pile against the ravages of weather'. Little wonder that an invasion of his home to free a chaffinch might have caused anger on the teacher's part. (Fr O'Regan also built a little wooden church, St Columbkille, at Kinlocheil.)

5 John 'the post' MacDonell and others of the last generation of Gaels

1. The sasine (record of land transfer) dates to 13 March 1784 when the general's representatives confirmed the land's passing to Frasers of Lovat, and Simon's successor, Archibald Campbell Fraser. Archibald at that point owned outright both North and South Morar, the general having bought North Morar in the 1760s.

2. By at least one writer of the South Morar affairs in the late eighteenth and early nineteenth century its oddness was resolved by writing 'Maybole'. Some time before 1947 the postman had to walk at least three times a week to Kinlochbeoraid to pick up outgoing mail, but he had to go every working day on which there was incoming.

3. Alasdair Roberts, *Tales of the Morar Highlands,* pp. 29–41.

4. See letter from Tearlach MacFarlane, 13 April 2007.

5. In May and December 2006 Allan Campbell of Mountain Bothies Association took digital photographs of an old-modern stone house up Gleann Dubh Lighe. In front stands an old cherry tree. Workers for MBA had unearthed a neatly built old path to

the house; I have no memory of that.

6. Story from Tearlach MacFarlane, 13 April 2007.

7. There were prominent Protestant Gillieses in Lowland Scotland: a judge and learned men. There was a Gillies in St Kilda in the early twentieth century. Those in Inverness county are Catholics from North Morar.

6 Sarah MacVarish, the old Cameron man and Calum Lowrie at Callop

1. On the other hand, the 1841 census for Achaphubuil shows a twelve-year-old boy, John Gibson, living there, of whom, as an old man, a young Sarah Henderson may not have been unaware.

2. A Duncan Henderson, Auchacharr, fought as a Jacobite in the Appin Regiment in 1745–6, and a Duncan MacHerioch, Achosrigan, with him. *No Quarter Given,* pp. 14, 15. The same sources gives two MacErich Jacobite officers in the Glencoe regiment (the piper and his nephew), and four MacKendricks (an Archibald, a Donald, and two Duncans). *No Quarter Given,* pp. 153, 154.

3. From the incomplete list of Jacobites serving in 1745–6 in *No Quarter Given,* there is a record of the military service of James MacLean, son of Ardgour, and three brothers, John, Hugh and Lachlan MacLean, brothers of MacLean of Kingairloch (p. 193). Those MacLeans who rose and fought gravitated to the MacLeans to their south, not to the Camerons. The same source shows an Alexander Stewart, son of James, Ardgour, who was an active Jacobite (*No Quarter Given,* p. 13).

4. Unidentified. NRAS3583, bundle 2 describes Allan Cameron of Inverscaddle as being drowned, probably in 1812.

5. NRAS3583, bundle 22. The Cameron–Glencoe link was a marriage one. Mary Cameron, daughter of Ewen of Fassifern, and sister of Colonel John who was killed at Quatre Bras (1815), was married to Alexander MacDonald of Glencoe, and the partners were cousins. Ewen of Fassifern was living in Inverscadale in 1771.

   NAS GD176/1430, a tack given by 'The Mackintosh' to Alexander MacDonell of Glencoe, shows that the latter tenanted the mains of Keppoch, Inverroymore, Inverroybeg and Boline from Whitsun 1804 for nineteen years. The document was registered in the court of Inverness on 11 August 1802.

6. I have found no later Patrick Henderson in the readily available censuses consulted (1841, 1861 and 1881), and only one earlier one (Patrick MacGillendrick, from Scardoish in Moidart, one of the rank and file in Clanranald's regiment in 1745, mentioned in Charles MacDonald's *Moidart or Among the Clanranald,* and cited in *No Quarter Given,* p. 149).

   NB The later two censuses (1861 and 1881) that I have read on the internet include only northern Ardgour (where most if not all of the relevant Hendersons and Boyds lived). Also the concept of locally born in 1841 was reduced to a Y or N reply. In the later censuses the actual parish is given.

7. Duncan Henderson, crofter and husband of Ann Kennedy, died on 27 July 1868 at Blaich; given age 72. He was a son of Allan Henderson, crofter, and Mary (Henderson) Henderson, no place given. The death notice was given by Duncan's son Allan on 28 July 1868, at Fort William. Allan (son of Duncan, son of Allan) Henderson was unable or unwilling to write his name in signing the death notice. See 1868 Deaths for the parish of Kilmallie, County of Argyll, p. 11, entry no. 31.

8. Reflecting a spotty official/church record availability, the 1841 census did not give exact ages for people ten and over. As valuable as the document is, some census takers in some Highland areas where travel was arduous relied on informants who were not always accurate. All four of these Ardgour Hendersons were born during the long English-French war.

9. The New Statistical Account drawn up by Donald M'Gillivray in 1835 describes a poor list in Kilmallie parish and gives the average paid out to the poor as between five and seven shillings per year. M'Gillivray noted the local generosity in food given to the needy, but also door-to-door begging. The census term, which, like others, appears to have been deliberately insensitive and derogatory, was the equivalent of old age pensioner for many older Highland people.

10. She was born on 12 March 1881. See Tearlach MacFarlane, correspondence, 5 Jan. 2007.

11. Sophia Henderson, see Marriages in the District of Kilmallie, 1928, p. 8, entry no. 15, at Corpach.

12. Rory MacDonald at Blarour wrote that the two little 'Poor's Houses' at Stronaba were built by Andrew Belford to house elderly employees of his Glenfintaig estate and their overseer. Belford bought Glenfintaig *c.* 1835 and died 1863, having built the hospital in Fort William but also having become hated by local Gaels as a clearer. The houses were taken over by the old Inverness County Council but reverted to the estate. I have found no home records but Mrs Sarah MacVarish seems to have been employed there during the war years. Since the end of the war the poor houses lay vacant and were neglected until recently when they were adapted for tourist occupation. Personal communication from Rory MacDonald, 24 December 2005.

13. Although she lived in much less luxurious times, she reminds me of Margaret 'Blue' MacLean from River Denys (who belonged to the Free Church, then the United Church, and who helped me through a very difficult time in Melford, Cape Breton *c.* 1978).

14. See Marriages for 1902, Registration District 520, entry no. 3, Kilmallie.

15. See Deaths for 1931, Registration District 098/B1, entry no. 34, Kilmallie, Argyll.

16. Ewen MacVarish, deer-stalker, aged 28, born at 'Drumfin, Kinlocheil', married, 3 November 1933, in Glasgow, Catherine Gordon (24), Glasgow. See Marriages of 1933, Hillhead, Glasgow, reg. dist. 644/12, entry no. 397. Their family were: Ewen Duncan MacVarish, born 17 July 1935, at Dalcattaig, Invermoriston; Alasdair, born 8 October 1939, at Cairnsary, South Gairloch; Gordon, born 26 November 1944, at

Achranich, Ardtornish, Morvern. See birth entries for Ewen MacVarish.

17. An IGI record shows that Allan Henderson, son of Duncan, was born 22 February 1837. Another, citing the OPR (Old Parish Records) shows that his parents, Duncan Henderson and Ann Kennedy, were married in Kilmallie, 22 February 1831.

18. Donnchadh (10) mac Alain 'ic Dhonnchaidh 'ic Alain.

19. See Deaths in the parish of Kilmallie, p. 16, entry no. 46. His wife was Sophia McMillan and he was a son of Donald McPherson (crofter, deceased) and Ann (McDonald) McPherson (deceased). The informant re. Martin McPherson's death was his son-in-law, Allan Henderson, still signing with his mark.

20. See Births, Kilmallie, 1886, p. 6, entry no. 16. On 13 August 1928, at the Corpach Free Church, Sophia Henderson (42), a spinster living at Blaich, daughter of the late Allan Henderson and Catherine (McPherson) Henderson, married Alexander Boyd (41), fisherman and bachelor living at Garvan. He was son of John Boyd, crofter, and Ann (MacKinnon) Boyd. See Marriages in the District of Kilmallie, 1928, p. 8, entry no. 15.

    The 1881 census for home 28 at Blaich shows a Duncan Boyd (60), his wife Ann (45) and four unmarried sons including John Boyd, aged 20; all were born in Kilmallie parish. The same census 1881 census for home 9 in Garvan shows Angus MacKinnon (63) and his wife Flora (59) and a twenty-two year old daughter Annie, a cattle dairymaid. All again were born in Kilmallie parish. MacKinnon is not a common name in Ardgour.

21. Martin son of Donald, probably grandson of Catherine MacPherson aged 70–4 in 1841. See census.

22. Where people of less status than 'farmer' in northern Ardgour in 1861 are concerned, the movement detectable involving the parish of Ardnamurchan, was away from there to the parish of Kilmallie. (At Drumfern, in the third house enumerated, Mary Cameron, a widow aged 51, i.e. b. *c.* 1811, born in Kilmallie parish, lived with her eight children all of whom were born in Ardnamurchan parish. She was described as a 'farmer'. She was a returnee.) Duncan Henderson appears to have come from Ardnamurchan alone of his family. He and his wife surely had older children than Allan, but they are unidentifiable. The Ardnamurchan presence in Ardgour was of several families but I have no arrival dates against which to check causes for movings. In all of this, the number of families at the most populous crofting township in Ardgour, Blaich declined from 47 in 1841, to 41 in 1861, to 33 in 1881. The population declined from 286, to 196, to 159 over the same years, 44.4 per cent over forty years.

23. The listing method in the 1841 census appears to have dictated the placing of the oldest adult male first. In this case it was Martin MacPherson (25) who heads the eighth home at Sallachan, Ardgour. His name is followed by Isabella's (25), then three MacPherson children's (Alexander, Ewan and Sarah), then Catherine MacPherson (70) and Christian (20).

24. Personal correspondence, 5 January 2007.

25. Letter and chart from *Tearlach* MacFarlane, Glenfinnan, 8 November 2006. Citing John 'Ton' MacDonald, Mingarry, he gave me one long MacVarish *sloinneadh* for Hugh MacVarish, Gaskan, Loch Shiel, b. *c.* 1775: Eoghann mac Iain, 'ic Iain, 'ic Iain, 'Raoghaill, 'ic Aonghais, 'ic Dhubhghall. Mr MacFarlane retold a MacVarish tradition linking Hugh with the MacVarish that lived at Corryhully in the first half of the nineteenth century.

26. Tearlach MacFarlane's work shows that the Morar and Àrasaig MacVarishes were descended from brothers Iain Bàn and Niall MacVarish who left Gasgan, via Langal nearby about 1790. The Coire Thollaidh MacVarishes, perhaps including brothers John and Eoghann, also came from Gasgan and neighbouring Annat (to the south-west). MacFarlane, letter, 8 Nov. 2006.

27. For some of those who came to Cape Breton see J.L. MacDougall's *History of Inverness County,* and James MacKay's *Genealogical History St Mary's Parish, Glendale, N.S.* (The Mingarrypark MacVarishes and Stewarts emigrated to PEI in 1834, via Fort William.)

28. Angus MacVarish, died at Callop, 22 August 1877, aged 54. He left his widow, Isabella (McIntosh) MacVarish (58) and a son Duncan (b. *c.* 1855) and daughter Mary (b. *c.* 1860) living in the third home canvassed in Callop in 1881 census – none were in Callop in 1861. See, Tearlach MacFarlane genealogy dated 8 November 2006, citing death register for Angus MacVarish, and the 1861 census.

29. MacFarlane letter, 8 Nov. 2006, citing the register of St Mary's Church, Fort William.

30. The 1861 census shows a Kennedy family in Muic, headed by Angus (32), shepherd, born in Kilmonivaig parish. Besides his wife and children there was also a servant, Marjory Kennedy (16), born at Laggan (Achadrom?).

31. See letter from Tearlach MacFarlane, 13 April 2007, in which he cited Iain MacMaster.

32. Letter to JGG from Tearlach MacFarlane, 27 April 2007.

33. In 1776 McCaskill got the ten-penny lands of Galmsdale, for the period of his incumbency. He also got the eight-penny lands of Sandyvig, and the five-penny lands of Sandyvoir for thirty years. This must at least have seemed ominous to the Catholic population. See GD201/5/1178. More to a point whose power is often overlooked was Clanranald's blatant favouring of the Presbyterian minister who had been settled at Kilmallie in 1751 by the barons of the exchequer. McCaskill began work as minister of the Small Isles on 14 January 1757. From his pre-1751 missionary days in Sunart, his prime purposes included 'the promoting . . . the Protestant Religion, Good Government, Industry and Manufactures.' E768, for-feited estates papers for the Lochiel estate.

34. PEI is 'the Island'; Newfoundland is 'the Rock'.

7 *The road from the Lochy Ferry to Àrasaig (1796–1812)*

1. Item 9 of NAS GD253/176/1 (Highland Roads and Bridges) records repairs to the 'bridge across the river Finnan in Glenfinnan' in 1837. The six-inch map of 1875 shows the bridge in its present position.

2. GD201/5/1231. There is some indication that the road had been begun in 1796. NB NRAS 2177/1523 contains correspondence from a Malcolm MacPherson at Borrodale to Clanranald's factor, Robert Brown, 9 April 1804, showing that 'bridges' had fallen down and that he, MacPherson, was not prepared to rebuild them, preferring to refund money paid him already and to delete the bridge-building clause from his contract. A rood could have been 16.5' 1.5' (br) 1' (d).

3. GD201/5/1231/23.

4. This could have been achieved without risk of salinity to Loch Shiel by diverting Allt Dubh Lighe and/or the Callop.

5. GD248/671/6/8.

6. Beef may have been in greater demand than mutton during the war, but later, bridges were of greater value to the drovers of sheep. South of the Callop farm there is an 'island' called *Dail Lagach* between the tributaries, Allt an Fhaing and Allt na Cruaiche in which sheep were contained. See OS six-inch sheet.

7. The brig *Friends* was to dock at Fort William 'on or about the tenth of June where is to continue ten running days to receive the passengers.' From an unpublished, typescript copy of the document of charter signed by Archibald McMillan of Murlagan and William Auld (for himself and the brig's owners), at Fort William, 3 July 1802. *Friends* was expected to carry 120 full passengers. Typed document from the collection of Hugh P. MacMillan, Ottawa, 25 May 2007.

8. Two documents from late 1811, pertaining to two MacDonald countries, emphasise the grim plight of many ordinary Gaels. On 24 August 1811 John Gillies and Hugh MacLean wrote an appeal to Lord MacDonald's commissioners on behalf of about 300 people in Fladda (Raasay) who, they believed, were to turned out of their traditional holdings to make way for one new occupant. (NRAS3273/1354) On 6 October a Duncan Shaw at Bay, factor for Clanranald's trustees on his Long Island estate (South Uist etc.), wrote to Clanranald's factor Robert Brown that 'Rhudinan' had 'sailed for America without clearing out of at any Custom house,' adding, 'I hardly think it possible he can escape our Cruizers.' (NRAS2177, bundle 1568) All cleared; nowhere to go.

9. NAS GD201/5/1231/1/41.

10. If the Kirkwoods' map of 1810 is correct (and there is little reason to think it was) then this was a stretch that was not even done in 1810.

   Dick and Readdie naïvely expected to be finished road and bridges from Àrasaig Inn to Lochy Ferry on Martinmas 1806. The work took six more years to complete and the firm found that they had underbid on the contract. In November 1809, for example, Readdie found he couldn't get the work done at 'Loch-an-Anugal Sea' end because of short days and lack of accommodation for his workmen, so he moved to work on an alteration on the east side of Borrodale. 'He's then like to go on with the road at the Inn of Arisaig.' NRAS2177, bundle 1550, from a letter from a Mr Easton to Thomas Telford, a copy of which is in the Robert Brown correspondence.

11. The old low road in my time, not much travelled, continued east from the big house along the north bank of the Finnan, past the sheep fank on the north side.

12. Dick and Readdie had difficulties with bridge building on both the Glenfinnan and on the Glengarry road. By autumn 1805 one had fallen on the latter. See Haldane, *New Ways,* p. 120. NB A John Livingston at Ardnafuaran, Àrasaig, made an offer to Robert Brown, Clanranald's factor, for the Àrasaig public house and croft on 18 April 1805. NRAS2177, bundle 1528.

13. The print room of the Royal Library at Windsor Castle holds, among many, an inked in pencil sketch by HRH dated 15 September 1873 of 'Charles Edward's monument, looking towards Ft. William.' K.43, f.5 (a)

14. I never saw it till 2002 when Seumas and I were shown it by its finder, Tearlach MacFarlane. I have not seen the sketches.

15. I have always thought of John Ford as old, and for a boy he may have seemed so. The only record I have found in the NAS death records gives a 'John Cameron Ford, Fort William, Aluminium Fitters Mate, died 21 January 1975, aged 54, usual residence, 59 Abraich Road, Inverlochy.' In 1950 he was still not thirty. 'Parents: John Ford, Still Man (deceased) and Mary Tod or Cameron (deceased).'

16. A recent photograph (internet) shows a square-ended rough stone, one-storey house at Coire Thollaidh, which has a chimney at each gable (and a sheet-metal roof), reminiscent of the late eighteenth-century tacksmen's homes in Morvern and elsewhere.

17. This was known as the Stagehouse Inn in the late 1940s and, for some unexplained reason, is now called the Prince's House.

8 Cregag/Craigag and Calap in a deeper historical perspective

1. The Cregag farm includes one tributary of the Dubh Lighe (which drains indirectly into salt Loch Eil). This tributary joins the Dubh Lighe at Dail na Sgainneal just north of the bridge that I knew in the trees.

2. So serious and risky was the Campbell commitment in the seventeenth century that two were beheaded for their gambles: Archibald, eighth earl (1661, by Charles II), and his oldest son Archibald, ninth earl, who gamely joined the rebellious Monmouth (a bastard son of Charles II) and went to his execution in 1685, at James VII's order. (Archibald, tenth earl, came ashore with William of Orange and got the estate back in 1696). Recent archaeological work in Culloden is revealing that the battle was a much more tight-run thing than the victors, for generations, have wanted everyone to believe. 'Hail the conquering hero comes' contained a deal more relief than crowing.

3. Also involved was the Norman family of Gordon, a female of which line, Lady Jane Gordon, was married to Archibald Campbell's heir, Colin Campbell, third Earl of Argyll.

4. See Jean and R.W. Munro, *Acts of the Lords of the Isles,* p. 108. I have chosen not to include alternative spellings of places that were used in *Origines Parochiales Scotiae* (Bannatyne Club, 1851–5) and which the Munros gave in squared brackets. I have yet to see copies of the original documents.

5. *Na h-uamhachan?* The little caves?

6. Callop is not visible in the MacCulloch photograph of *c.* 1951, which was taken from about the hundred-foot contour line. See MacMillan, *Bygone Lochaber,* pp. 90, 91. Roy's map gives the knoll as Tòrr an Tairbeirt.

7. Munros, *Acts of the Lords of the Isles,* p. 109.

8. Munros, *Acts of the Lords of the Isles,* p. 224.

9. Munros, *Acts of the Lords of the Isles,* p. 198. Clachfyne is unidentified. It may have been a property whose drainage was into the *Dubh Lighe* (rather than into the Callop), which, perhaps, lay between 'Clachak' and 'Drumnasall'.

10. Lady Margaret Douglas, daughter of the second Earl of Morton, married Archibald Campbell, eighth Earl of Argyll, Lord Lorn, and first Marquis of Argyll, main acquirer of Ardnamurchan from Clann Iain [Dòmhnullach], beheaded in 1661.

11. A similar case is given by Alastair Campbell in his *History of Clan Campbell* (vol. 2, p. 119), also without source. Writing of John Dubh MacConnochie, a violent cattle thief (and tutor to his nephew Campbell of Inverawe), *c.* 1595, like MacMillan and his superior, he faced a problem. 'Neither Argyll nor Glenorchy would willingly own him to be their man because they would then have to bear the responsibility [for his thievery].'

12. Ewen's son Allan, tenth of Ardgour, was served heir to his father in 1698. Fiona MacLean of Ardgour, E-communication, 12 March 2007, citing, informally, the work of a MacLean aunt by marriage.

13. NRAS3283, bundle 348.

14. NRAS3283, bundle 375. NB a 'John Cameron of Inverscaddel' was described as deceased in 22 July 1763. See RH15/44/201. Was this John Cameron, third of Glendessary?

15. There is also, on the Callop side of the watershed, a Clach mhic Bheathain, marked on the six-inch OS map.

16. The pass over Feadan Mhic Bheathain is marked on the 1872 surveyed six-inch map. 'Beallach n Gerridh' appears earlier on the Thomson *Atlas* that Johnston surveyed in 1820. NB There is another *feadan* place name on the six-inch map, Feadan a' Chreimh [Stream of the Gentian(?)], marked on a tributary of the Fionn Lighe, north of Torebane at Kinlocheil.

17. MacMillan cited no source for MacMillan cattle raiding to their westward.

18. See MacMillan, *Bygone Lochaber,* p. 61. The refusal of cash compensation may have been involved in this case (although little or nothing is known of that practice at that

date in Gaelic Scotland). NB It was an effort reportedly of the Macgillonie Camerons in the mid eighteenth century to take the Lochiel lands in which the acquisitive, non-Jacobite John Cameron of Fassifern was implicated, and for which he was banished beyond Scotland.

19. The war was brutally concluded with the Williamite massacre of the non- and anti-Presbyterian MacDonald of Glencoe, and members of his family and of his Gaelic and Jacobite clan in the early winter of 1692. The MacDonalds in Glencoe were geographically isolated from their MacDonald brethren, Gaelic guardians of a land approached from inland garrisons to the south-east, but nonetheless in a dangerous cul-de-sac of old clan Donald east of the Great Glen (hemmed in by Stewarts, Camerons and Campbells). The Keppochs over the mountains to the north were both more numerous and less easily cut off. If the war of 1688–1713 is seen as a diminishing of Dutch guilder world power, the little irony for Highland people lay in the transfer of Nova Scotia (as it then was defined) to Britain.

20. The 'Very Desirable' farm of Biallid, on Cluny MacPherson's estate, near New-townmore in the parish of Kingussie, was advertised to let starting Whitsun 1880 in *The Scotsman* of 8 October 1879. Its main selling point was its herd of between 2,300 and 2,500 black-faced ewe stock. It remains in the hands of the old MacPherson family.

21. By Scots law of 1597 the payment of blackmail was a capital crime. See Erskine, *Principles,* p. 509.

22. More eloquently than any other documents, maps allow us knowledge of where the fringes were. Timothy Pont's map of *c.*1610 shows the ignorance of non-Gaels of the geography of the Highlands west beyond Kinlocheil. William Roy's work just after 1750, while showing the rig systems near Castle Urquhart, is innocent of detail in North Morar and not very informative even about Callop. The coastal and sea charts did not coincide with science either, by and large, until long after the Forty-five.

23. Chambers, in his *Domestic Annals,* led into the William Bane MacPherson cattle raid story with a report of a complaint lodged officially to the Scottish Privy Council by Lord Rollo on 22 January 1691 of a cattle raid made on his own lands. Chambers did not link the two events, but Rollo's disposition at Aberdeen in September 1689 as the head of a troop of horse, and his known resentment at Dundee's efforts to catch him earlier in the year (not to mention open divisiveness in rural Perthshire over the civil war) point to him as the man who would have not been frightened by a Highland cattle thieving operation, almost anywhere. The principal thieves involved are nowhere named. It is important to add too that no less an authority on the history of the cattle business in Scotland that A.R.B. Haldane, author of *The Drove Roads of Scotland,* wrote that the Scottish Privy Council records showed monotonously, repeatedly, the amount of cattle theft going on in the country, Highland and Lowland alike, from 1550 to 1650. Scotland was regarded in 1650 as England's pastureland. Rustling, something that Colonel John Hill at Fort William could not in conscience countenance in 1691 and on, was certainly not confined to

Gaelic Scotland.

24. The Exchequer Records, army musters in the E100/25 series show that from May to October 1697 Colonel Sir John Hill's regiment of foot at 'Fortwilliam' included the following officers/leaders of companies: Lieutenant Colonel Forbes, Major Anderson and captains Allan Cathcart, Francis Farquhar, Charles Forbes, Hamilton, Lord Kilmaur (an Ayrshire Cunningham whose major title was Earl of Glencairn), John McCulloch, John McKenzie, Menzies and Richardsone. The same companies were at Fort William in November 1697 with one of Hill's two Stewart companies (James's or John's). Hill's own company, from May to July 1697, was serving in Sir William Douglas's regiment of foot at Leith Links (E100/31/295).

25. I don't believe this example, taken from over a century earlier, is inappropriate. On 18 October 1548, Archibald Campbell, 4th of Argyll used the following phrase in the ending of a letter to his relative, John Campbell of Glenorchy, 'We haif shawin our mynd at lenth in yis mater to our servand Archibald MacKewir[/n?] to quhom ze pless to gif credence.' See Jane Dawson's *Breadalbane Letters 1548–83*. See also GD112/39/1/1.

26. The development of square-rigged shipping capable of cannon broadside was also a fundamental element in the final break between the Gaels (in Ireland and Scotland), as representations on early-seventeenth-century maps show.

27. NRAS26/14. The entire citation is of the abstract of the contents. The subordinate citation offered within, marked '–', are Simon Fraser's/Lord Lovat's words to Donald Cameron of Lochiel. Lovat, Lochiel, the Duke of Perth, and the Earl of Traquair had signed a Jacobite association in 1740 when Britain declared war on Spain. Their continental agent was Drummond of Balhaldie, Lochiel's uncle by marriage. NB Permission to read the original documents, NRAS26/14, was formally denied through the assistant registrar, 29 March 2007 (see NRAS ref. NAS4/AB3/459.3/Part 1, NRAS26).

28. From Maggie MacDonald, Clan Donald library, Armadale, Sleat, 12 April 2007. At £2 each, nearly double what Fassifern claimed in compensation, there would have been 2,500 beasts.

29. From Maggie MacDonald, Clan Donald library, Armadale, Sleat, 12 April 2007. A letter from Lovat to Lochiel, dated 21 June 1743, written by Lovat's son, was carried by Lovat's chamberlain to whom Lochiel was told he could talk freely. The bearer was the real source of thought transfer, not the paper.

30. Sir Walter Scott's noble description of Donald Cameron of Lochiel in *Tales of a Grandfather* is of questionable value, from an educated Presbyterian point of view.

31. See MacMillan, *Bygone Lochaber,* p. 174. MacMillan may have included the remark out of some honest and innocent deference to some other possibility that his text ignores.

32. Erskine, *Principles,* p. 518.

33. From the claims for losses in 1746, from Drumsallie to Banavie, there had been 343 cows, 170 horses and well over 1,000 sheep and goats. See *Bygone Lochaber.* (I do not

remember beasts along the same road in 1950, although there must have been several.) I am unaware of any similar claims for losses from any other Jacobite area. This place was set down for retribution.

34. NAS E768/1 Forfeited estates papers, rental and survey of Lochiel by David Bruce, January 1749.

35. 'Alexander McConchie vc Dhuill alias McOlonich', 'Donald McConchie vc Dhuill alias McOlonich' and 'Dugald mcDhonichie roy alias McOlonich in Acharacle'. NAS SC54/17/2/65/6.

36. NAS SC54/17/2/65/8.

37. *No Quarter Given,* p. 37. Source, Seton and Arnot, *Prisoners of the '45.*

38. Livingstone, *No Quarter Given,* p. 39.

39. As in similar-scale losing actions, truth about the defeated is difficult to assess, especially from any written record not taken in the heat of war. What appears, from Marjorie Macdonald's 'Letters of the Clanranald Family (1746–1752)' to be Young Clanranald's unshakeable adherence to his people and their Catholic tradition on the estate until he died in 1777, is called into question by John MacDonald of Glenaladale's letters in the 1770s – Glenaladale was feeling insecure about his holding, perhaps from when non-Jacobite Old Clanranald died in 1766, perhaps earlier. At great expense Captain John managed a large emigration in 1771–2.

His attitude may be defended using other parts of today's paper trail, the sisters-in-law, Old Ranald Clanranald's wife Margaret (MacLeod), and Boystill's wife Margaret, for example, left a signed letter, dated 25 March 1740, suggesting what amounted to the de-traditionalising of the Clanranald estate. The letter expressed their 'regret that no missionary has been sent to South Uist wherein the providence of ane allwise God has ordered our lot.' See NAS CH1/2/73. General Assembly [Church of Scotland] Papers, 1736–1740. If, conceivably, there were diverting cunning behind such a letter, there is another alarming suggestion of the collapse of tradition even under Clanranald (d. 1766). That was the Presbyterian-conducted specifically religious McNeill census of Eigg 1765. See, McNeill, 'Census of the Small Isles'.

40. Electronic notes from Dr Robert Cameron, Australia, 18 and 19 May 2007.

41. I am indebted to Sally MacPhee, Brisbane, for this information.

42. Any seventeenth-century pro-Cameron sentiment on the part of Argyll withered with the 1745 Rising, against the failing of which Cameron of Lochiel very specifically insured himself with Prince Charles. The Lochiel estate was thoroughly robbed in 1746 and the Campbell presence became dominant almost immediately. Campbells controlled the forfeited Cameron estate and against that power there was no recourse.

43. Gaelic system subtleties like fosterage and kindly tenancy made this society reluctant to tender to the powerful claims for democratic rights much beyond crofts on the poor lands until long after the majority had melted away.

44. Duncan MacMillan and his brothers, Myles, Ewen, and John, at Kinlocharkaig had tended John's, first Fassifern cattle from 1745–50. Where the herd was is not known

and the number claimed as having been taken by the redcoats from the Kinlocharkaig area strongly suggests Fassifern had his in safer pastures. (Myles and John
were suspected cattle thieves after 1746, Myles was caught in August 1750 for goat-
theft in 1748, and Fassifern's patronage of them must have raised serious suspicions.)
Duncan MacMillan's son Ewen (*c.* 1736–1781) had fostered John's grandson John
Cameron the colonel, and Duncan's grandson (and Ewen MacMillan's son)
Eoghann Bàn Chalpa had been the colonel's personal servant and foster brother
at Quatre Bras in 1815. See *Bygone Lochaber,* pp. 86, 87.

45. Another John Cameron wrote that the existence of steelbow land occupation in
    Gaelic Scotland was a late reflection of ancient, pre-Christian Irish law (but a system
    of land use found in rural France until the Revolution in 1789). See Cameron, *Celtic
    Law,* p. 74.

46. In the 1774 survey of farms on the Locheil estate in the forfeited estates there is no
    Cregag. After 'Coribeg' (farm no. 30) there are Kinlocheil (31), 'Drimscallie' (32),
    Stronlia (33) and then Auchintore (south of Fort William). E786/50.

47. M.E.M. Donaldson in *Scotland's Suppressed History,* p. 142, wrote that Sir Ewan
    Cameron of Lochiel [Eoghann Dubh], an anti-covenanter, wrote that 'Every parish
    had a tyrant who made the greatest lord in his district stoop to his authority,' and that
    each had 'twelve or fourteen soure, ignorant enthusiasts, under the title of elders,'
    composing his council. 'If any of what quality soever, and the assurance to disobey
    his edicts, the dreadful sentence of excommunication was immediately thundered
    out against him, his goods and chatels confiscated and seazed, and he himself as being
    looked upon as actually in the possession of the devill and irretrievably doomed to
    eternal perdition.'

48. On 18 August 1800 Campbell gave advice to Clanranald's factor Robert Brown at
    Àrasaig to winter his stots (NRAS2177, bundle 1508). In the letters received by
    Brown, there is one dated 16 March 1804 from a 'Ewen McMillan, cattle drover,
    Garvan, Ardgour, wanting farm of Nuntown.' (NRAS2177, bundle 1522) It was
    cusp time for cattle.

49. An eloquently virulent opinion of Clanranald's clearing policies is found in Dr John
    R. MacCormack's *Highland Heritage & Freedom's Quest.*

50. NRAS3583, bundle 12, 'Miscellaneous Papers'.

51. NRAS3583, bundle 19.

52. According to Fiona MacLean (9 May 2006), Alexander MacLean was gazetted
    ensign in the 2nd Battalion The Royals (The Royal Dragoons) in 1780; he
    proceeded to serve as a lieutenant in the 63rd regiment, the West Suffolk Regiment
    of Foot. From the War Office army list of 1789 a Captain Alexander MacLean is
    shown to have been a captain in the 'Eighth (or the King's Royal Irish) Regiment of
    (Light) Dragoons', with his service in the regiment dating to 30 September 1787. He
    ended his military career as lieutenant-colonel in the 3rd regiment of Argyll Militia;
    a letter to Lord Neville from MacLean, at Oban, 22 July 1811 (GD51/1/998),
    shows him as commandant.

The 63rd regiment had fought at Bunker Hill (1776), at Brandywine and Germantown, and then at Charleston (1780) in the South. A segment became mounted and fought under Banastre Tarleton (British Legion), at Waxhaws (May 1780) and at Camden (Aug. 1780) and at the defeat at Cowpens on 17 Jan. 1781, among other actions. What remained of the regiment would have told stories of the American campaign when Alexander Lindsay (1752–1825), 6th Earl of Balcarres, in Fife, became colonel in 1782. Tarleton's influence in royal circles is well known.

Where the 8th Dragoons are concerned, in 1787, when MacLean began to serve the regiment as a captain, the colonel was General Charles Grey (1729–1807), first Earl Grey, who did a two-year stint from 1787 to 1789. His son Charles Grey, second earl, was British foreign secretary in 1806, Whig leader in the House of Commons, and prime minister from 1830 to 1834 when the government finally ended empire slavery (Reform Bill of 1832). MacLean's potential for gaining patronage was not inconsiderable.

53. NRAS3583, bundle 2. The fourth Earl of Hopetoun, Sir John Hope (1765–1823), from whom Ardgour also leased Keith House, was another half-brother of Ardgour's wife, Margaret Hope (1772–1831) – the marriage took place in 1793. Sir John had fought with Abercromby at Alexandria (1801) and had evacuated Corunna after the death of John Moore (1809). For an hour or two he hosted George IV at Hopetoun House in 1822. Sir John's son John was the fifth earl from 1823 till 1843. As an example of the tartan fashion set by George IV, the fifth Earl of Hopetoun married the oldest daughter of Godfrey MacDonald, third Lord MacDonald of Slate.

54. As some measure of MacLean of Ardgour's locally perceived commercial acumen, Col. David Robertson Macdonald of Kinlochmoidart wrote to Clanranald's factor in mid 1806 noting that MacLean had advised him that he should be seeking rents three times what they had been in 1791.

   Socially, although MacLean resigned from the Lothian hunt some time before 13 February 1811, that he had been a member at all indicates the tightness of his Saxon socialising (NRAS3583, bundle 2). In 1826 he held a £45 share in the steamboat comet. His situation in an undeniable economic system forced him into the commercial world – I have found no evidence that he ever resisted.

55. On 21 November 1823 there were 27 impoverished crofters at Blaich, the first of Ardgour's crofting communities. According to the then ex-factor, John Cumming (at Achdalieu on the north shore of Locheil, presumably the fifth of Achdalieu) their holdings would only yield £2 10s. per annum each, and that only from sea-ware. With canal and road work finished the crofters could afford to pay no rent (NRAS3583, bundle 8). Ardgour's purchase of Inverscaddle cannot be disconnected from steady rental income from, *inter alia*, crofters working on the road and canal projects.

   The ordinary people on the Keppoch farmlands that Alexander MacDonald of Glencoe had obtained in nineteen-year tack (Whitsun 1804–Whitsun 1823) probably were aware of the same vice. The tack document (GD176/1430,

registered on 11 August 1802 in Inverness) is bundled with subsequent correspondence about a dispute of payments by Glencoe to Mackintosh and about the
valuation of the property (mains of Keppoch, Inverroymore, Inverroybeg and
Boline). The dispute continued in 1824 and 1825, now between the trustees of
Glencoe and the Mackintosh. See GD176/990.

56. Somerled MacMillan, *Bygone Lochaber,* p. 239. From nearby Cameron country there
was one man from 'Lochielhead' (Alex. Cameron), one from 'Kinlochiel' (John
Cameron), a man and his (unnamed) from Drimnassalie (Duncan Cameron), and a
man and his wife (unnamed) from 'Drimnasallie', who also emigrated in 1802
(NAC, MG 24, I 183). See *Lochaber Emigrants to Glengarry,* pp. 7–13. For many years
I assumed wrongly that Donald MacMillan's leaving marked the end of a tenanting
MacMillan presence in Callop. Donald MacMillan may have been a family servant
at Callop.

57. His reason(s) for vacating Glasforin are not known.

58. Sally MacPhee, Brisbane, Australia, noted that John MacVean (d.1826) had the
Drumfern tack from Whitsun 1821 for eleven years and that there may be grounds
to suspect collusion between John and his son Alexander in division of wealth to the
near exclusion of Alexander's sisters. Electronic communication, 23 April 2007.

59. Blàr nan Cléireach is not marked on Timothy Pont's (Adv.MS.70.2.9, Pont 13.
1583–96) map, or Robert Gordon's (Adv.MS.70.2.10, Gordon 37. 1632–52) both
of which were made not long after the Reformation. It is not included in Herman
Moll's map of 1745. It is among the farms sketched in 1774 for the forfeited estates
managers. It is marked also on John Thomson and William Johnson's map of 1820 as
'Blairnaclerach'. On the Bartholomew half-inch map of 1972 the place is not
included, but there is a hill, Meall nan Cléireach.

60. The 1861 census shows a James MacGregor, writer (lawyer) aged 66 living in
Duncan's Square, Fort William. He was born in Knockbain north of Inverness. His
son Ronald (30), W.S. was born in Kilmallie parish.

61. NRAS3583, bundle 6.

62. NSA, vol. 7, p. 123. Parish of Ardnamurchan. The only fishing station marked on
the Langlands map of Argyllshire in 1801 is 'Tobermorry Fishing Station'. NB The
presence of outside tinsmiths at Corpach and Scardoish in the 1841 census
emphasises Samuel Lewis's reporting that there were salmon canneries at both
places in 1846. See Lewis, 'Excerpts from a Topographical Dictionary of Scotland'.
The recorded presence of only five boatbuilders in the same census hints at the
overseas nature of this business – a MacIntyre at Lochyside, three Rankins in one
home in Achintore, and a boat carpenter MacDonald at Dalilea.

63. See GB 0248 UGD 008/6, 'Records of the Edinburgh & Glasgow Railway Co.,
Scotland.'

64. No buildings are shown in the photograph, and no expressed defence of the
approximate year, presumably assumed from clothing and the keeper's accoutre-
ments.

65. See Search Sheet, county of Inverness, 1568, folio 223, 'Disp. By John Guthrie . . . Scarborough and Conaglen . . . to West Highland Woodlands . . . Gloucestershire.' Affixed is the second description, 'The Old Forge, Craigegg, Glenfinnon.' (NB The copies of the Search Sheets claim not to have any evidential status.)

66. The only home that I visited in late 2002 was so modern and comfortable that thinking back to Sarah MacVarish's little bothy must have been almost unimaginable for those who had been there in the 1940s.

67. Clerk, *Memoir*, p. 98. *Fraxinus excelsior* (?). The stump was measured in 1764 and showed a girth of fifty-eight feet. Given the ancient practice of daubing hot ash sap on a newborn as protection from the devil, one here perhaps finds a last relic of older religion and confirmation of this place as holy. See Cameron, *Gaelic Names of Plants*, p. 47.

68. One of Robert Adam's photographs of a Highland farm in the Hebrides shows an area protected from animals by a bank with fencework on top pointing outwards.

69. In 1834 there is a record of falling wood prices in Scotland caused by imports. A report from Alexander Mackintosh, former tacksman (presumably in Lochaber) to the Mackintosh chief, offers advice on tree care and on how to get best prices in a falling market. See NAS GD176/1589. How much pressure this exerted on the ordinary Gael is not yet calculable. I have no idea when the *'doirean'* on the Callop farm were last managed.

70. *Amnicola*, dwelling or growing by a river; from *amnis, —is*, m. (anciently feminine), a river. In Scottish Gaelic *amhuinn* is feminine.

71. OED gives rushy and grassy for 'benty'. If the cover had not changed between 1813 and 1945 the word meant heathery and brackeny.

72. I am indebted to Sally MacPhee, Brisbane, for genealogical information on the MacVeans. Mary MacBean's gravestone was found by Canadian Cedric Macvean.

73. A Captain James Dallas of Cantray was killed at Culloden, serving in Lady Macintosh's regiment. See *No Quarter Given*, p. 183. For more general information, see OSA, vol. 4. Entry for the parish of Dallas by Revd Mr David Milne.

74. Huie's letter (8 Feb. 1848) included the observation that Allan's command of Scottish Gaelic would be best spent in 'destitute parishes of the Highlands or the shepherdless flocks of Nova Scotia. In Australia we have very few who would profit by your preaching in Gaelic.' He added that Allan MacVean would be wasting 'that rare and estimable gift . . . in the Australian soil.'

   In a letter sent almost a year later, on 6 February 1849, things had changed. There had been a tide of immigration of Highlanders to Port Phillip and 'a great many of whom' spoke no English. Allan MacVean suddenly was a coveted man.

   NB Revd Thomas Davidson left his Church of Scotland position in Kilmallie (where he had been presented 23 November 1835) to join the new Disruption Church in 1843. See NRAS26/50/2/bundle 1. He began the Kilmallie Free Church where he was minister in April and May 1845. See GD112/51/82. MacLean of Ardgour faced a determined Disruption group to whom he denied

land near his own home. Allan MacVean must have been influenced by the
breakaway thinking.

75. The part, if any, played by the teacher and catechist Neil MacLean at neighbouring
Corriebeg (see 1841 census), in instructing the MacVeans in religious and other
matters, is unknown.

76. Clanranald, who chose to profit personally and directly by kelp, using next to slave
labour on his properties, is far from forgotten by the descendants of those Gaels,
many of whose lives ground to nearly economic nothing and hopelessness before
they came to Nova Scotia and Prince Edward Island. See, John R. MacCormack,
Highland Heritage.

77. The summer make-work and unemployment insurance system that existed (and still
exists) in Nova Scotia, while it is not allied to subsistence farming and the sustaining
of a Gaelic culture, is a latter-day variant.

78. Admiralty Chart 1426 (surveyed in 1841) shows a road from the northward ending
at 'Stroncrigan' farm and another from a little to the north of 'Inverscardale' Point.
There were also roads in the Corran area.

79. *Inverness Courier*, 30 May 1838. There is no mention here, or in the NSA, of the
outbreak of cholera in Scotland in 1832–3 – it was essentially an urban phenomenon. A note in the New Statistical Account describes destitution in the parish of
Morvern in 1837 and 1838 and the failure of the herring fishery in Loch Sunart 'of
late years' (relative to date of NSA, *c.* 1843). See Revd John MacLeod, entry for
Morvern, NSA, vol. 7, pp. 173 and 194.

80. These assisted emigrations fall generally within the category of (post-1836) individual Gaels rather than family emigrations (as in the tacksman/community
emigrations of the last three decades of the eighteenth century) but this is an
oversimplification. The *Inverness Courier* article noted, for example, that a problem
for colonial authorities in Australia was that the Highland immigrants would not
split up in the new land, preferring social cohesion to opportunity.

81. Not included are Giusachan, Scamodale, Gorstanvorran, Polloch and Glen Hurich
all of which are on or drain into the south-east side of Loch Shiel. Polloch and Glen
Hurich may have been part of Sunart. The term 'Cligvullin' occurs in NRAS3583,
bundle 12. Fiona MacLean of Ardgour first drew my attention to the fact that
Clovulin began as Cladh a' Mhuilinn. She also noted that the old graveyard has lain
beneath a new road for many decades. E-mail, 16 January 2006. (The Admiralty
chart cited above gives 'Chlavoulin'.)

82. Nearby is another gentleman's seat at Aryhoulan (to which no name is attached).

83. The Duke of Argyll divested himself of his farms in Morvern in 1819, which
encouraged even more sheep-farming. (Patrick Sellar, the clearer, bought Ardtornish in 1838.) See Maudlin, 'Tradition and change', pp. 180, 181.

84. *The Scotsman*, 9 September 1849, p. 3. *The Scotsman*'s source was a correspondent for
the *Inverness Advertiser* who wrote that 'the hills of Lochaber, from the quiet bosom
of which they were thus unkindly wrenched,' carefully did not state that these

people were evicted.

85. He induced, by discussion and education, many sub-tenants on the estate to accept enclosed, personal farms on Loch Eil in 1802, surveyed out of four earlier large farms. The surveying was done in 1801 and the Langlands map of Argyll, 1 August 1801, shows nine shorefront holdings on Loch Eil extending almost three miles, where Blaich is today. The Langlands map also marks four farm buildings, two on either side of one river in the middle of what was given as 'Blaichs'. The occupiers had until 1805 to build stone houses and head and side dykes. MacLean held Blaich of the Crown. By about 1818 many of the crofters there were becoming impoverished and their rents had to be forgiven by MacLean. About 1818, a new manse had been built at Kilmallie. By 1825 the Blaich rents, for two years, had become a legal subject as the church teinds had to be assessed correctly, based on the estate rental – there was no escaping the money system since 48 Geo III, c. 138, sect. 11 (1808) dictated that the minister's stipend could no longer be paid in grain; it had to be in money. Blaich was part and parcel of the sale to Morton in 1858. See *inter alia* Alexander MacLean's address to his sub-tenantry at Ardgour House, 31 August 1850 (when he was 86).

86. NRAS3583/B, bundle 21.

87. When old Ardgour died she married a John Campbell (another Highlander?) and in 1806 received a 'jointure' from her son Alexander MacLean of £150 per annum.

88. The relationship between Colonel Alexander MacLean and the Camerons of Fassifern was friendly. In 1805 MacLean put in a good word for John Cameron, future hero of Quatre Bras, with Major General John Hope (Alexander's brother-in-law) (Clerk, *Memoir of Colonel John Cameron*, p. 33); the Ardgour family papers record the drowning in 1812 (?) of Allan Cameron of Inverscaddle (NRAS3583, bundle 2). Allan Cameron is not identified (perhaps a Glendessary). Also when Ewen Cameron's son Peter Cameron, HEIC, died 4 October 1843 it was at Blaich, on Ardgour soil.

89. Much of Cameron of Locheil's extensive forest 'was cut down about twenty years ago' according to Revd Donald M'Gillivray, see OSA, vol. 14, p. 120. Did the wood float to the mill at Camusasaig?

   A James MacAlpin was tenant at Inverscaddle from 19 July 1817 to 28 August 1818 (NRAS3583, bundle 21). He was described as general merchant and trader at Corpach on 13 November 1822 when, at Inverary, he made out 'an abstract State and Value of debts due to and by the Sequestrated Estate.' MacAlpin interestingly enough was holder of the 'farms of Inverscadle and Glashoran.' (NRAS3583, bundle 22) Sequestration was a court of session ordered placing of the management of an estate into a competent factor's or other's hands. Glaschoran presumably was part of James Riddell's Sunart estate.

90. *Fias* suggests a bend or a crook and Druim Leathad nam Fias is a distinctly crooked ridge of hills, separating Cona Glen and Glen Scaddle. Sheet 40 of the OS

Landranger one-inch series, and the Bartholomew half-inch map (1972), show the first hill/mountain to the west of the ridge as Stob Mhic Bheathain, the first of three *stoban*.

91. According to the rules for census takers in 1841, persons aged from 15 to 20 were listed as '15' but unfortunately the earlier youth's age of 17 confounds the purpose.

92. The *Inverness Advertiser* for Christmas day 1868 notes the death of a John Mitchell at Stronchreggan. A John Mitchell, 'factor to Hon Mrs Stewart Mackenzie of Seaforth' is mentioned in a newspaper cutting of the *Journal of Agriculture* for October 1854 and the suspicion that it is probably the same John Mitchell that comes from the document's source, NRAS3583, bundle 11 (Ardgour papers).

93. Dalindrein is marked on the Thomson *Atlas* of 1832. It lies next to and south-west of Stronachreggan, on what was still called Loch Eil (which ran as far as the Corran Ferry). The 'dal' here, and in 'Dalreoch' and Dail na Sgainnir, suggests a Norse connection, but, best of all might be Glen Scaddle, which Somerled MacMillan gives as from Gleann Sgarbh Dal [Glen of Cormorant Glen]. See MacMillan, *Bygone Lochaber,* p. 259.

NB Norse occurs in place names on both shores of Loch Shiel, at Acharacle, Dalnabreac, Glenaladale, Dàil Beag (below the viaduct in Glenfinnan) and Scamadale. With significant, rich Norse burials found at Colonsay and Oronsay, and with the naming of Sunart, there is reason to suppose Norse exploration to Loch Eil, perhaps also into Loch Shiel. See Laing, *Archaeology of late Celtic Britain and Ireland,* p. 201.

94. The two Glendinning factors' records for the Conaglen estate continue until Sholto died in 1884.

95. The 1841 census rules dictated that people between the ages of 15 and 20 should be noted as age 15, and those 20–25 as twenty, so Donald Cameron could have been fifty and Marjory seventy-five. There were obviously exceptions, however.

96. The 1829–30 rent for Cregag was £50 per annum while that for Callop was £78.

NB Angus MacInnis's widow, Christian (1841)/Catherine (1861) was living as head of a household of seven on Low Street, Fort William in 1861 and working as a fifty-three year old 'washer-woman'. (See 1861 census.) An Angus MacInnis (15) was a servant in 1841 to the inn-keeper, locally born Donald MacDonald (25) in Glenfinnan – the inn was the first house recorded and probably was the slated, two-storey house represented in the John Fleming painting of in or pre-1834. The MacInnis family at Callop in 1841 may have figured in Angus MacDonald of Glenalladale's plans for greater Glenfinnan before he himself moved there, after 1861.

97. There is a letter of offer to lease Craigag estate for £45 per annum, dated 16 April 1851, from Ranald P. McDonell, Keppoch. See NRAS 3583, bundle 20. The 1861 census for Keppoch shows the principal farm headed by Ronald MacDonell (56). Eighteen people were listed living there, including 3 ploughmen, 1 herd, 1 dairymaid, 4 shepherds, 1 gamekeeper, 2 domestic servants (and a housekeeper, Ronald's widowed sister-in-law, and her 3 scholar daughters). According to Rory

MacDonald, Blarour, he (Ranald P.) was a grandson of *Aonghus Bàn Innse*. Ranald P. died in 1864 at Keppoch after succeeding his older brother at Keppoch in 1855.

98. The lands and estate of Conaglen consisted of the 'lands and Farms of Inverscadle, Conaglen or Corraglen, Corlarich and Candellich, North and South Suiskie or Duisky, North and South Garbhan or Garvan, Calp, Cregag, Altlaig, Drumfern, Dalriach and Mealdabh and lands and Farms of Dalindrein, Stronchrigan or Strongregane, Auchenfobell or Auchphubill, Tronselk or Trinslaig and Blaich, with Mills, Salmon and other Fishings as well in salt as in fresh water, in Parish of Kilmalie and Counties of Argyll and Inverness, being the portion of Entailed lands, Barony and Estate of Argour and others, lying to north of line of southern marches of Carlarich & Crandellich and Inverscadle.' See Search Sheet, county of Inverness, 1568, folios 543 and 544.

99. In Drumsallie and Callop in 1891 there were nine homes and a population of thirty-three people. Of these two were unilingual Gaelic, twenty-two bilingual Gaelic and English, and the remaining nine, presumably, unilingual English. See Duwe, *'Alba 1891* no. 016.'

100. Alexander is unidentified but probably was a son of either John or Ewen MacVarish.

101. Of the twenty-eight, those from the south shore of Locheil area were two from North Garvan, two from Treslaig, two from Achafubil and nine from Duisky. The *Derry Castle* was built in Montreal.

9 The Callop River and the road and the Glenfinnan station

1. From 1883 to 1924 the owner of the Moidart estate was Francis Edward Fitzalan-Howard, Lord Howard of Glossop, a powerful English Roman Catholic whose estate included Dorlin and Dalilea in the east-west tail of Loch Shiel further around than the guardian Eilean Fhianain (the family had bought Moidart in 1871 from Catholic barrister James R. Hope-Scott). With the coming of the railway to Fort William in 1894 there was clear potential for delivery of goods, people and mail to the communities on the banks of Loch Shiel by boat. Francis Howard began a steamer service on Loch Shiel in 1898, calling his steam launch the *Lady of the Lake* in memory of Hope-Scott's first wife, a granddaughter of Sir Walter Scott. It ran six days a week and was a success. When the Mallaig branch line opened in 1901 the *Clanranald II* was handling the Loch Shiel passengers, mail and freight, with the Glenfinnan pier at the big house (where an anchorage of some sort surely was in 1745). Sometime in or after 1908, Colonel John MacDonald (2nd Batt. Camerons, dsp 1916 aged 79), whose base was the big house in Glenfinnan, moved the pier to the Callop, where I remember it in the 1940s. (In the 1940s, before MacBrayne was approached to take over the Loch Shiel service in 1951, local landowners formed the Loch Shiel Steamboat Service Company.)

2. Only a few years ago I was told in Mabou by a visitor from South Uist that Angie had only recently died and I felt a pang of sorrow. I had visited him once in the 1970s. The South Uist person knew Angie as Angie the gate. Nicknames change, like place names.

3. Dr Hugh A. MacMaster, Judique, the fiddler, born in 1924.

4. With Gaelic almost safely out of the way, and tourism beginning to seem a lucrative potential, Route 19 became the Ceilidh Trail, fitting in with the Glooscap Trail, the Sunrise Trail and many others in the province. The symbol on the Route 19 sign is a stylised piper, tastefully drawn.

10 On the old roads in October 2002

1. The last of the great eastern deciduous is in the Codroy in Newfoundland.

2. See MacDougall, *History of Inverness County*, p. 154. Dr Robert Cameron, in 'Cameron Genealogies' (internet) described Donald Cameron as 'Donald Dhu of Glenpean' implying that he was a Macgillonie, originally Strone people. They were known, according to Somerled MacMillan, as Clann Dhòmhnaill mhic Dhùghaill. Dr Cameron continued to note that Donald Cameron of Glenpean was a great Scottish swordsman and the man who trained Allan Cameron of Erracht before the latter's famous duel with Cameron of Muirshearlaich in 1772. Dr Cameron gave Donald Cameron's wife as Marjorie Cumming of 'Artlewn' and daughter of George Cumming and Christina McLachlan.

   NB Somerled MacMillan cited the compearing of a George Cumming in Achdalieu at a land court in Bunarkaig in 1755. *Bygone Lochaber*, p. 171.

   NB An internet source consulted on 3 March 2007 stated that Ewen Cameron had brothers who emigrated to Australia where one, Donald, died at Deniliquin in New South Wales in 1881. The same source, citing Port Hastings cemetery records gave Ewen's death in 1868 when he was 87. He also had a son Alexander, b. 1818 (who married an Isabel Laidlaw), and a son George, born in Àrasaig (no date).

3. MacDougall, *History of Inverness County*, p. 155. Dr Robert Cameron's 'Cameron Genealogies' (internet) adds that George Cameron was baptised at Kilmallie 28 June 1820 and died 16 June 1897. Cameron also gives Ewen Cameron's dates as 1783 to 14 April 1869, and Ewen's wife Christina Laidlaw's dates as *c*. 1794 to 6 May 1873.

4. Until 1824 a Scotch mile was 1976.5 yards.

5. See MacDougall, *History of Inverness County*, pp. 156–8.

6. His father, Ewen the third Achdalieu, had been robbed by Cumberland's soldiery despite, as far as I am able to tell, like Fassifern his more powerful neighbour, staying out of the Jacobite war Lochiel could not resist. John, future fourth, himself protected Fassifern.

7. NAS CC2/8/59, an edict from the Argyll Commissary court during the years 1706–1825.

11 *The train journey north and straggling thoughts*

1. *The Scotsman* newspaper of 24 May 1897 reported a 'Moor fire near Glenfinnan,' a 'serious moor & timber fire at Craigag, on Lord Morton's estate.' This fire consumed an area of three miles by one mile and destroyed 'a valuable quantity of growing timber, and ruined for several seasons a large extent of grouse moor.' Part of the Craigag holding was a deer shelter. Damage was done also on Lochiel and Glenaladale land. There was fear that Craigag Lodge might be burned but well directed efforts saved it. Damage was estimated at between £800 and £1,000. This was the fourth moor fire in the area within 'the past few days'. A tramp, Francis Thomas Dennis, was suspected of arson.

2. On 9 October 2006 an old Gaelic-speaker, Flora Christina (MacInnes) MacIsaac, died at the Milford Haven Home for special care in Guysborough, Nova Scotia aged ninety-one. She had been born on 11 January 1915 at Kinloch Rannoch in Perthshire. She became the wife of Alex Tando MacIsaac, a provincial politician in Nova Scotia. Her memories of her early years are not generally known yet. A Rannoch couple, Archibald Stewart (*c.* 1796–1833) and wife, Ann McNaughton (*c.* 1797–1849), are buried at Barney's River in east Pictou county, NS.

3. There were three 'passes' on Rannoch Moor, Gorton in the south, Rannoch, and Corrour in the north. See John Thomas, *The West Highland Railway,* pp. 20 and 21.

4. Loch Treig was dammed and its waters tunnelled through Ben Nevis between the two twentieth-century German wars. Its level according to Thomas, was raised thirty-three feet, necessitating a shifting of the West Highland's track and the creation of a railway tunnel. The British Aluminium Company at Fort William now had water and power enough. M.E.M. Donaldson found somewhere that eagles' feathers from birds from Loch Treig were the most sought in bow-and-arrow times. See *Wandering*, p. 98. The old West Highland went right past the by-then-submerged Eadarloch crannog but no one knew to tell me about it. (See Ritchie, 'The lake-dwelling or crannog in Eadarloch . . .' PSAS, 1941–2.)

5. 'The owners of the Glenfinnan Estate, who saw 500 acres of their moorland damaged last month by a fire believed to have been started by sparks from the Hogwarts Express during filming for *Prisoner of Azkaban* are to sue for £100,000 damages.' Mr (Alistair) Gibson, the estate's forestry manager, said that 200 acres of the total damaged 'was a plantation of native trees such as Scots pine.' He specified that 50,000 trees were lost. Taken from 'The Hogwarts Wire' on the internet on 19 December 2005. NB The Hogwarts Express is known to non-fantasy filmgoers as the *Jacobite*, the reintroduced tourist attraction on the old West Highland line.

Bibliography

Published texts

Act to Attaint, 19 Geo. II, cap. 26 (1746). The act against treason (7 Anne, c. 21 ([post-Union], 1707) is cited from Erskine.

Acts of the Parliaments of Scotland, volume 5, 1625–1649.

A List of the Officers of the Army and Marines, 1789.

Allardyce, Col. James, LL.D. (ed.). *Historical Papers Relating to the Jacobite Period 1699–1750.* 2 vols. Aberdeen: New Spalding Club, 1895 and 1896.

Anderson, John. *A History of Edinburgh from the earliest period to the completion of the half century 1850, with brief notices of eminent or remarkable individuals.* Edinburgh: A Fullarton & Co., 1856.

Ashley, Maurice. *General Monck.* London: Jonathan Cape, 1977.

Barrow, G.W.S. *Robert Bruce and the community of the realm of Scotland.* London: Eyre & Spottiswoode, 1965.

Botting, Douglas. *The Saga of Ring of Bright Water: The Enigma of Gavin Maxwell.* Glasgow: Neil Wilson Publishing, 2000.

Brown, Jennifer M. *Scottish Society in the Fifteenth Century.* New York: St Martin's Press, 1977.

Brown, Mike. *Evacuees: Evacuation in Wartime Britain 1939–1945.* Gloucester: Sutton Publishing, 2000.

Buchan, John. *The Massacre of Glencoe.* New York: G.P. Putnam's Sons, 1931.

Burt, Edward. *Letters from a Gentleman in the North of Scotland (1727–1736).* 2 vols. London, 1754.

Caimbeul, Aonghas Pàdraig. *West Highland Free Press,* 27 October 2006 and 23 February 2007.

Cameron, Donald [alias Alasdair MacLean]. *The Field of Sighing: A Highland Boyhood.* London: Green and Co Ltd, 1966.

Cameron, John. *Celtic Law: The 'Senchurs Mór' and 'The Book of Aicill,' and the traces of an early Gaelic system of law in Scotland.* London, Edinburgh and Glasgow: William Hodge and Company Limited, 1937.

Cameron, John. *Gaelic Names of Plants*. Edinburgh: William Blackwood, 1893.

Cameron, Neil. 'A Romantic folly to Romantic folly: the Glenfinnan Monument reassessed,' in *Proceedings of the Society of Antiquaries of Scotland*. vol. 129 (1999), pp. 887–907.

Campbell, Alastair. *A History of Clan Campbell From Flodden to the Restoration*. volume 2. Edinburgh: Edinburgh University Press, 2002.

Chambers, Robert. *Domestic Annals of Scotland, From the Reformation to the Revolution (From the Revolution to the Rebellion of 1745)*. Edinburgh: W. & R. Chambers, 1858–61.

Clerk, Revd Archibald. *Memoir of Colonel John Cameron, Fassifern, K.T.S., Lieutenant-Colonel of the Gordon Highlanders, or 92nd Regiment of Foot*. Printed for Sir Duncan Cameron, Bart., of Fassifern. Second edition: Glasgow, Thomas Murray & Son, 1858.

Cowan, E.J. 'The Looting of Lochaber', in Fleming, *Lochaber Emigrants,* below.

Dawson, Jane. 'Breadalbane Letters 1548–83'. http://www.div.ed.ac.uk/scottish-lett_1.html.

————. *Campbell Letters 1559–83*. Edinburgh: Scottish History Society, 1999.

Donaldson, M.E.M. *Scotland's Suppressed History*. London: John Murray, 1938.

————. *Wandering in the Western Highlands and Islands Recounting Highland & Clan History, Traditions, Ecclesiology, Archaeology, Romance, Literature, Humour, Folk-Lore, etc.* Paisley: Alexander Gardner Ltd, 1923.

Dunbar, John Telfer. *'Herself': The life and photographs of M.E.M. Donaldson*. Edinburgh: William Blackwood & Sons Ltd, 1979.

Duwe, Kurt C. '*Alba 1891: Gàidhlig* (Scottish Gaelic) Local Profile' (no. 016). November 2006. Internet (www.linguae-celticae.org).

Dwelly, Edward. *The Illustrated Gaelic–English Dictionary*. Glasgow: Gairm Publications, 1971.

Dye, John. 'High Mingarry', for *Comann Eachdraidh Mhùideirt*. Undated internet source (www.moidart.org.uk).

Emmerson, George. *Ranting Reed and Trembling String: a History of Scottish Dance Music*. Montreal: McGill-Queen's University Press, 1971.

Erskine, John. *The Principles of the Law of Scotland, in the order of Sir George MacKenzie's Institutions of that law*. 11th edition. Edinburgh, 1820.

Fenton, Alexander and Bruce Walker. *The Rural Architecture of Scotland*. Edinburgh: John Donald Publishers Ltd, 1981.

Fleming, Rae (ed). *Lochaber Emigrants to Glengarry*. Toronto: Natural Heritage/Natural History Inc., 1994.

Galbraith, Paul. *Beloved Morar,* unknown binding, 1994.

Gaskell, Philip. *Morvern Transformed: A Highland parish in the nineteenth century*. Cambridge: Cambridge University Press, 1968.

Gibson, John G. *Old and New World Highland Bagpiping*. Montreal and Kingston: McGill-Queen's University Press, 2002.

Grant, James. *Thoughts on the Origin and Descent of the Gael: with an account of the Picts,*

Caledonians, and Scots; and observations relative to the authenticity of the poems of Ossian. Edinburgh: Archibald Constable and Co., 1814.

Haldane, A.R.B. *The Drove Roads of Scotland.* Edinburgh: Edinburgh University Press, 1968.

————. *New Ways through the Glens.* London, Edinburgh: Thomas Nelson and Sons Ltd, 1962.

Inverness Courier. 30 May 1838, 17 August 1847.

Inverness Journal. 16 September 1825.

Kelly, Fergus. *A Guide to early Irish Law,* Dublin: Advanced Studies, 1988.

Keltie, Sir John Scott (ed.). *A History of the Scottish Highlands, Highland Clans and Highland Regiments.* 2 vols. Edinburgh and London: A. Fullarton, 1875.

Laing, Lloyd. *The Archaeology of Late Celtic Britain and Ireland c.400–1200 AD.* London: Methuen & Co. Ltd, 1975.

Lewis, Samuel. *Topographical dictionary of Scotland comprising the several counties, islands . . . with historical descriptions.* 4 vols, 1846. (I used an edited ten-page excerpted version from 'Clan Cameron Archives' taken from internet.)

Livingstone, Alastair, with Christian W.H. Aikman and Betty S. Hart. *No Quarter Given: The muster roll of Prince Charles Edward Stuart's Army, 1745–46.* Glasgow: Neil Wilson Publishing, 2001.

MacAulay, Murdo. *Hector Cameron of Lochs and Back: the story of an island minister.* Edinburgh: P. Knox, 1982.

MacCormack, John R. *Highland Heritage & Freedom's Quest.* Halifax, NS: Kinloch Books, 1999.

Macdonald, Marjorie. 'Letters of the Clanranald Family (1746–1752)', In *Clan Donald Magazine No 6 (1975).* http://www.clandonald.org.uk/cdm06/cdm06a07.htm.

McDonald, R. Andrew. *Outlaws of Medieval Scotland: Challenges to the Canmore kings, 1058–1266.* Phantassie, East Lothian: Tuckwell Press, 2003.

MacDougall, John L. *History of Inverness County Nova Scotia.* Belleville, Ontario: Mika Publishing Company, 1976. Canadiana Reprint Series No. 43. (Originally published in 1922.)

MacKay, James, et al. *Genealogical History of St. Mary's Parish Glendale, N.S.* n.f.i.

MacKenzie, John. *Sar-Obair nam Bard Gaelach: or the Beauties of Gaelic Poetry.* New edition, Edinburgh: Norman MacLeod, 1904.

MacLean, Alasdair. *Night Falls on Ardnamurchan: The Twilight of a Crofting Family.* London: Victor Gollancz Ltd, 1984.

MacLean, Calum Iain. *The Highlands.* London: B.T. Batsford Ltd, 1959 (and several subsequent editions).

MacLeod, Revd John. Entry for the parish of Morvern, NSA, vol. 7, 173 and 194.

MacLeod, Norman. *Caraid nan Gàidheal.* New edition. Edinburgh: Norman MacLeod, 1899.

MacMillan, Somerled. *Bygone Lochaber.* Glasgow, 1971.

McNeill, Neill. 'Census of the Small Isles 1764–65, at Canna 20th March 1765'.

Mason, David. *Shadow over Babylon.* London: Bloomsbury Publishing, 1993.

Mason, Michael Henry. *Deserts Idle*. London: Hodder & Stoughton, 1928.

Maudlin, Daniel. 'Tradition and change in the age of improvement: a study of Argyll tacksmen's houses in Morvern' in *Proceedings of the Society of Antiquaries of Scotland*, vol. 133 (2003), 359–74.

Munro, Jean and R.W. Munro (eds). *Acts of the Lords of the Isles 1336–1493*. Scottish Historical Society: Edinburgh, 1986.

Murray, Alexander. *The true interest of Great Britain, Ireland and our plantations . . . and a new method of husbandry by greater and lesser canals*. London: printed for the author, 1740.

Neat, Timothy. *When I was Young. Voices from the Lost Communities in Scotland*. Edinburgh: Birlinn, 2000.

Niven, David. *The Moon's a Balloon*. London: Hamish Hamilton, 1972.

Old and New Statistical Accounts of the parishes of Scotland. (OSA, vols 4, 7, and 14; NSA, vols 7 and 14). Edina: Edinburgh University data library (available on the internet).

Parry, M.L. 'Climate change and the agricultural frontier: a research strategy', in Wigley et al, *Studies in Past Climates* (see below), pp. 319–336.

Prebble, John. *Glencoe: the story of the massacre*. New York, Chicago and San Francisco: Holt, Rinehart and Winston. 1966.

Prunier, Clotilde. *Anti-Catholic Strategies in Eighteenth-Century Scotland*. Frankfurt-am-Main, Berlin, Bern, Bruxelles, New York, Oxford and Wien: Peter Lang Europäischer Verlag der Wissenschaffen, 2004.

Ritchie, James. 'The lake dwelling or crannog in Eadarloch, Loch Treig: its traditions and its construction', *Proceedings of the Society of Antiquaries*, vol. 76 (1941–2), seventh series vol. 4, pp. 8–78.

Roberts, Alasdair. *Tales of the Morar Highlands,* Edinburgh: Birlinn, 2006.

Robertson, Tim. 'Arisaig and Moidart Parish Council Minutes 11 April 1895–30 March 1906'. *Comann Eachdraidh Mùideart*, internet source (www.moidart.org.uk).

Rogers, Charles. *The Scottish Minstrel: The Songs of Scotland subsequent to Burns, with memoirs of the poets*. Edinburgh: William P. Nimmo, 1873.

Scott, Hew. *Fasti Ecclesiae Scoticanae,* vols 4 and 8. Edinburgh: Oliver and Boyd, 1928.

Sellar, W.D.H., O'Donnell Lecture 1985. 'Celtic Law and Scots Law: Survival and Integration', *Scottish Studies* 29, (1989), pp. 1–27.

Seton, Bruce and Jean Gordon Arnot (eds). *Prisoners of the '45*. 3 vols. Volume 14 of the third Scottish History Series. Edinburgh: Constable, 1928 and 1929.

Seymour, W.E. (ed.). *A History of the Ordnance Survey*. Folkstone, Kent: William Dawson & Sons Ltd, 1980.

Shaw, John. *The Blue Mountains and Other Gaelic Stories from Cape Breton* (*Na Beanntaichean Gorma agus Sgeulachdan Eile à Ceap Breatainn*). Montreal and Kingston: McGill-Queen's University Press, 2007.

Speck, W.A. *The Butcher: The Duke of Cumberland and the Suppression of the '45*. Caernarfon: Welsh Academic Press, 1995.

Thomas, John. *The West Highland Railway*. Colonsay: House of Lochar, fourth edition, 1998.

Wigley, T.M.L., M.J. Ingram and G. Farmer (eds). *Studies in Past Climates and their Impact on Man*. Cambridge: Cambridge University Press, 1981.

Williams, Scott. 'Sandy Boyd', in Atlantic Canada Pipe Band Association publication, 2005.

Wood, Wendy. *Mac's Croft*. New York: E.P. Dutton & Co., Inc., 1949.

Letters

Cameron, Dr Robert S. Australia Electronic mail, 2006 and 18 and 19 May 2007.

Cradock, Caroline. Scottish Catholic Archives, 16 Drummond Place, Edinburgh, to the author, 26 June 2006.

Duwe, Kurt. Hamburg, Germany. Electronic mail, 12 November 2006.

Gray, Alistair. Blaich, Ardgour. Electronic mail, 8 November 2005.

MacBrayne, Pat. Edinburgh, 21 April 2007.

MacDonald, Maggie. Clan Donald library, Armadale, Sleat, 12 April 2007 (re. 1743 drove).

MacFarlane, *Tearlach*. *Innis a' Bhorbhain*, Glenfinnan, 8 November 2006 (letter and speculative genealogical chart of one Clanranald MacVarish family), and letters, 5 January, 13 April and 27 April 2007.

MacPhee, Sally. Brisbane, Australia, E-mail, 23 April 2007.

O'Rua, Eileen. Glenfinnan, E-mails, 25, 30 and 31 August 2006, and 19 April 2007.

Electronic records

Clan Cameron Archives (citing NLS17527/97, Donald Campbell of Aird's, 'Scheme for Civilising the Clan Cameron'.

Cameron, Dr Robert. Leura, New South Wales, 'Cameron Genealogies'.

Campbell, Allan. Digital photographs of the mountain bothy at *Gleann Dubh Lighe,* 2006.

Hardie-Stoffelen, Annette. 'The rise of the Flemish families in Scotland'. amg1.net/ Scotland/flemfam.htm

MacLean, Fiona. Ardgour. E-communications, October 2006, and 12 March 2007, the latter citing, informally, the work of a MacLean aunt by marriage.

Sackler Archive of the Royal Society, Carlton House Terrace, London. GB117 EC/ 1868/08.

The Scottish Record Society's 'Commissariot of Edinburgh Consistorial Processes and Decreets 1658–1800'.

Stewart, Martin. Diary of travel in Sunart.

Archival material

48 Geo III, c. 138, sect. 11 (concerning teinds or tithes).

GB 0248 UGD 008/6, 'Records of the Edinburgh & Glasgow Railway Co., Scotland', (held at Glasgow University).

National Archives of Canada, MG24, I 183. List of Emigrants per Mr Archibald MacMillan [1802].

National Archives of Scotland (NAS)

NAS CH1/2/73. General Assembly [Church of Scotland] Papers, main series, royal bounty papers, 1736 to 1740. Lady Clanranald and Lady Boistill's letter (NAS presumption, to the moderator of the committee for reformation of the Highlands and Islands).

NAS CH1/5/119. 'A State of Popery in Scotland containing an Hint of the Reasons of its continuance there, Places where, and proposing some Remedies for removing these Evils 1736'.

NAS CS96/3377. (1811–1812) and 3378 (1812–1817). Sederunt books pertaining to James MacDonald, drover and cattle dealer.

NAS E768. Forfeited estates papers for the Lochiel estate, 1749–1784.

NAS E100/12/8a (Exchequer records). 'Certificate anent muster of Lord Rollo's troop: Aberdein'. September 1698.

NAS E100/14/3. Muster of Argyll's regiment, 24 August 1689.

NAS E100/25 series. Musters of Colonel John Hill's regiment, May to October 1697.

NAS E100/31/295. Musters of Colonel John Hill's company, May to July 1697.

NAS E768/1. Rental of the estate which pertained to Donald Cameron, the younger of Lochiel . . . taken up by David Bruce, one of the surveyors of the forfeited estates in Scotland. Presented to the barons of the exchequer. Dated Edinburgh, 23 January 1748/9.

NAS E786/50. Forfeited estates papers for the Locheil estate, 1774.

NAS GD51/1998. Letter to Lord Neville from MacLean, at Oban, 22 July 1811.

NAS. GD112 The Breadalbane Muniments, pertaining to the decade of 1690–1700.

NAS GD112/3/9. Remission under the great seal, 19 October 1488.

NAS GD112/11/3/3/85. Complaint of Donald MacArthur, Portbane on Loch Tay, 4 November 1793.

NAS GD112/39/1/1. Argyll to Glenorchy, 18 October 1548.

NAS GD112/51/182. Petition of Revd Thomas Davidson, Kilmallie Free Church, April 1845.

NAS GD201/1/273. Clanranald's tack of 1749 to forfeited estates surveyor David Bruce.

NAS GD201/1/281. Clanranald papers, title deeds, contracts, bonds etc., 1520–1859. (Sale of wood for charcoal to Hartlie, Aitkenson and Co., Cumberland.)

NAS GD201/1/341. Precept of *Clare Constat* (16 June 1835) to Angus MacDonald of Glenalladale, of lands of Dalilea, Langall and others in the parish of Ardnamurchan.

NAS GD201/5/1178. Tack from Clanranald to Revd Malcolm McCaskill of lands in Eigg, 30 August 1776.

NAS GD201/5/1188. Twelve-year missive tack of Drimloy, near Dalilea, Moidart, from John MacDonald of Clanranald to John McVarish.

NAS GD201/5/1231.

NAS GD201/5/1231/1/23. Letter of John MacDonald of Borrodale to H. Macdonald Buchanan concerning Thomas Telford's proposed alterations to the Àrasaig to Lochy Ferry road, 15 September 1814.

NAS GD201/5/1231/1/41. Road contract between commissioners for Highland roads and bridges and Messrs. Dick and Readdie, Perth, August 1804.

NAS GD201/5/1231/1/42. Abstract of James Donaldson's survey and report of the Loch-na-Gaul road, 1804.

NAS GD201/5/1231/1/43. Specifications for the bridges on the Loch-na-Gaul road, 1804.

NAS GD248/671/6/8. Telford's instructions.

NAS GD253/129/19, 20 and 21.

NAS GD253/176/1. Item 9. (Highland Roads and Bridges) records repairs to the 'bridge across the river Finnan in Glenfinnan' in 1837.

NAS RH4/93/1. Loch Etive Trading Company Records 1729–1754. (RH4/93 LETC papers cover 1729–1789).

NAS RH15/44/201, 'Signet letters of horning' against Marjory, d/o 'deceased John Cameron of Inverscaddel' and her husband, Coll MacDougall of Creganich (Lismore). 22 July 1763.

NAS RH15/105/9. Revd William Grant, correspondence to William Ross.

NAS RHP6591 'Plan of part of the annexed estate of Lochiel south of Loch Arkaig' by William Morison, surveyor, 1772.

NAS RHP747/1–3, three copies of 'the lands of Inverscadale, Strongrigan and others', in 1858, in the papers of the Earl of Morton, drawn by T. Strachan in Edinburgh and lithographed by Schenck and Macfarlane of Edinburgh.

NAS SC54/17/2/65/6. Argyll justiciary court records, 1664–1748 (theft of lead).

NAS SC54/17/2/65/8. Argyll justiciary court records, 1664–1748 (theft of lead from Lochnell).

NAS SC54/17/3/2 and SC54/17/4/8/1, Argyll Justiciary Court processes, 1664–1748 (re. Rev John MacCalman).

NAS4/AB3/459.3/Part 1, NRAS26. Electronic communication from assistant registrar, T. Spencer, dated 29 March 2007.

National Register of Archives of Scotland

NRAS26/50/2, bundle 1; 26/50/3, bundles 3 and 5 (Revd Thomas Davidson).

NRAS656, bundle 1/15. Plans of the lands of Achranich in Morvern, 1815.

NRAS2177, bundles 1508, 1522, 1532 (concerning Kinlochmoidart rentals *c.* 1806), 1550 (from a letter dated 9 November 1809, from a Mr Easton to Thomas Telford, a copy of which is in the Robert Brown correspondence), 1554 (John MacVarish to Robert Brown, re. Glenuig holding), 1568 (miscellaneous correspondence to Robert Brown, re. illegal emigration, 6 October 1811).

NRAS3273/1354 (Gillies and MacLean to the commissioners of Lord MacDonald, 24 August 1811).

NRAS3273/4249. Duncan Macqueen's complaint over cattle straying at Haughgary, North Uist. From 'Tenants' Petitions, offers . . . 1783–1799' in papers of Macdonald family. Barons Macdonald.

NRAS3583/B. 47 bundles of records and papers of the MacLeans of Ardgour.

NRAS3583, bundles 2, 8 (re. Ardgour place names, and the Blaich crofters in 1823 and 1825), 11, 12, 19, 20, and 28, 348 and 375.

Sasine Register (from a newspaper column held in handwritten materials). 'Memorandum between NIALL DIARMID CAMPBELL, DUKE of ARGYLL, and sold [sic] acting Trustee under Deed of Trust by SHOLTO GEORGE WATSON DOUGLAS, EARL of MORTON . . .' Dated 25 November 1924, in Search Sheet, county of Inverness, 1568., H545.

The Scotsman archives (1817–1950). Issues of 7 April 1826, 2 May 1835, 16 Sept. 1837, 9 Sept. 1849, 4 Sept. 1872, 11 and 16 Sept. 1873, 26 Jul., 17 Sept., and 8 Oct. 1879, 27 Mar. 1889, 10 Sept. 1895, 24 May 1897, 3 Mar. 1898, 28 Apr. 1934, and [Angie 'the bar'] Jan or Dec. 1949.

State papers, June–December 1695 (sic), part of the Breadalbane Muniments.

The photographs of Robert Moyes Adam, held by Special Collection of St Andrews University, including RMA H-922 and H-11106A.

The photographs of A.J. Valentine, including photograph JV-D2503 (Library University of St Andrews).

Censuses of Fort William and surrounding area, 1841, 1861, and 1881, taken from an internet site hosted by www.rootsweb.com.

Births, marriages and deaths

IGI and OPR records

Births in the parish of Kilmallie, county of Argyll, 1886, page 6, entry no. 16 (Sophia Henderson).

Deaths for the parish of Kilmallie, county of Argyll, 1868, page 11, entry no. 31 (Duncan Henderson); and for 1883, page 16, entry no. 46 (Martin MacPherson).

Birth entries for the family of Ewen MacVarish and Catherine Gordon: Fort Augustus, reg. no. 092/A2, entry no. 6; Gairloch, southern, reg. no. 066/2, entry no. 15; and Morvern, reg. no. 528/00, entry no. 5.

Deaths for 1931, Registration District 098/B1, entry no. 34, Kilmallie, Argyll (Duncan MacVarish).

Deaths for 1976, Registration District 239, entry no. 14, Fort William (Sarah MacVarish).

Death record for John Cameron Ford, Fort William, d. 21 January 1975 (from NAS).

Marriages for 1902, Registration District 520, entry no. 3, Kilmallie (Sarah Henderson and Duncan MacVarish).

Marriages in the District of Kilmallie, 1928, page 8, entry no. 15 (Sophia Henderson and Alexander Boyd).

Marriages of 1933, Hillhead, Glasgow, reg. dist. 644/12, entry no. 397 (Ewen MacVarish and Catherine Gordon).

Births at the maternity hospital, Glasgow, 1907, ref. no. 644/10 537 (George Stewart Oliver).

Marriages at Arisaig 91B, 1938, ref. no. Arisaig 5 (George Oliver and Margaret McLennan).

Deaths in Fort William 239, 1975, ref. no. Fort William 11, George Oliver, and Fort William 239, 1982, ref. no. Fort William 90.

Births, Kilmallie, 1904, ref. no., 52, Margaret McLennan.

Deaths, Inverness 231, 1983, ref. no. 167 (John Monaghan).

Privately held archival material

Murlagan and Glen Pean MacMillan and other family papers sought and found in North America and held by Hugh P. (Dall) MacMillan, D. Litt., Ottawa, Ontario, in May 2007. (I was kindly given access to typed transcripts, not all of whose typographic errors were correctable.)

Maps and Atlases

Admiralty. Chart 1426. Loch Eil leading to the Caledonian Canal (surveyed in 1841). NLS.

————. Chart 2155. The Sound of Mull (surveyed in 1851). NLS.

Arrowsmith. Aaron Arrowsmith (1750–1823). 'Map of Scotland constructed from original materials.' London, 1807. NLS, EMS.s.253.

Bartholomew. Half-inch map series, no. 50, *Arisaig and Lochaber*, 1972.

Bruce. Alexander Bruce. *Plan of Loch Sunart*, 1733.

Cowley. John Cowley. Map of the Duke of Argyll's heritable dukedom and justiciary territories, islands, superiorities and jurisdictions. EMS.s.738(16); London, 1734.

Elphinstone. John Elphinstone (1706–1753). 'A new and correct map of North Britain.' London: And. Millar, 1745. EMS.x.16.

Gordon. Robert Gordon (1580–1661). 'A mapp of Scotland', corrected and improved by R. Morden. London, *c.* 1690. (This document contains a 'table of shires or shreifdoms with the counties *[sic]* in Scotland'.)

————. Robert Gordon. 'Lochabre Glencooen.' Adv.MS.70.2.10 (Gordon, 37 and 38), imprint 1636–52.

Johnson. Robert Johnson. 'A Plan of Fort William with the Country ajasent', *c.* 1710. NLS maps, MS.1646 Z. 02/24a.

Kirkwood. James Kirkwood (1745/6–1827) & Sons. 'This map of Scotland constructed and engraved from the best authorities'. 1804 (Edinburgh and London): NLS EMS.s.74, and 1810 (n.p), NLS EMS.s.b.2.118.

Kitchin. Thomas Kitchin. 'A new and complete map of Scotland and islands thereto belonging'. 1773 (London). NLS EMS.s.188.

————. Thomas Kitchin. 'North Britain or Scotland divided into its counties corrected from the best surveys & Astronomical Observations by Thos Kitchin Hydrographer to his Majesty London' in a geological map published in London, 1 December 1778, attributed to Necker de Saussure.

Langlands. George Langlands & Son, Campbeltown. 'This map of Argyllshire Taken from Actual Survey'. London, 1801. NLS EMS.s.326.

MacCulloch John MacCulloch (1773–1835). A geological map published in 1840.

Moll. Herman Moll 'Geographer' (d. 1732). 'A pocket companion of ye roads of ye North part of Great Britain called Scotland containing all ye Cities, Market Towns, Boroughs &c. the principal Roads, with ye Computed Miles from Town to Town'. NLS EMGB.b.1.35(4).

————. 'Scotland divided into its Shires'. London, 1745. EMS.b.2.1/2.

Necker. Louis Albert Necker (de Saussure)(1786–1861). 'Scotland, coloured according to the rock formations . . .' 1808. NLS, no designation.

Ordnance Survey. Six-inch maps, 1870s.

Sheet IV, an area on the south shore of Loch Shiel from *Camas na Craoibhe Daraich* and *Sgéir Ghiusachan* (56° 50′), to the Callop River (56° 52′), in Argyllshire. Surveyed in 1874, published Southampton, under the directorship of John Cameron, RE, CB, FRS, 1875.

An area of Kilmallie [parish] including Craigag, Callop and east to Kinlocheil, with land to the north and south. Surveyed in 1872, engraved in 1874, Southampton.

Sheet CXXXVII. Glenfinnan and Corryhully *[Coire Thollaidh]*, engraved in 1875, published Southampton, 1877.

Ordnance Survey. one-inch maps,

Ordnance Survey, one-inch maps, 1898–1904. Parishes distinctly coloured.

Sheet 62, Loch Eil, surveyed in 1898. Published 1902.

Sheet 35, Loch Arkaig. 1967 reprint of the fully revised 1954 version.

Ordnance Survey. 1:50,000, Landranger series,

Series M 726, Edition 3-GSGS, Sheet 40, Mallaig & Glenfinnn Loch Shiel. Published in 1997.

Pont. Timothy Pont (fl. *c.* 1560–*c.* 1585). Map no. 13, 'A description of Maimoir in

Lochabir wt ye places adionying', with possible additions by Robert Gordon. NLS Adv.MS.70.2.9.

————. Timothy Pont. Map no.16.

Raif. Mahmoud Abdurrhaman Raif. 'Ascozia'. Uksküdar, Muhenduishame Press, 1803/4. EMS.s.750.

RHP89887. Sketches of Cregag and Callop farms, parts of the plan of the Ardgour estate. 1815.

Roy. William Roy (1726–1790). Maps from his military survey of Scotland, 1747–1755. Sheet 12/4, 12/5, 23/1 and 23/2. From black and white A3 extract copies held by NLS; the original is held by the British Library.

Thomson. John Thomson (1777–*c.* 1840), with William Johnson. *The Atlas of Scotland* 1832. 'Southern part of Inverness-shire,' imprint 1820, NLS, EMS.s.712(24a), and 'Northern part of Argyll Shire', imprint 1820, EMS.s.712(17).

Walker. John Walker (1759–1830). 'Geographical and statistical map of Scotland'. London, 1828. Shelf-mark, NLS, Marischal 86.

Index

BIRLINN LTD (incorporating John Donald and Polygon) is one of Scotland's leading publishers with over four hundred titles in print. Should you wish to be put on our catalogue mailing list **contact**:

Catalogue Request
Birlinn Ltd
West Newington House
10 Newington Road
Edinburgh EH9 1QS
Scotland, UK

Tel: + 44 (0) 131 668 4371
Fax: + 44 (0) 131 668 4466
e-mail: info@birlinn.co.uk

Postage and packing is free within the UK. For overseas orders, postage and packing (airmail) will be charged at 30% of the total order value.

For more information, or to order online, visit our website at **www.birlinn.co.uk**

Birlinn Limited
IMPRINTS: JOHN DONALD · POLYGON